DISPENSATIONAL THEOLOGY

A TEXTBOOK ON ESCHATOLOGY IN THE TWENTY-FIRST CENTURY

By

Reid A. Ashbaucher

RAP

REID ASHBAUCHER PUBLICATIONS
Toledo, Ohio U.S.A.

REID ASHBAUCHER PUBLICATIONS
Toledo, Ohio U.S.A.
https://ra-publications.us

RAP

DISPENSATIONAL THEOLOGY

A Textbook on Eschatology in the Twenty-First Century

Library of Congress Control Number: 2019942806
ISBN: 978-1-7331399-1-5

Printed in the United States of America
U.S. Printing History
First Edition: June 2019
Corrections: July 2022 (p. 66, 67, 193)

Table of Contents

Acknowledgements

Based on the subject of Premillennialism, this book is built on the outline of a two semester course syllabuses developed by Temple Baptist Seminary (now part of Piedmont International University). I want to express my appreciation for their permission to use these syllabuses as an outline and resource in the development of this work.

I want to thank all those who provided permission to use their copyrighted material for quotes and summarizations of their content, which greatly enhanced the content of this work.

Reid Ashbaucher
Reid Ashbaucher

Philosophy behind Resource Choices

The collection and handling of resources for *Dispensational Theology* was based on the following principles:

- Articles referred to in this work, were written by those holding either a Th.D., D.D., alternative doctorate degrees, or by those holding a Ph.D. in the field the articles were written.

- The referenced Internet resources were based on information provided, the subject matter fitting the criteria of the scope and sequence of this work, and the accuracy of the source.

- First choice preferences for resources on early Church Fathers come from the historical leaders themselves as their works were translated and made accessible in English.

- Internet Encyclopedias were preferred for this work based on the relevance of information presented within the articles and the reliability maintained by the Encyclopedia entities.

Examples:

The *Internet Encyclopedia of Philosophy* was created in 1995 and has over a million visitors per month with over 20 million-page views per year, based on self-reporting by the website. Submitted articles are written by those holding doctorate degrees and are professors at universities around the world—approximately 300 in number.[1]

The *Stanford Encyclopedia of Philosophy* chooses their writers through their board management system. Those who take part must hold a Ph.D. degree in their perspective fields of writing and shown scholarship through other published works in respected venues.[2]

Theopedia, an Encyclopedia of biblical Christianity states the following about themselves: "*Theopedia* openly maintains a bias, or a Particular-point-of-view, that being 'conservative evangelical Protestant Christianity.' This bias is to be expected in *Theopedia* content." This resource was chosen when the content was accurate and best supported the scope of information within this work.[3]

The *Catholic Encyclopedia* was a choice of practicality based on scholarship. It is reasonable to assume that those directly involved in early Church History, as recorded through a

---

[1] Resource of information from https://www.iep.utm.edu/home/about; accessed 14 December 2018.
[2] Resource of information from https://plato.stanford.edu/info.html#policies; accessed 14 December 2018
[3] Resource of information from https://www.theopedia.com/about; accessed 14 December 2018

written record, would seek to keep accurate records and have first-hand knowledge of any subject it maintains.

- First-hand sourcing was maintained, when possible, through eyewitness accounts and by written works of authors on the subject matter.

- The closest record to the source was the first choice for published works of the authors, based on the belief that the closest record should produce the least amount of error. Therefore, in foot notations you will see dates of publications going as far back as 1703 A.D. They have obtained translations representing the original copies of the Early Church Fathers as far back as the first century.

- The rest of the source material comes from those holding doctorate degrees in the areas of Theology and Philosophy as they have proven themselves over the years to be authorities and major contributors to the subjects discussed within this work. This also includes online library sources that have collected data on our subject and made it available to the public, to which we should be grateful.

- Internet resourcing was chosen for the benefit of those students living in the twenty-first century who are very comfortable with this environment and may not have access to library systems and resources, due to their circumstances in the world.

- We have taken advantage of the public library system, as they have digitized many older works and made them available for public use. They have also made older materials classified as *public domain* available online as original content resources. This is especially true in relation to University Journals and book materials written over seventy-five years ago.

The realization that those within the time and sequence of events associated with the subject matter of this work have been reasonable individuals, living through their circumstances, experiences and education. These factors influenced them toward one common goal—to please their God in life. Through this study, we can trace God's progressive revelation as he moved individuals to preserve his Word and guide God's Church towards a better understanding of his original intent through biblical translations and God's wise leadership influencing his servants.

An attempt was made to provide information that would bring a better understanding of events and theological perspectives, while maintaining respect for others and their valuable contributions to this subject within each individual's lifetime.

No individual or institution has all the truth, but by collectively gathering truths discovered from each individual's study of the Word, a better picture of the whole can emerge for all to benefit from.

We should understand this realization of combined truth as being a product of the Holy Spirit, our ultimate teacher who reveals truth to both the educated such as the Apostle Paul, or those less educated such as the Apostle Peter.

Because of this, a show of bias toward anyone who may have God's truth to share was consciously avoided. Exceptions were made regarding educational standards on re-sourcing when those resources were found reasonable, appropriate and aligned with God's Word.

It is not this author's intent to defend or disparage any Eschatological viewpoint, but to seek a better understanding of the truth within Theology using the Grammatical-historical approach.

Within this work, the author believes Dispensational Theology represents the best understanding of truth when studying the discipline of Eschatology based on this simple principle: "There are no contradictions in Scripture. For biblical truth to be true it must agree with all other biblical truth." If there are genuine contradictions within any theological system that cannot be harmonized with the Scripture as a whole, then this truth has yet to be realized, hence requiring further study.

This is the bar for this work, and this author will always pursue the truth until Christ returns. Jesus said, "Sanctify them in the truth; Thy word is truth." (John 17:17)

RECOMMENDED SUPPLEMENTAL READING

SECTION I

- *The Letter and the Spirit: A History of Interpretation from Origen to Luther* by Wai-Shing Chau | Published by Peter Lang Publishing, Inc.

- *The Interpretation of Prophecy* by Paul Lee Tan | Published by Assurance Publishers (Available through TanBible.com)

- *Dispensationalism* by Chares C. Ryrie | Published by Moody Publishers

SECTION II

- *Dispensationalism* by Charles C. Ryrie | Published by Moody Publishers

- *The Millennial Kingdom* by John F. Walvoord | Published by Zondervan Publishing

- *Things to Come* by J Dwight Pentecost | Published by Zondervan Publishing

Explanation of General Format

Footnotes:

- Footnote numbering runs from the beginning to the end of the book and is not associated with chapter breaks. They will provide credit for quotes or original thought from original sources and may provide additional information on any subject. Footnote content is reflected in the Bibliography found at the end of the book.

- Footnote and Bibliography formats follow Turabian Sixth Edition.

Quotations:

- Quotes over six lines use special standalone formatting.
- Quotes under seven lines use standard quotation marks.
- Quote Spellings—Some quotes are from sources dating back to the days of Old English spellings or from authors originating in other English-speaking countries using different spellings from American English. In most cases the author's original spelling was left intact, but in some cases, changes were made to U.S. English spellings to aid in recognition of terms for the reader.

Square Brackets: [ ]

- Square Brackets used in the body of the text, designate the summarization of material that expanded over more than one paragraph. Brackets are then followed by a footnote providing the source of the material summarized.

Introduction

The subject of Eschatology has been studied and written about for centuries. The various viewpoints based on differing hermeneutical perspectives have driven this subject in many directions, causing confusion as to how we should view *end-times* doctrine from a Biblical perspective.

Eschatology should not be disassociated from the subject of Biblical Hermeneutics, which allows for a better scriptural interpretation that provides the foundation to anyone's theological perspective. If we ignore the hermeneutical principles behind any interpretation of *end-time* events, we will lose continuity to the flow of arguments supporting an interpretation or position on any issue.

Within the subject of Eschatology, many sub points developed over the years have led us to differing perspectives and interpretations of *end-time* views. Within the last few centuries there have been numerous books written on these views, leaving Christendom confused as to how someone should approach such a subject, let alone how to understand what they read on the topic.

As one reads on this subject the question may arise, what do the Scriptures really teach? This brings us to the purpose of writing this book, which is to provide a textbook on the views of Eschatology as they relate to a dispensational perspective that is presented systematically.

Within this single volume, a comprehensive perspective on *Dispensationalism* will be developed and compared to other *end-time* views existing in other theological systems, such as Reformed or Covenant Theology, Roman Catholicism, and from within its own system as related to Ultra-dispensationalism and Progressive Dispensationalism.

When we talk about a dispensational theological system, we should understand this to mean the harmonization of biblical principles and events that are not isolated but seen as a collection of truths working together towards a single common goal that God has established for his glory. The system itself represents a tool that organizes these truths into a coherent systematic structural approach to the Scriptures, that can then be used to aid in better understanding God's revealed revelation concerning his eschatological plans.

Our discussions in Section One will cover: Historical Background, Hermeneutics of Prophecy, Dispensations and Biblical Evidence for Premillennialism. This scope will include views expressed by many of the early Church Fathers, along with B. B. Warfield, O. T. Allis, Joachim of Floris, Daniel Whitby, Charles Hodge, A. H. Strong, Loraine Boettner, Thomas Aquinas, Martin Luther, John Nelson Darby, C. H. Spurgeon, George Eldon Lad, J. Dwight Pentecost, Charles Ryrie, John Walvoord, Nathaniel West, Milton S. Terry, and Paul Lee Tan—among others.

Section Two will cover: The distinction between the Church and Israel and major elements in God's prophetic program, which will include discussions on: The Day of the LORD and the Day of Christ, The Tribulation Period, The Rapture and Related Events, The Second Advent, and The Millennium.

The material covered in the two major sections of this book can represent two semesters of course work and will allow its readers to understand the subject of Eschatology and the positions of Dispensational Theology in particular, as the subject is presented in a systematic, concise and comprehensive way. It is hoped this will clear up any confusion on this subject with a better understanding of *end-time* prophecies from a Dispensational perspective.

It is not the intent of this book to disparage other theological perspectives, but to show the differences and the whys and wherefores regarding eschatological viewpoints within the Christian Faith, while showing the strengths and the positive influences Dispensational Theology can have on the Christian Faith in the Twenty-First Century.

As time has passed over the years, new theological perspectives in eschatology have been developed, moving us past early interpretations on the Scriptures and older views expressed by John Nelson Darby in the 1800s on the doctrine of Eschatology.

It is the view of this author that the study of Theology is progressive in nature; God can and has revealed new insights into a better understanding of the Scriptures as a whole for the edification of all saints. It is this author's position that there are no contradictions in Scripture, therefore, for Biblical truth to be true, it must agree with all other Biblical truth. This is the standard of this book, and those who pursue God's truth should settle for nothing less.

SECTION I

CHAPTER ONE

Premillennialism: Defining the Terms

INTRODUCTION

There are four ways the subject of Premillennial Eschatology shows its importance in theological studies.

First, it provides a system of interpretation that brings a systematic approach to understanding major biblical doctrines as they relate to the Scriptures as a whole. This is accomplished through harmonization of Scriptural Revelation as presented through the written Scriptures by creating a structural system to build on. This approach helps resolve apparent conflicts between various doctrines within the Scriptures.

Second, it is important because it provides protection against a liberal approach to theology and religious cults that do not adhere to an historical Christian orthodox view that holds to the original teachings of Christ, his Apostles and early Church Fathers from the beginning of the Church, as referenced in Acts Chapter 2.

This provided protection comes in three forms: (i) It protects by the hermeneutical method used—The Grammatico-Historical Method—a literal method of interpretation which will be further discussed throughout this book.

(ii) It protects by allowing the individual the right to interpret and understand their own interpretations as the Holy Spirit directs, in contrast to the Catholic tradition. (1 John 2:27; John 14:26)

(iii) It protects by nature of the hermeneutical approach used, relying on the authority of the Scriptures as a whole versus spiritualization, personal experience or past traditional allegorizations (2 Timothy 3:16-17).

Third, it provides the Christian stability in their understanding of prophesied events reflected through the Scriptures as they unfold in the future (Colossians 2:1-5).

Fourth, it promotes and produces holy living through the hope expressed within its message as expressed here:

> Beloved, now we are children of God, and it has not appeared as yet what we shall be. We know that, when He appears, we shall be like Him, because we shall see Him just as He is. And everyone who has this hope fixed on Him purifies himself, just as He is pure. (1 John 3:2-3)

> For the grace of God has appeared, bringing salvation to all men, instructing us to deny ungodliness and worldly desires and to live sensibly, righteously and godly in the present Age, looking for the blessed hope and the appearing of the glory of our great God and Savior, Christ Jesus; who gave Himself for us, that He might redeem us from every lawless deed and purify for Himself a people for

His own possession, zealous for good deeds. (Titus 2:11-14)

FEATURES OF DISPENSATIONAL PREMILLENNIAL ESCHATOLOGY

Dispensational Theology is a system based on six featured principles represented within dispensational premillennial eschatology, as reflected in the following summary.

First, the hermeneutical principles applied in support of its thesis are foundational to its structure. Paul Lee Tan (Th.D.) defines that method as the Grammatico-Historical Method and explains it this way:

> To "interpret" means to explain the original sense of the speaker or writer. To interpret "literally" means to explain the original sense of the speaker or writer according to the normal, customary, and proper usages of words and language. Literal interpretation of the Bible simply means to explain the original sense of the Bible according to the normal and customary usages of its language.
>
> In order to determine the normal and customary usages of Bible language, it is necessary to consider the accepted rules of grammar and rhetoric, as well as the factual Historical and Cultural data of Bible times. Therefore, the literal Method of interpretation is also called the Grammatico-Historical Method.[4]

Second, this view requires a literal fulfillment of Old Testament prophecies, requiring a literal future time period to fulfill those prophecies such as the millennium.

Third, this view requires a clear recognized distinction between the Nation of Israel and the New Testament Church, supported through the logic that if prophecies about the Nation of Israel are interpreted literally, then fulfillment of those prophecies must be literally fulfilled by the same entity the prophecies speak about—the Nation of Israel.

Fourth, this view supports a pre-tribulation Rapture, while recognizing this may not be true for those who do not hold to the concept of Dispensationalism.

Fifth, this view requires a literal millennial kingdom, arguing a literal kingdom that is still future is required to fulfill both Old and New Testament prophecies.

Sixthly, "What dispensationalists do believe is that salvation is always by grace through faith and that the dispensations are rules of life, never the basis or cause of salvation." [5]

TERMINOLOGY USED WITHIN PREMILLENNIAL ESCHATOLOGY

Eschatology—The study of future things, with an emphasis on *end-time* events within the discipline of Christian Theology.

Millennium—A term originating from Latin, which means thousand. Within the context of Eschatology, it refers to a future period of one thousand years, when Christ establishes his kingdom on earth to fulfill covenant promises to Israel.

Premillennialism—This view believes in a literal millennial period, with Christ

---

[4] Paul Lee Tan, *The Interpretation of Prophecy* (Winona Lake, Indiana: Assurance Publishing, 1974), 29.

[5] Ibid., 255.

returning to the earth before this period begins for the purpose of ruling and reigning over his Kingdom on earth.

Postmillennialism—This view holds to a period labeled millennium in which the Gospel can be preached worldwide. After which, Christ will return at the end of this period.

Amillennialism—This term comes from the Greek—meaning *no millennialism*. This view denies a literal millennial kingdom on earth. It holds to a view that Old Testament promises for a future kingdom will be fulfilled as a *spiritual kingdom*. This view also holds this *spiritual kingdom* could manifest itself in one of two ways. One, the Church represents this kingdom between the first and Second Advent. Second, the Church is in heaven with Christ ruling.

Amillennialism will be explored in more detail in Chapter 2.

Present or Realized Millennialism—A twentieth-century term that represents a belief in a millennial period currently being realized between the first and second advents. This view does not hold to no millennialism, but to a present or realized millennialism—taking place now—spiritually.

Many holding to the Reformed tradition of John Calvin also hold to *Realized Millennialism*.

Rapture—This term represents the concept of being taken or the catching away of living saints, along with the resurrection of the dead in Christ during the Church Age, with the Church Age represented as the time between the day of Pentecost and the future Rapture which takes place before the Second Advent.

The concept of the Church age is supported within the interpretation of the *mysteries* spoken of in the New Testament and the understanding of certain prophecies.

More will be discussed on the issue of mysteries in later chapters.

The Tribulation—A future seven-year period, which is considered an unprecedented time of trouble on earth when God will pour out his wrath in judgment upon the nations of the world.

The Great Tribulation—A reference to the last three and half years of the seven-year Tribulation period where God's judgment becomes more severe.

Pre-tribulation Rapture View—This view holds that the Rapture will take place before the seven-year tribulation period, thus protecting the Church, also referred to as the body of Christ, from God's coming wrath (God's wrath—Revelation 6:15-17; 14:19-20; 16:1; 19:15-16; 1 Thessalonians 1:9-10; Colossians 3:5-7).

The Partial Rapture View—This view holds to the belief that those actively looking for the Rapture will be taken at that time, and all other Christians will remain behind and live through the seven-year tribulation period.

Mid-tribulation Rapture View—This view believes that the Church will be raptured at the midpoint of the Tribulation period and be saved from the Great Tribulation that takes place during the final three-and-a-half years.

Post-tribulation Rapture View—This view holds to the Rapture taking place after the seven-year tribulation period with the

Second Advent taking place immediately afterward.

Second Advent—This term represents the second coming of Jesus Christ to the earth with his saints at the end of the tribulation period.

The Revelation of Christ—This term is associated with the Greek word *Apokalupsis* (ἀποκάλυψις) and carries the idea to *uncover* or *unveil,* as used many times in the New Testament in both noun and verb form.

Within the context of Eschatology, the term *The Revelation of Christ* represents the unveiling of the Glory of Christ as it relates to both the Rapture and the Second Coming of Christ, also referred to as the Second Advent[6] (Scriptural references to the second coming—1 Peter 4:13; 2 Thessalonians 1:7; Luke 17:30) (Scriptural references to the Rapture—1 Corinthians 1:7; Colossians 3:4; 1 Peter 1:7, 13).

This term is specifically referenced in First Corinthians 1:7-9 which reads: "so that you are not lacking in any gift, awaiting eagerly the Revelation of our Lord Jesus Christ, who shall also confirm you to the end, blameless in the day of our Lord Jesus Christ."

Imminence—This term carries the meaning of *impending.* When this word is used regarding the *Rapture,* it means the event could take place at any time, versus the idea of something that could happen soon.

The Church—Within the context of Dispensational Theology, *The Church* is represented by all the saints who ever lived from the day of Pentecost to the time of a future Rapture. This period is also referenced as the Church Age.

Within other theological systems, the term *Church* may include Old Testament saints covering other periods.

Dispensation—Scripturally, we may define dispensations as an economy or stewardship implemented by God for his purpose at any point in human history—past, present or future. These economies rarely overlap—but they do on occasion.

The term *economy* as expressed in the previous paragraph is defined by Merriam-Webster's 11th Collegiate Dictionary in three ways: (3 a: "The arrangement or mode of operation of something: Organization." b: "a system especially of interaction and exchange." (4: "The structure or conditions of economic life in a country, area, or period.") [7]

When placing these three definitions into the discussion, they become helpful in aiding our understanding of dispensations by providing a clearer picture of purpose and functionality of the designated dispensational periods.

The discussion on dispensations will continue more extensively in Chapter 7.

Chiliasm—The word itself means *Millennialism.* This word is used in older writings—pre-twentieth Century—when referencing the doctrine of the millennial kingdom based on Revelation 20:1-3.

---

[6] John F. Walvoord, "New Testament Words for the Lord's Coming," *Bibliotheca Sacra* 101 (July-September 1944): 283; available from Theological Journal Library, Vol. 1-5, (Faithlife Corporation product available from Logos.com.)

[7] *Merriam-Webster's 11th Collegiate Dictionary,* s.v. "economy." [CD-ROM] © 2003. (www.merriam-webster.com)

PROGRESSIVE UNDERSTANDING AND DEVELOPMENT OF DOCTRINE

Biblical doctrines have been developed over the years, bringing us to a better understanding of the Scriptures as a whole.

One reason for this is because of progressive Revelation within the Scriptures themselves.

This progression is showed through the mysteries revealed concerning Christ and the Church as spoken of by the Apostle Paul in Colossians 1:25-27 and Ephesians 3:4-13. Jesus reveals the mystery concerning the Holy Spirit in John 14:16-17, 26-27, and in 16:13-14.

The purpose of these new revelations can be explained as fulfilling the conditions of the New Covenant as found in Jeremiah 31:31-34.

Therefore, it could be said that the prophets and others throughout the Old Testament did not fully understand what God was doing in relation to his eschatological plans.

This concept, called progressive Revelation, could be better understood from the following perspective.

God, over time, reveals new doctrinal concepts by building on one concept at a time. This is evident through Christ's comments in Mark 12:29 when he quoted what the Jewish leadership of his day believed about God as expressed in the Old Testament. "Hear, O Israel! The Lord our God is one Lord…," reflecting that the religious community of Jesus' day did not understand God as triune.

The concept of understanding the full dynamics of who the Holy Spirit was during the time of Christ came through Christ himself, as he expressed in John Chapter 14.

We can also see dispensations in similar ways. Humanity went from perfection to its fall, thereupon requiring governance by conscience, then formal government, and then strengthening the existing government by adding the Law. Within this mix, God added covenants to help reinforce commitments to right living. This is offered only as an analogy to help stimulate our thinking on how and perhaps why God implements progressive Revelation.

God knows we learn about life in stages, building knowledge upon knowledge until we understand the whole picture. This concept is demonstrated in the humanities approach to Science. One experiment leads us to understand aspects of some concept, then subsequent experiments add to that knowledge base until we come to a more complete understanding of any given concept.

Paul Lee Tan (Th.D.) explains the Doctrine of progressive revelation this way:

> The Doctrine of progressive revelation teaches that the complete revelation of God was unfolded to man progressively and gradually, not all at once in a complete and final form. God revealed Himself to man in progressive stages and periods. Even during New Testament times, Christ was still telling His disciples, "I have yet many things to say unto you, but ye cannot bear them now" (John 16:12). It was only after the writing of the last New Testament book, the Apocalypse, that formal revelation was finally closed with this clear warning— "If any man shall add unto these things, God shall add unto him the plagues that

are written in this book" (Rev. 22:18).[8]

Church history provides us with another example of progressive understanding.

Before the Reformation in 1517 A.D., the primary method of Scriptural interpretation was allegorical. After the Reformation, a more literal method of interpretation was realized. This changed how individuals understood the Scriptures, allowing people to come to a better understanding of God's truth from behind the shadows of allegorization.

Because of the mysteries revealed in the New Testament, we now have a better understanding of the Trinity, who the Holy Spirit is, who Christ is, what the Church is, and how the Church (the body of Christ) came into existence.

These same things could be said regarding the history of dispensational thinking.

Later on, as we develop this topic, it will be shown that there were always individuals who held to dispensational concepts since the first century; but almost from the beginning, the Church was more focused on other issues. The organized Church focused on more important issues in their current day, such as the recognition of a triune God coexisting as one entity, and the deity of Jesus Christ as equal in nature with God the Father.

The culmination of this focus came to a head through agreements established by early Church leadership in the third and fourth centuries.

These agreements manifested themselves through the Nicene Creed of 325 A.D., the Nicene/Constantinople Creed of 381 A.D., and the Chalcedonian Creed in 451 A.D.

On top of this focus, extending from the third century, the Method of how someone saw and interpreted the Scriptures began to develop into an allegorical methodology, supported by early Church Fathers.

It was not until Martin Luther ushered in the Reformation in the sixteenth century that the method of interpretation began to become clearer through a literal single tier approach, therefore allowing a fresh look at old doctrines lingering under the shadows of more important issues of earlier times.

Following the Reformation, a literal method of interpretation began to allow a new look at dispensational concepts. This leads us to the next chapter, beginning with a survey of the history and characteristics of hermeneutics and other principled views.

---

[8] Tan, *The Interpretation of Prophecy*, 111-112.

CHAPTER TWO

The History and Characteristics of Amillennialism

INTRODUCTION

The history of Amillennialism can be traced through the lives of those who had a significant influence on its development and advancement.

As alluded on the Introduction page, hermeneutics plays a major role in the development of the doctrine of Eschatology. Therefore, the historical timeline's starting point will begin with those persons who helped facilitate the hermeneutical approach used for scriptural interpretations.

The nature of developing a historical perspective can be helpful if we remember the following principles, as expressed by Wai-Shing Chau (Th.D.).

It is dangerous for a historical study to pass judgment. Often it is dismissed as being subjective and biased. But as it is doubtful, there is any history that is not interpretative, it is especially important for a history of the development of ideas to assess the contribution of each figure to the whole development.[9]

It is not the intent of this study to pass judgment on any historical figure or entity,

but only to help in understanding the questions of how and possibly why things are the way they are.

The starting point to understanding any interpretation of Scripture begins with the history of past practices by the early church Fathers. J. N. D. Kelly provides us some insight in this area.

…this principle of interpretation was no invention of the early second century. The apostles, as we shall see, had employed it, and there is every reason to suppose that our Lord Himself set the precedent—a fact which Justin explicitly acknowledged. In the days of the Apostolic Fathers and the Apologists it was already traditional in the Church, a tradition for which (again Justin is the first to avow it) the Church was on the human plane indebted to the apostles.[10]

This history leads us to the beginning of the second century.

---

[9] Wai-Shing Chau, *The Letter and the Spirit: A History of Interpretation from Origen to Luther* (New York: Peter Lang Publishing, Inc., 1995), 5.

[10] J. N. D. Kelly, *Early Christian Doctrines*, rev ed. (San Francisco: Harper & Row Publishers, 1978), 32.

PRE-THIRD CENTURY VIEWS ON ESCHATOLOGY

JUSTIN MARTYR—A.D. 100-165

Justin Martyr was an apologist and self-taught philosopher who studied several systems of philosophy, to include that of the Old Testament prophets.[11] The reason for becoming a philosopher came about through a chance meeting he had with a wise stranger he met while walking on a beachfront near where he was staying. Part of that conversation follows:

> When he had spoken these and many other things, which there is no time for mentioning at present, he went away, bidding me attend to them; and I have not seen him since. But straightway a flame was kindled in my soul; and a love of the prophets, and of those men who are friends of Christ, possessed me; and while revolving his words in my mind, I found this philosophy alone to be safe and profitable. Thus, and for this reason, I am a philosopher.[12]

With regard to understanding how first-century philosophy fits into the theology of his day, we read the following conversation between Justin and a Jewish man named Trypho:

> **Justin:** And in what would you be profited by philosophy so much as by your own lawgiver and the prophets?
>
> **Trypho:** Why not? Do not the philosophers turn every discourse on God? And do not question, continually arise to them about His unity and providence? Is not this truly the duty of philosophy, to investigate the Deity?[13]

Trypho's comments reflect the reality Hellenistic philosophy had on Jewish theology. This was seen in the life of Philo, a first century Jewish scholar.

> Philo (c. 30 B.C.–c. A.D. 45), who, as well as being a scholarly man with a decidedly mystical bent, was a considerable personage in the Jewish community at Alexandria and headed the delegation which it sent to Emperor Gaius in A.D. 40. An inflexible Jew in faith and practice, he was drawn to the Greek philosophers, especially Plato, accepting wholeheartedly the Platonic distinction between the ideal, or intelligible, and the material worlds. But maintained that all their best ideas had been anticipated in the Jewish Scriptures. The Pentateuch was his favorite study, and the majority of his voluminous works are devoted to expounding it. He regarded the Bible as fully inspired in the sense that God used its authors as passive instruments for communicating His will.[14]

When reading Justin's own accounts, with relation to himself and the Jewish sect,

---

[11] Justin Martyr Dialogue with Trypho 1-8. *Ante-Nicene Fathers*, vol. 1, ed. Alexander Roberts, James Donaldson, and A. Cleveland Coxe, trans. Marcus Dods and George Reith. (Buffalo, NY: Christian Literature Publishing Co., 1885), rev. ed. for New Advent by Kevin Knight. http://www.newadvent.org/fathers/01281.htm.

[12] Ibid.

[13] Ibid., 1.

[14] Kelly, *Early Christian Doctrines*, 8.

we learn that he supported the reliability of the Septuagint over other Jewish Old Testament translations. The reasons are provided within his discussion with Trypho.

Justin expressed his concern over words and other syntaxes missing in Jewish translations in relation to the Septuagint. He believes this was because of the Jewish translators' bias in opposition to the Christian sect of his day. These missing references were primarily associated with Old Testament messianic prophecies such as Isaiah 7:14 and Psalm 96:10.[15]

Within Justin's arguments over the reliability of translations of the Old Testament Scriptures, he sees the prophecies as being literally fulfilled in the life of Christ. This was the beginning of Justin Martyr's hermeneutical approach of interpretation.[16]

IRENAEUS OF LYONS—A.D. 130-201

Irenaeus of Lyon was born around 130 A.D. in Proconsular Asia and died around 201 A.D. Irenaeus served as bishop of Lugdunum (Lyon). As a young man he had connections with Bishop Polycarp and viewed as a disciple of the Apostle John. Irenaeus wrote extensively in Greek, which secured his place in Christian literature, of which only a few full versions of his works translated into Latin survived. The more important writings are explained here:

A treatise in five books, commonly entitled Adversus haereses, and devoted, according to its true title, to the "Detection and Overthrow of the False Knowledge" (see GNOSTICISM, sub-title Refutation of Gnosticism). Of this work, we possess a very ancient Latin translation, the scrupulous fidelity of which is beyond doubt. It is the chief work of Irenaeus and truly of the highest importance; it contains a profound exposition not only of Gnosticism under its different forms but also of the principal heresies which had sprung up in the various Christian communities and thus constitutes an invaluable source of information on the most ancient ecclesiastical literature from its beginnings to the end of the second century.[17]

Irenaeus' writings indicate that he understood the Old Testament prophecies to be fulfilled during the timeframe of the Apostle John's prophecies in a literal not allegorical way. Irenaeus writes,

And of this tabernacle Moses received the pattern in the mount; Exodus 25:40 and nothing is capable of being allegorized, but all things are steadfast, and true, and substantial, having been made by God for righteous men's enjoyment. For as it is God truly who raises up man, so also does man truly rise from the dead, and not allegorically, as I have shown repeatedly. And as he rises actually, so also shall he be actually disciplined beforehand for

---

[15] Justin Martyr Dialogue with Trypho 71-73.
[16] Ibid., 7.
[17] *The Catholic Encyclopedia*, vol. 8, s.v. "St. Irenaeus," by Albert Poncelet (New York: Robert Appleton Company, 1910.) 26 Apr. 2010 http://www.newadvent.org/cathen/08130b.htm.

incorruption, and shall go forwards and flourish in the times of the kingdom, in order that he may be capable of receiving the glory of the Father. Then, when all things are made new, he shall truly dwell in the city of God. For it is said, "He that sits on the throne said, Behold, I make all things new. And the Lord says, Write all this; for these words are faithful and true. And He said to me, They are done." Revelation 21:5-6 And this is the truth of the matter.[18]

Irenaeus' position on the binding of Satan is also taken in its literal context as we read:

> But when this Antichrist shall have devastated all things in this world, he will reign for three years and six months, and sit in the temple at Jerusalem; and then the Lord will come from heaven in the clouds, in the glory of the Father, sending this man and those who follow him into the lake of fire; but bringing in for the righteous the times of the kingdom, that is, the rest, the hallowed seventh day; and restoring to Abraham the promised inheritance, in which kingdom the Lord declared, that "many coming from the east and from the west should sit down with Abraham, Isaac, and Jacob." Matthew 8:11[19]

Irenaeus' statement supports the view of the Abrahamic covenant being fulfilled through an eternal earthly future kingdom after the Great Tribulation; thereupon supporting a literal approach to a Scriptural interpretation versus an allegorical one.

POST SECOND CENTURY VIEWS ON ESCHATOLOGY

ORIGEN ADAMANTIUS—A.D. 185-254

Edward Moore (Ph.D.) wrote an article about Origen for *The Internet Encyclopedia of Philosophy*. Through its summarization, we can learn the following.

[Origen of Alexandria was the first Christian theologian and philosopher to create a systematic approach in the establishment of some basis of orthodoxy. Origen found this necessary at a time in church history where there was widespread persecution and little consensus among the churches on biblical doctrine. Other Christian intellects confined themselves to apologetic and moralizing works—such as Clement of Alexandria (215 A.D.). Origen was developing a defense against Gnosticism and a pagan philosopher called Celsus, who mounted an attack on Christianity. This idea of creating some resemblance of a system or systematic approach came from his observations of the well-organized and systematic approach the Gnostic sect took to support their arguments.

Origen's response came through his theological treatise called, *On First Principles*, while his defense against the philosopher

---

[18] Irenaeus of Lyons *Against Heresies* 5, 35.2. *Ante-Nicene Fathers*, vol. 1. ed. Alexander Roberts, James Donaldson, and A. Cleveland Coxe, trans. Alexander Roberts and William Rambaut (Buffalo, NY: Christian Literature Publishing Co., 1885.)

Revised and edited for New Advent by Kevin Knight. http://www.newadvent.org/fathers/0103535.htm.

[19] Ibid., 5, 30.4.

Celsus came through his treatise called, *Against Celsus*.] [20]

Origen's Hermeneutical Principles

The key to understanding hermeneutical principles in church history between early and medieval times lies with the letter/spirit antithesis based on the reading and interpretation of Romans 2:25-29, 7:1-7, and Second Corinthians Chapter 3.

This connection is clearly made by Wai-Ching Chau (Th.D.) in his book *The Letter and the Spirit: A History of Interpretation from Origen to Luther*. He explains the concept this way: "To put it into a more testable form, it is our assumption that there are correspondences between one's understanding of the letter/spirit antithesis and hermeneutics and theology." [21] Chau's assumption is supported in Ernest Kasemann's article, *The spirit and the letter*, in which he writes, "it is well known that the letter/spirit antithesis has been used by the early and medieval church as the scriptural guarantee for the importance of the allegorical interpretation." [22]

The letter/spirit antithesis is based on the Scriptural use of the term found in Romans Chapters 2, 7 and Second Corinthians 3:5-6, which reads:

> Not that we are adequate in ourselves to consider anything as coming from ourselves, but our adequacy is from God, who also made us adequate as servants of a

new covenant, not of the letter, but of the Spirit; for the letter kills, but the Spirit gives life.

It is argued that the letter represents the law and the old covenant while the spirit represents the concepts of all the New Covenant stands for in Christ.

This argument leads to another argument over the doctrine of justification with respect to works within the New and Old Testaments. In the end, the argument of how one views the letter/spirit antithesis and applies it to their understanding of hermeneutical principles will determine how they interpret the Scriptures as a whole.

Another influential factor in Origen's hermeneutics is the philosophical base he was grounded in. Chau makes this observation, "It is apparent on reading *On First Principles* that its author operates according to a Middle-platonic scheme." [23]

Chau ties this influence to how Origen applies the letter/spirit antithesis in his treatise, *On First Principles*. [24]

Origen believed in the strict concept of the verbal inspiration of Scripture, stating, "Christ, the Word of God, was in Moses and the prophets." [25] In addition, he believed Christ was in the apostles. Therefore, there is no concept of progressive revelation with Origen.

Chau goes on to develop the argument that Origen's hermeneutic is the product of his twofold understanding of verbal

---

[20] *The Internet Encyclopedia of Philosophy*, s.v. "Origen of Alexandria (185—254 C.E.)," by Edward Moore. ISSN 2161-0002; available from https://www.iep.utm.edu/ origen-of-alexandria/; Internet; accessed 1 December 2018.

[21] Chau, *The Letter and the Spirit*, 3.

[22] Ernest Kasemann, "The Spirit and the Letter," in *Perspectives on Paul*, trans. M. Kohl (Philadelphia: Fortress, 1971), 139, quoted in Wai-Shing Chau: *The Letter and the Spirit* (New York: Peter Lang Publishing, 1995), 1.

[23] Chau, *The Letter and the Spirit*, 16.

[24] Ibid., 19.

[25] Origen De Principiis Preface 1. *Ante-Nicene Fathers*, vol. 4, ed. Alexander Roberts, James Donaldson, and A. Cleveland Coxe, trans. Frederick Crombie (Buffalo, NY: Christian Literature Publishing Co., 1885.) Revised and edited for New Advent by Kevin Knight; available from http://www.newadvent.org/fathers/ 04120.htm.

inspiration as it relates to his use of the letter/spirit antithesis. This is seen in his writing of the *Hexapla*. Chau makes this observation: "But interestingly, and seemingly paradoxically, this is also the basis for his allegorical interpretation of the Scripture." [26]

To understand the history of how the letter/spirit antithesis helped develop Scripture interpretations, consider the life of Theodore of Mopsuestia.

THEODORE OF MOPSUESTIA—A.D. 350-428

Theodore of Mopsuestia was born in 350 A.D. in Antioch, Syria and died around 428 A.D.

Theodore was a Syrian theologian, educated in classical literature and studied philosophy and rhetoric, serving as Bishop of Mopsuestia for thirty-six years.

Through the writings of his commentaries, Theodore primarily demonstrated the prevailing historical and grammatical method of the Antiochene School through his highly exegetical skill sets.[27]

Theodore of Mopsuestia Hermeneutics

Antiochene hermeneutics developed in opposition to the hermeneutics of the Alexandrian School took a different interpretable approach to the letter/spirit antithesis.[28]

By summarizing Wai-Ching Chau's (Th.D.) research, we learn that [Theodore of Mopsuestia was also its bishop between A.D. 392 and 428. He was honored by the Antiochenes as their interpreter and considered to be the most consistent in his application of Antiochene hermeneutical principles.

Theodore's version of hermeneutics interprets the letter/spirit antithesis in the following way. The letter represents the past and the spirit as the future, bringing about an historical attribute to this view. The letter is also seen as providing knowledge of good and evil, but without the power to do the right thing. The spirit represents the power to fulfill the law, acknowledging the knowledge that the letter brings.

From a hermeneutical perspective, the most obvious attribute related to Theodore's exegesis is an interpretation with strict historic literalism. This is also true regarding his allegorical interpretations, which he viewed as a language skill versus the approach of the Alexandrian School, which he opposed.

Theodore believed in the holy inspiration of the Scriptures, with two qualifiers that led him to believe the Old Testament could not be spiritualized, it could only be interpreted in the context of the writers and their history. This in turn created a problem for him, leaving the Old Testament irrelevant to the New Testament.

In recognizing this issue, he ties the two testaments together through typology and prophecy, reflecting on the words of the New Testament that became evident in the words of the Old Testament prophets.

Despite his efforts to harmonize the two testaments, Theodore had issues with his own views and ultimately held that Old Testament prophecies, due to their historical setting, remained in the Old Testament with very few exceptions, and

---

[26] Chau, *The Letter and the Spirit*, 20.

[27] *The Catholic Encyclopedia*, vol. 14, s.v. "Theodore of Mopsuestia," by Chrysostom Baur (New York: Robert Appleton Company, 1912.) 26

Apr. 2010 http://www.newadvent.org/cathen/14571b.htm.

[28] Chau, *The Letter and the Spirit*, 43.

believed very few prophecies were considered messianic.

This worked against the Christian claims of a new revelation found in Christ. It also made Alexandrian allegories null and void for lack of harmonization of both the Old and New Testaments.

All of this was a direct result of Theodore's view that the letter represented the past of the Old Testament and the spirit as the future, as represented by the New Testament. Theodore could not find how the two could be harmonized and become one unit through his philosophical hermeneutic.

The positive that came out of his work was the progress made in understanding of the Scriptures. The Pauline message of the Gospel was recognized as new, establishing the primary purpose of the law. In addition, the case for justification by grace in Christ alone would become even clearer in time.]
[29]

We find within *The Catholic Encyclopedia* conformation of Theodore's hermeneutic, as it expresses some of his history in the following way: "In his explanation of the Holy Writ Theodore employs primarily the prevailing historical and grammatical method of the Antiochene School." [30]

With his relationship to Justin Martyr and Irenaeus of Lyons, we begin to see the support for the literal versus the allegorical, but we also see the loss of understanding the literal fulfillment of Old Testament prophesies in the New Testament, even though Theodore took a literal approach to

his hermeneutics. These difficulties begin to work themselves out, as the historical timeline of hermeneutical development will reflect.

AUGUSTINE OF HIPPO—A.D. 354-430

The background of Augustine of Hippo is provided through several sources.

Augustine of Hippo was born November 13, 354 A.D. in Tagaste, Numidia—now Souk Ahras, Algeria, and died August 28, 430 A.D. in Hippo Regius—now Annaba, Algeria.

Augustine served as bishop of Hippo from 396 to 430 A.D. He was a Catholic theologian/philosopher who infused Christian doctrine with Neoplatonism.

Augustine wrote numerous works, of which the more important were, *Confessions*, written in 400 A.D., and *The City of God*, written between 413 and 426 A.D., which helped shape the practice of biblical exegesis while laying a foundation for medieval and modern Christian thought.[31]

"One of the decisive developments in the western philosophical tradition was the eventually widespread merging of the Greek philosophical tradition and the Judeo-Christian religious and scriptural traditions." [32]

A response given on Augustine's defense to the question of his dedication to

---

[29] Chau, *The Letter and the Spirit*, 48-65.

[30] *The Catholic Encyclopedia*. vol. 14, s.v. "Theodore of Mopsuestia," by Chrysostom Baur (New York: Robert Appleton Company, 1912); available from http://www.newadvent.org/cathen/14571b.htm; Internet; accessed 13 October 2018.

[31] *The Internet Encyclopedia of Philosophy*, s.v. "Augustine (354—430 C.E.)," by J. Mark Mattox. ISSN 2161-0002; available from

https://www.iep.utm.edu/augustin/ #H7; Internet; accessed 1 December 2018.

[32] *The Stanford Encyclopedia of Philosophy* (Winter 2016 Edition), s.v. "Saint Augustine," by Michael Mendelson, ed. Edward N. Zalta available from https://plato.stanford.edu/archives/win2016/entries/augustine/; Internet; accessed 9 October 2018.

his faith versus his views in Greek philosophy follows:

> The object of his philosophy is to give authority the support of reason, and "for him the great authority, that which dominates all others and from which he never wished to deviate, is the authority of Christ;" and if he loves the Platonists it is because he counts on finding among them interpretations always in harmony with his faith (Against the Academics, III, c. x).[33]

Augustine's Hermeneutical Principles

Augustine's hermeneutics developed over his lifespan, changed at different points in his life. Chau comments: "It is a well-known fact that Augustine's ideas are constantly in process during his lifetime. A study of his doctrine on the letter and the spirit involves nothing less than tracking of his development." [34] Chau goes on to say that between 391 and 395 A.D., Augustine believed the spirit and letter antithesis represented a literal and figurative interpretation of the Old Testament, with Christ being the key to understanding the figurative. However, this changed in 396 A.D.,[35] as Augustine writes,

> The law is 'letter' to those who do not fulfill it in the spirit of charity to which the New Testament belongs. So those who are dead to sin are freed from the letter which holds guilty those who do not fully

obey what is written. The law is nothing else than a 'letter' to those who can read it but cannot fulfill it….

> Hence 'the letter killeth, but the spirit giveth life.' The law, when merely read and not understood or fulfilled, killeth. In that case, it is called 'the letter.' But the spirit giveth life because the fulfillment of the law is charity shed abroad in our heart by the Holy Spirit which is given to us.[36]

Augustine as a theologian/philosopher held a dualism in his religious beliefs. He confessed to being part of the Manichaeism sect, a third-century religion based on multiple religious views held at the time, that died out around the tenth century. In 397 A.D., Augustine was confronted with a philosophical position held to be a part of Manichaeism that shed light on his faulty thinking on the subject of the letter and spirit antithesis. This caused him great distress, leading him to abandon Manichaeism for the Catholic doctrinal position.[37]

After evaluating Augustine's life experience on this matter, it is clear his doctrinal position on the letter and spirit antithesis reverted to his views prior to 396 A.D.[38]

Through his writing of *On Christian Doctrine*, Augustine defines his hermeneutics on literal and allegorical

---

[33] *The Catholic Encyclopedia*, vol. 2, s.v. "Life of St. Augustine of Hippo," by Eugène Portalié (New York: Robert Appleton Company, 1907); available from http://www.newadvent.org/cathen/02084a.htm; Internet; accessed 9 October 2018.

[34] Chau, *The Letter and the Spirit*, 75.

[35] Ibid., 76.

[36] Augustine, "To Simplician on Various Questions" (I.1.17), Augustine: Early Writings,

p.385, quoted in Wai-Shing Chau: *The Letter and the Spirit* (New York: Peter Lang Publishing, 1995), 77.

[37] Augustine Confessions 5, V24. *Nicene and Post-Nicene Fathers*, First Series, vol. 1, ed. Philip Schaff, trans. J.G. Pilkington, (Buffalo, NY: Christian Literature Publishing Co., 1887.) Revised and edited for New Advent by Kevin Knight. http://www.newadvent.org/fathers/110105.htm.

[38] Chau, *The Letter and the Spirit*, 84.

interpretation, expressing his views in the following manner:

> But in addition to the foregoing rule, which guards us against taking a metaphorical form of speech as if it were literal, we must also pay heed to that which tells us not to take a literal form of speech as if it were figurative. In the first place, then, we must show the way to find out whether a phrase is literal or figurative. And the way is certainly as follows: Whatever there is in the word of God that cannot when taken literally, be referred either to purity of life or soundness of doctrine, you may set down as figurative. Purity of life has reference to the love of God and one's neighbor, soundness of doctrine to the knowledge of God and one's neighbor. Every man, moreover, has hope in his own conscience, so far as he perceives that he has attained to the love and knowledge of God and his neighbor. Now all these matters have been spoken of in the first book.[39]

The result of Augustine's life work stabilized the concept of how and when literalism and allegory should be used in relation to Origen's hermeneutical approach, which was much more frequent.

Augustine's Contribution to Amillennialism

Augustine held to five theological views that are characteristics of Amillennialism.

1. Augustine believed the millennium could only be interpreted two ways: First, the last part of this age, up to the Second Advent, represents the millennium. This was based on his allegorical interpretation of the concept of six days we work, followed by the Sabbath—the day of rest. Second, the millennium represents all generations based on his allegorical interpretation of Psalm 105:8: "He has remembered His covenant forever, The word which He commanded to a thousand generations...." Consequently, Augustine concludes "to a thousand generations," represents all generations since the enactment of the New Covenant, beginning at the time of Christ.[40]

2. Augustine rejects the concept of a literal millennial reign of Christ because of the mishandling of Scriptures by carnal believers, whom he called *Millenarians*.[41]

3. Augustine, through these two previous positions, recognized a literal thousand-year period.

4. Augustine believed the binding of Satan found in Revelation 20 took place during Christ's ministry on earth.[42]

[39] Augustine On Christian Doctrine III.14. *Nicene and Post-Nicene Fathers*, First Series, vol. 2, ed. Philip Schaff, trans. James Shaw, (Buffalo, NY: Christian Literature Publishing Co., 1887.) Revised and edited for New Advent by Kevin Knight. ttp://www.newadvent.org/fathers/12023.htm.

[40] Augustine The City of God 20.7. *Nicene and Post-Nicene Fathers*, First Series, vol. 2, ed. Philip Schaff, trans. Marcus Dods (Buffalo, NY: Christian Literature Publishing Co., 1887.) Revised and edited for New Advent by Kevin Knight. http://www.newadvent.org/fathers/ 120120.htm.

[41] Ibid.

[42] Ibid.

5. Augustine believed what the Scriptures called *The Great Tribulation*—a 3 ½ year period, occurs after the millennial period is completed.[43] This is based on his dealing with Revelation 20 through an allegorical interpretation of Matthew 12:29: "Or how can anyone enter the strong man's house and carry off his property, unless he first binds the strong man? And then he will plunder his house." This story appears in all three synoptic gospels. Augustine's interpretation is lengthy and repeated several times throughout his writings in *The City of God*.[44]

Following Augustine, the historical timeline for hermeneutical development flows into how others viewed the Scriptures. This can be seen in the *Glossa Ordinaria*.

GLOSSA ORDINARIA—COMPILED BETWEEN THE 9TH AND 14TH CENTURIES

The *Glossa Ordinaria* is a collection of glosses or individual notes giving an explanation of how church Fathers and other biblical Medieval Time scholars interpreted the meaning behind words and passages of the Scriptures. How these glosses influenced modern-day biblical hermeneutics begins with the following explanations:

The historiography of recent decades has largely shown the importance of the glosses on the Bible for medieval culture, profane as well as religious. Among them, the Glossa Ordinaria, originating at the cathedral school of Laon at the threshold of the 12th century, played a capital role in the history of exegesis, preaching and theology, at least until the end of the Middle Ages.[45]

As Scriptural commentaries, there are two celebrated glosses on the Vulgate. The former is the "Glossa Ordinaria," thus called from its common use during the Middle Ages. Its author, the German Walafrid Strabo (died 849), had some knowledge of Greek and made extracts chiefly from the Latin Fathers and from the writings of his master, Rabanus Maurus, for the purpose of illustrating the various senses—principally the literal sense—of all the books of Holy Writ. This gloss is quoted as a high authority by St. Thomas Aquinas, and it was known as "the tongue of Scripture." Until the seventeenth century, it remained the favorite commentary on the Bible; and it was only gradually superseded by more independent works of exegesis.[46]

---

[43] Augustine *The City of God* 20.13.

[44] Ibid., 20.8.

[45] Glossae.net, "A project for the electronic edition of the Glossa Ordinaria of the Bible," [database online]; available from http://glossae.net/ en/content/project-electronic-edition-glossa-ordinaria-bible; Internet; accessed 22 October 2018.

[46] *The Catholic Encyclopedia*, vol. 6, s.v. "Scriptural Glosses," by Francis Gigot (New York: Robert Appleton Company, 1909.) 26 Apr. 2010 http://www.newadvent.org/cathen/06586a.htm.

The Hermeneutics behind the Glossa Ordinaria

Wai-Shing Chau's (Th.D.) analysis of the *Glossa Ordinaria* is expressed as follows:

> As might be expected, the *Glossa Ordinaria* mainly follows Augustine's trend of thought in interpreting the letter and the spirit. In fact, Augustine's treatise *On the Spirit and the Letter* is often quoted. Following this doctor of grace, the *Glossa Ordinaria* understands the spirit as the grace of the new testament bestowed in Christ, pertaining to all the three categories of knowledge, delight, and charity. Thus the human predicament is understood as being defective simultaneously in mind, will, and power. Again, the distinction between the old and the new testament is clear-cut. The newness of the gospel is upheld at the expense of the old.[47]

The Glossa is seen to break away from Origin's allegorical interpretations of the Old Testament, but instead, through its own version of allegory, upholds the historical setting of Old Testament passages, upholding the concept that "only through faith in Christ that the law is fulfilled." [48]

Some conclusions drawn from the Glossa are supported by Christ's statement found in Matthew 5:17: "Do not think that I came to abolish the Law or the Prophets; I did not come to abolish, but to fulfill."

The next significant person in the historical timeline of hermeneutics is Thomas Aquinas.

THOMAS AQUINAS—A.D. 1225-1274

Thomas Aquinas, philosopher, theologian, Doctor of the Church (Angelicus Doctor), patron of Catholic universities, colleges and schools. Born at Rocca Secca in the Kingdom of Naples, 1225 or 1227; died at Fossa Nuova, 7 March 1274.

The principles of St. Thomas on the relations between faith and reason were solemnly proclaimed in the Vatican Council. The second, third, and fourth chapters of the Constitution "Dei Filius" read like pages taken from the works of the Angelic Doctor. First, reason alone is not sufficient to guide men: they need Revelation; we must carefully distinguish the truths known by reason from higher truths (mysteries) known by Revelation. Secondly, reason and Revelation, though distinct, are not opposed to each other. Thirdly, faith preserves reason from error; reason should do service in the cause of faith. Fourthly, this service is rendered in three ways:

- reason should prepare the minds of men to receive the Faith by proving the truths which faith presupposes (praeambula fidei);
- reason should explain and develop the truths of Faith

---

[47] Chau, *The Letter and the Spirit*, 113.

[48] Ibid.,115-116.

and should propose them in scientific form;

- reason should defend the truths revealed by Almighty God.[49]

Ralph McInerny, author of *St. Thomas Aquinas*, and John O'Callaghan (Ph.D.), who has research interests in Medieval Philosophy, Thomas Aquinas, and Thomistic Metaphysics, co-authored an article posted online with *The Stanford Encyclopedia of Philosophy*.

The article provides some insight into how Thomas Aquinas fits into church history and his handling of the issues of faith and reason through the mix of philosophy and theology.

The following is an excerpt from that article.

Thomas Aquinas (1225–1274) lived at a critical juncture of western culture when the arrival of the Aristotelian *corpus* in Latin translation reopened the question of the relation between faith and reason, calling into question the *modus vivendi* that had obtained for centuries. This crisis flared up just as universities were being founded. Thomas, after early studies at Montecassino, moved on to the University of Naples, where he met members of the new Dominican Order. It was at Naples too that Thomas had his first extended contact with the new learning. When he joined the Dominican Order, he went north to study with Albertus

Magnus, author of a paraphrase of the Aristotelian *corpus*. Thomas completed his studies at the University of Paris, which had been formed out of the monastic schools on the Left Bank and the cathedral school at Notre Dame. In two stints as a regent master, Thomas defended the mendicant orders and, of greater historical importance, countered both the Averroistic interpretations of Aristotle and the Franciscan tendency to reject Greek philosophy. The result was a new *modus vivendi* between faith and philosophy, which survived until the rise of the new physics. The Catholic Church has over the centuries regularly and consistently reaffirmed the central importance of Thomas's work, both theological and philosophical, for understanding its teachings concerning the Christian revelation, and his close textual commentaries on Aristotle represent a cultural resource, which is now receiving increased recognition.[50]

It is evident that the battle over which philosophical system would have the biggest influence on Christian theology in the medieval period was coming, and Thomas Aquinas played a major role in reshaping how the Christian world would build its hermeneutical principles up to the time of the Reformation and far beyond.

The Hermeneutics of Thomas Aquinas

Thomas' interpretation of the letter/spirit antithesis differs from Origin, as he adopts

[49] *The Catholic Encyclopedia*, vol. 14, s.v. "St. Thomas Aquinas," by Daniel Kennedy (New York: Robert Appleton Company, 1912.) 26 Apr. 2010 http://www.newadvent.org/cathen/14663b.htm.
[50] *The Stanford Encyclopedia of Philosophy*, Summer 2018 Edition, s.v. "Saint Thomas Aquinas," by

Ralph McInerny and John O'Callaghan, ed. Edward N. Zalta; available from https://plato.stanford.edu/archives/sum2018/entries/aquinas/; Internet; accessed 24 October 2018.

the Augustinian tradition with some changes based on understandings of his own.[51]

Chau expresses these changes as a combination of applying philosophical thought to Thomas' theological understanding.

> Thus it seems that Thomas' understanding of the letter and the spirit is a synthesis of Augustine and Paul, Plato, and Aristotle. He modifies Augustine's understanding of Paul's strong emphasis on the death and resurrection in Christ and the newness of the gospel. And he supplants the lower levels of Platonic metaphysics with an Aristotelian one.[52]

This mixture of philosophy affected Thomas' theology, as Chau explains:

> 'The letter' is the imperfect figure of the old law, which is fulfilled by Christ, in whom true knowledge, 'the spirit,' is granted. He also seems to have extended the notion of 'letter' to include all knowledge gained through natural senses, as opposed to the true knowledge, the eternal vision, that is granted in 'the spirit.'[53]

Why is all this important? Because it allowed Thomas, as a theologian, a more valid interpretational view of the Scriptures, versus those of the past, this is seen through Thomas' interpretation of Second Corinthians Chapter 3, with relation to how it relates to others in the past, applying the letter/spirit antitheses test.

Chau summarizes Thomas' view this way:

> 'The letter' is apparently taken here as equivalent to the written Mosaic law, which cannot offer help to sinners. 'the spirit' is referred to as the Holy Spirit who gives new life to those in Christ. The letter gives way to the spirit and is abandoned. But Thomas does not mean that there is no law in the spirit. Rather, the Holy Spirit perfects the mind by imprinting the law in the hearts, and molds it with charity, so that doing good work according to the law becomes a natural habit that no longer requires guidance by external precepts. Thomas understands this as the freedom of the Christian.[54]

This interpretation falls more in line with the New Covenant as expressed in Jeremiah 31:31-34, and more specifically with verse 33, which states: "'But this is the covenant which I will make with the house of Israel after those days,' declares the Lord, 'I will put My law within them, and on their heart I will write it; and I will be their God, and they shall be My people.'" Christ in Matthew 5:17-20 supports this concept:

> Do not think that I came to abolish the Law or the Prophets; I did not come to abolish, but to fulfill. For truly I say to you, until heaven and earth pass away, not the smallest letter or stroke shall pass away from the Law, until all is accomplished. Whoever then annuls one of the least of these

[51] Chau, *The Letter and the Spirit*, 130.
[52] David Knowles, *The Evolution of Medieval Thought* (Baltimore: Helicon, 1962), 257, quoted in Wai-Shing Chau: *The Letter and the Spirit* (New York: Peter Lang Publishing, 1995), 132.
[53] Chau, *The Letter and the Spirit*, 129.
[54] Ibid., 128.

commandments, and so teaches others, shall be called least in the kingdom of heaven; but whoever keeps and teaches them, he shall be called great in the kingdom of heaven. For I say to you, that unless your righteousness surpasses that of the scribes and Pharisees, you shall not enter the kingdom of heaven.

Thomas Aquinas also believed in progressive revelation, that is, God's revelation comes to us in stages,[55] which supports the dispensational position within the study of Eschatology. This also seems to be the same pattern reflected in the history of hermeneutics, as its development has come to us in stages.

Thomas also held the position that "Justification is by grace alone because the power to turn, to believe, to hope, and to love are all bestowed only in Christ. Thomas emphasizes that salvation involves nothing less than the death and resurrection." [56]

Thomas' Scriptural interpretations fall under two hermeneutical principles, the literal and the spiritual. By combining all other interpretational concepts like historical or literal, tropological or moral, allegorical, and anagogical, into his two principles, he creates a system that gets him closer to a more reasonable approach that falls in line with understanding the original intent of the Scriptures.

This is borne out through his interpretations being more in line with today's interpretations then those of Origin or even Augustine's.

He combines historical, etiological, analogical and parabolic and includes them into his version of a literal concept.[57]

This is similar to Milton S. Terry (S.T.D.), in his book *Biblical Hermeneutics* (1883), which creates two approaches similar to Thomas Aquinas, referencing them as General and Special Hermeneutics.[58]

Paul Lee Tan's (Th.D.) approach in his hermeneutic book *The Interpretation of Prophecy* (1974) combines all forms of interpretation under one umbrella called the Grammatico-Historical Method.[59] Tan states:

> To "interpret" means to explain the original sense of a speaker or writer. To interpret "literally" means to explain the original sense of the speaker or writer according to the normal, customary, and proper usages of words and language. Literal interpretation of the Bible simply means to explain the original sense of the Bible according to the normal and customary usage of its language.
>
> In order to determine the normal and customary usage of Bible language, it is necessary to consider the accepted rules of grammar and rhetoric, as well as the factual historical and cultural data of Bible times. Therefore, the literal method of interpretation is also called the Grammatical-Historical Method.[60]

Thomas, not having any knowledge of the future development of hermeneutics,

---

[55] Chau, *The Letter and the Spirit*, 129.

[56] Ibid., 131.

[57] *The Summa Theologiæ of St. Thomas Aquinas*, Sacred Doctrine, 1.10, 2d. rev. ed., 1920, trans. Fathers of the English Dominican Province [Online Edition]; available from

http://www.newadvent.org/summa/; Internet; accessed 27 October 20018.

[58] Milton S. Terry, *Biblical Hermeneutics* (New York: Eaton & Mains, 1890), 17.

[59] Tan, *The Interpretation of Prophecy*, 29.

[60] Ibid.

unwittingly provides Tan's work some support as he states:

> Since the literal sense is that which the author intends, and since the author of Holy Writ is God, Who by one act comprehends all things by His intellect, it is not unfitting, as Augustine says (Confess. xii), if, even according to the literal sense, one word in Holy Writ should have several senses.[61]

Under one sense called literalism, Tan recognizes parts of valid speech, such as the various classifications in the figures of speech listed here: Simile, Metaphor, Metonymy, Synecdoche, Irony, Personification, Apostrophe, Allegory, Hyperbole, Parable, Riddle and Fable, all falling under Tan's definition of literal interpretation.[62]

As this study progresses, these concepts will be developed more fully.

NICHOLAS OF LYRA—A.D. 1270-1349

Nicholas Of Lyra was born in 1270 A.D. in Vieille-Lyre, Normandy, and died in Paris in October 1349 A.D.

Nicholas was "sometimes hailed as the greatest medieval exegete."[63] Nicholas had a long-time teaching relationship with the educational institution Sorbonne. "The College of Sorbonne (French: Collège de Sorbonne) was a theological college of the University of Paris, founded in 1253 by Robert de Sorbon (1201–1274), after whom it was named." [64]

The importance of Nicholas' work can be found in his 50-volume commentary on the whole Bible, which was the first of its kind to be printed. The significance of this work were the emphasis on literal versus an allegorical method of interpretation of the Holy Scriptures. "Though his influence on Luther has been rightly denied, the wide acceptance of his *Postilla Litteralis* suggests his great influence on exegesis in the following couple of centuries." [65]

The Hermeneutics of Nicholas of Lyra

Nicholas' hermeneutics build on Thomas Aquinas, as he takes on a similar approach to the understanding of the letter/spirit antithesis. However, Nicholas moves further towards a literal interpretation, not denying the spiritual sense but creating a new way of looking at how it is applied.[66]

Thomas' approach was to understand the Scriptures in a literal sense, and a literal spiritual sense, represented as the literal and the spiritual.[67] Nicholas advocated for a double literal sense. "Where Thomas distinguishes between the human literal sense and the divine literal sense, Nicholas lumps the two together as the double intention of a human author." [68] This meant Nicholas could interpret the Old Testament in its historical context as literal, but then apply a messianic spiritual meaning to the same text, tying it to the New Testament, thus providing context and continuity to the whole of scripture.

---

[61] *The Summa Theologiæ of St. Thomas Aquinas*, Sacred Doctrine 1.10.

[62] Tan, *The Interpretation of Prophecy*, 140.

[63] Chau, *The Letter and the Spirit*, 149.

[64] *Wikipedia*, s.v. "College of Sorbonne," [encyclopedia on line]; available from https://en.wikipedia.org/wiki/College_of_Sorbonne; Internet; accessed 29 November 2018.

[65] Chau, The Letter and the Spirit, 149.

[66] Ibid., 154.

[67] Ibid.

[68] Ibid.

This is similar to Paul Lee Tan's approach. Tan explains:

> Spiritualizers believe that since the Bible is spiritual in nature, the interpreter should penetrate behind the speech to the living Spirit. They believe that the written words of Scripture simply cannot contain all that is in the Spirit's mind, and that to interpret the words literally is to miss the true meaning of the Bible....[69]
>
> Literal Interpreters, of course, recognize that the Scripture contains spiritual truths which no uninspired Shakespeare could produce. The Bible is divine both in its origin and in its content, and, as such, it is certainly *spiritual*. The proper method of getting to know the spiritual truth, however, is not through *spiritualization*. Spiritual truths when revealed, are revealed as the written Word of God. Literal interpretation of that which is written brings out these truths.[70]

It would appear the issue with Thomas', Nicholas' and Tan's approach is resolved in the answer to the question, how should one understand the figurative language of the Scriptures. Tan gives the following explanation for dealing with this issue:

> The presence of figures in Scripture, however, does not militate against a literal interpretation. Since literal interpretation properly accepts that which is normal and customary in language—and figurative language is certainly

normal and customary—literal interpreters are not hindered by that which is figurative. There is no necessity to change to a different method of interpretation.[71]

This approach also worked for Nicholas, as Chau summarizes:

> This difference from Thomas correlates with their differences in the understanding of the letter as figure. For Nicholas, the Old Testament words also served as signs for the spiritual truth. Thus the spiritual meaning was already contained in the use of words in the Old Testament and was already revealed to the Old Testament author.[72]

To summarize our hermeneutical history, we see the struggle in how to understand the historical from the spiritual nature of the Scriptures has been an ongoing process. Through God's grace and help, a better understanding to this issue is emerging from the struggles of good men, as they pursue the best approach to biblical interpretation and how we should be interpreting the Holy Scriptures.

It should not be forgotten how we come to understand spiritual knowledge. From a human perspective, knowledge comes from one's culture, experience, and education. God then adds his wisdom to this knowledge, which produces true understanding, even truth based on his creation or the natural. We see this concept supported in First Corinthians 2:11-14, James 3:13-17, Proverbs 3:19-20, 4:7 and 2:6. Through understanding these passages,

[69] Gustav Friedrich Oehler, *Theology of the Old Testament*, rev, trans. George E. Day (New York: Funk and Wagnalls Pubs., 1883), 491, quoted in Tan, *The Interpretation of Prophecy*, 32.

[70] Tan, *The Interpretation of Prophecy*, 32.
[71] Ibid., 31.
[72] Chau, The Letter and the Spirit, 154.

the following statement becomes valid: "God's wisdom, plus knowledge equals understanding." [73]

Our historical understanding of the development of hermeneutics will conclude with Martin Luther and the reformation movement. This is not to suggest the discipline of hermeneutics has not been influenced by others throughout history, but for this study the more important points have been covered for understanding how the interpretive methods of our subject matter—Eschatology—has developed over time.

MARTIN LUTHER—A.D. 1483-1546

Martin Luther, the primary contributor in a key change to understanding the letter/spirit antithesis, was also a major player in changing the hermeneutical approach to the Scriptures.

This new approach resulted in how Luther saw and understood the doctrine of salvation, which was by faith through Christ alone.

Martin Luther was born November 10, 1483, in Eisleben, (Saxony Germany) and died February 18, 1546, in Eisleben.

Through summarizing Warren Quanbeck's lecture on Luther, we learn that [Luther was influenced primarily by three individuals, William of Occam, St. Augustine, and Faber Stapulensis.

William influenced Luther in several areas of thinking. First, in the area of epistemology, changing the emphasis of the times from the intellectualism of Thomas Aquinas to voluntarism. Second, his influence reaches into the area of establishing the truth of revelation and the authority of the church, which came through understanding the authority of the Scriptures instead of human reasoning. Thirdly, through the teaching of the absolute power of God, with the corresponding view of the issue of voluntarism, which promoted the idea of human power—man can do anything he wills.

Augustine's influence came through his understanding of the spirit and letter antithesis. "Augustine, and Faber after him, taught that the letter is dead until made alive by the Spirit's work. The Scriptures become God's Word only when the Spirit accomplishes a correspondence between the reader and the realities of the Spirit in Scripture" [74]

The breakthrough in Luther's theology came when he realized that the Gospel not only represented the wrath of God toward sin but the Grace of God toward the sinner. Therefore, God is not only judging, he is also justifying. This brings Luther to a new understanding of the Scriptures that could only be realized through faith in Christ. The work of God is found in Christ, foreshadowed by the Old Covenant.

Luther sums up his views by stating, "The Work and power of God is faith, for He himself makes men righteous and works all virtues." [75]

This discovery came not through men, or philosophical thought or reason, but through the Holy Spirit revealing truth directly from the Scriptures. This realization of God speaking directly from the Bible caused Luther to place all

---

[73] Reid A. Ashbaucher, *Made in the Image of God: Understanding the Nature of God and Mankind in a Changing World*, 2 rev ed. (Toledo: Reid Ashbaucher, 2017), 61.

[74] Warren A. Quanbeck, "Luther's Early Exegesis," in *Luther Today*, Martin Luther Lectures vol.1 (Docorah, IA: Luther College Press, 1957), 47.

[75] Ibid., 57.

authority for faith and practice in life on the Scriptures, leaving the Pope's, bishop's, and council's tradition secondary.

Luther was especially influenced by French humanist Lefevre d'Etaples who was also known as Faber Stapulensis.

Faber believed that the Holy Spirit was the true author of the Scriptures, that the literal sense is what the Holy Spirit intends for understanding, which included prophetic passages. He taught a system of a double literal sense, a literal-historical sense, and a literal-prophetic sense. Faber also believed that only the Holy Spirit could bring understanding to the Scriptures.] [76]

David Whitford (Ph.D.) wrote an article providing further insight between Thomas Aquinas and Martin Luther's view on the use of philosophy and reason within their theology.

German theologian, professor, pastor, and church reformer. Luther began the Protestant Reformation with the publication of his Ninety-Five Theses on October 31, 1517. In this publication, he attacked the Church's sale of indulgences. He advocated a theology that rested on God's gracious activity in Jesus Christ, rather than in human works. Nearly all Protestants trace their history back to Luther in one way or another. Luther's relationship to philosophy is complex and should not be judged only by his famous statement that "reason is the devil's whore."

Given Luther's critique of philosophy and his famous phrase that philosophy is the "devil's whore," it would be easy to assume that Luther had only contempt for philosophy and reason. Nothing could be further from the truth. Luther believed, rather, that philosophy and reason had important roles to play in our lives and in the life of the community. However, he also felt that it was important to remember what those roles were and not to confuse the proper use of philosophy with an improper one.

Properly understood and used, philosophy and reason are a great aid to individuals and society. Improperly used, they become a great threat to both. Likewise, revelation and the gospel when used properly are an aid to society, but when misused also have sad and profound implications. [77]

Through the summarization of Wai-Shing Chau's (Th.D.) research, we also learn [Martin Luther's hermeneutics started out just as it had for Augustine, in stages. Luther's understanding of Genesis 29:8-10 concerning Moses, allegorically, helped him see, "as the truth is veiled under language, it can be easily misunderstood if it is interpreted grammatically and historically instead of as a figure of some future truth." [78] This led Luther to understand the letter/spirit distinction to represent the old Law of Moses as the letter that kills, and his prophetic interpretations to represent the Spirit, much like that of his past predecessors. [79]

---

[76] Quanbeck, "Luther's Early Exegesis," in *Luther Today*, 42-64.

[77] *The Internet Encyclopedia of Philosophy*, s.v. "Martin Luther (1483—1546)," by David M. Whitford. ISSN 2161-0002; available from

https://www.iep.utm.edu/luther/; Internet; accessed 29 November 2018.

[78] Chau, *The Letter and the Spirit*, 164.

[79] Ibid., 166.

Things changed for Luther as he saw the spirit representing several things: it tied the word of God, the spiritual interpretation for understanding Christ and the church, to Christ; while at the same time the letter was seen to include "all veiled revelation of God, in contrast to the spirit which is the simple word of God." [80] In the end, how Luther saw the letter and the spirit became blurred, making the two terms relative.

Through his studies, he comes to realize that God is not just love, but also the God who loves.[81] These observations lead Luther to see God not just giving the power to keep the law, but also providing a love-motivating attitude to keep the law. This caused him to see the law in a new light.

In his lectures on Romans between 1515 and 1516, "he commented on Romans 2:25-29 that the true circumcision is not an external circumcision of the flesh, but an internal one of the heart. And a true Jew is one inwardly, not apparently. So the apparent Jew who is circumcised physically does not really keep the law,[82] 'because the law is spiritual. They, however, are keeping the Law only outwardly according to the letter.'" [83]

Luther began to see the law as spiritual when fulfilled in grace. "The law is no longer the law of the letter, but the law of the spirit, written on the hearts by the finger of God." Luther saw the law that points to grace, not the letter that kills.[84]

Now "the letter and the spirit cannot be distinguished objectively and outwardly. It all depends on how it is heard. Without the Holy Spirit, a proclamation of the gospel is nothing but empty letter. But with the infusion of the Holy Spirit, every law becomes spiritual and directs toward Christ." [85]

In 1521, Luther adds an element to his interpretations by tying the letter and spirit to conscience. After 1532, Luther finalizes his view on the letter/spirit antithesis and understood that grace is required for spiritual understanding, and knowledge is always seen as a divine gift.[86]

Luther made a major change in his views and began to see the law and the gospel in their functional capacity instead of an ontological identity.[87]

This change was more in methodology than content, leading Luther down a road that created this result in his thinking:

> The law is still seen to be fulfilled in faith, and the spirit enables the true keeping of the law. One significant consequence of such a change in methodology is the dismissal of the significatory notion of the letter. The letter is perspicuous and has to be understood according to the historical-grammatical meaning. In this way, the final barricade of allegorical interpretation is torn down.[88]

This left Luther with the view that "the law is such a peculiar thing that when one intends to keep it, one, in fact, violates it. In order to truly keep the law, one has to neglect it but fulfill it naturally out of

[80] Chau, *The Letter and the Spirit*, 166.
[81] Ibid., 168.
[82] Ibid., 169.
[83] *Luther*, vol. 25, "lectures on Romans," ed. Hilton C. Oswald, trans. Walter G. Tillmann and Jacob A. O. (St. Louis: Concordia, 1972), 23, quoted in Wai-Shing Chau: *The Letter and the Spirit* (New York: Peter Lang Publishing, 1995), 169.
[84] Chau, *The Letter and the Spirit*, 173.
[85] Ibid., 175.
[86] Ibid., 182.
[87] Ibid., 183.
[88] Ibid.

gratitude and love." [89] "The law is spiritually kept only when it is spiritually understood and fulfilled in grace." [90]

This is the true meaning behind the New Covenant when God says, "But this is the covenant which I will make with the house of Israel after those days,' declares the Lord, 'I will put My law within them, and on their heart I will write it; and I will be their God, and they shall be My people." (Jeremiah 31:33)

These concepts of Luther are similar to those expressed by Thomas Aquinas. The difference being Luther expanded his understanding to reformulate his hermeneutical application based on the understanding of charity, or the love of God as expressed in the gospel message.

Another consequence of Luther's hermeneutics resulted in things that affected his eschatological positions.

First, the literal interpretation shifts from Christ and the church as a subject and speaks to the actual Old Testament, pre-advent situation. Second, the prophetic is understood not as the church, but as the faithful synagogue awaiting Christ's coming.[91] The result is, the voice of the Old Testament is heard, and the historical is not opposed within the prophetic word.] [92]

Epilogue

The tradition of Luther's new hermeneutic lacked full acceptance by other reformers who followed, such as Philipp Melanchthon (1497-1560), Matthias Flacius (1520-1575), and John Calvin (1509-1564), whose defining difference with Luther laid with the concept of tying conscience to the hearing of the Word.[93] This concept eluded Calvin in his theological approach.

Later these differences will manifest themselves in the eschatological approaches of others.

Following the history of today's hermeneutical development, three major resources have emerged in the development of hermeneutical approaches, moving the development of biblical eschatological interpretations into the twenty-first century.

Thomas Aquinas' writings found in his systematic theology work are called *Summa Theologica*, which was twice endorsed by the Roman Catholic Church; once in 1879 by Pope Leo XIII, who "wrote the encyclical *Aeterni Patris* (Eternal Father), 'On the Restoration of Christian Philosophy according to the Mind of St. Thomas Aquinas, the Angelic Doctor.' Wanting to ensure coherence between philosophy and Roman Catholic theology, the Pope officially sanctioned the philosophy of Thomas Aquinas as the proper philosophy to carry out this program." [94] And a second time "in 1917, the Code of Canon Law, promulgated by Pope Benedict XV, required that the study of philosophy and theology in all institutes of higher education, including seminaries, must be carried out 'according to the arguments, doctrine, and principles of St. Thomas which they are inviolable to hold.'" [95] By the 1930s, Karl Rahner, who was and remains the most influential Roman Catholic

---

[89] Chau, *The Letter and the Spirit*, 184.

[90] Ibid., 169.

[91] James Samuel Preus, *Luther and the Old Testament*, trans. Eric W. and Ruth C. Gritsch (Philadelphia: Fortress, 1969), 227-248, quoted in Wai-Shing Chau: *The Letter and the Spirit* (New York: Peter Lang Publishing, 1995), 186.

[92] Chau, *The Letter and the Spirit*, 164-186.

[93] Ibid., 184.

[94] James C. Livingston, *Modern Christian Thought: The Twentieth Century*, 2d. ed., vol. 2 (Minneapolis, MN: Fortress Press, 2006), 197.

[95] Printed as a preface to *St. Thomas Aquinas, Summa Theologica*, vol. 1 (New York, 1920), xvi, quoted in Livingston, *Modern Christian Thought*, 2 ed., vol. 2, 197.

theologian of the twentieth century and wrote thousands of publications, became a major influencer of Catholic theology.[96]

In addition, Rahner edited collections of documents on the Vatican II and a multi-volume commentary on the Council that became the standard reference commentary. This editorial work enabled Rahner's theology to exercise a broad influence on Roman Catholic theology.[97]

Milton S. Terry

On the Protestant side, Milton S. Terry (S.T.D— Doctorate of Sacred Theology), Professor of Hebrew and Old Testament exegesis and Theology, wrote several books, including *Biblical Hermeneutics* in 1883, a 518 page book listed as volume II of a IX volume set that made up a collection called, *Library of Biblical and Theological Literature.*

Terry's approach to hermeneutics is the Grammatical-Historical Method as he explains:

> In distinction from all the above-mentioned methods of interpretation, we may name the Grammatico-Historical method as the method which most fully commends itself to the judgment and conscience of Christian scholars. Its fundamental is to gather from the Scriptures themselves the precise meaning which the writers intended to convey. It applies to the sacred books the same principles, the same grammatical process and

exercise of common sense and reason, which we apply to other books. The Grammatico-historical exegete, furnished with suitable qualifications, intellectual, educational, and moral will accept the claims of the Bible without prejudice or adverse prepossession, and, with no ambition to prove them true or false, will investigate the language and import of each book with fearless independence.[98]

Terry's approach divided his hermeneutics into two tiers, the first called general hermeneutics and the second was special hermeneutics, which handled all the issues of figurative and poetic language within the Scriptures. Terry writes, "If Special Hermeneutics serves any useful end, it must cultivate the habit of searching for what the Scripture has to say for itself, not of imposing upon its language the burden of whatever it is able to bear." [99] *Biblical Hermeneutics* is still used today and remains in print through current publishers, as well as bible software companies.

Another Protestant work is *The Interpretation of Prophecy* (1974) by Paul Lee Tan (Th.D.), who was Director of Asian Studies and Adjunct Professor at Dallas Theological Seminary and recognized as an authority on Biblical prophecy. His book on the subject contains over 430 pages and is still available through his ministry website at TanBible.com.

The difference between these two major works is their approach to interpretating figurative language. Terry divides the rules into two sections; while Tan sees all rules under a single umbrella, both fully support the Grammatico-Historical Method.

---

[96] Livingston, *Modern Christian Thought*, 2 ed., vol. 2, 207.

[97] Ibid., 206-207.

[98] Terry, *Biblical Hermeneutics*, vol. 2, 70.

[99] Ibid., 6.

Terry's book is more technical in nature and very helpful. Tan's book takes advantage of 100 years with no real updates to Biblical hermeneutics for prophecy in a major work; consequently, providing an update in modern terms, a biblical hermeneutic that focuses on biblical prophecy that is systematic, reasonable and sound in its approach.

KEY PARTICIPANTS IN THE POST-MEDIEVAL PERIOD

E. W. HENGSTENBERG—A.D. 1802-1869

Hengstenberg, Ernest Wilhelm (1802-1869), German Lutheran divine and theologian, was born at Frondenberg, a Westphalian village, on the 20th of October 1802. He was educated by his father, who was a minister of the Reformed Church, and head of the Frondenberg convent of canonesses (Fräuleinstift).

Entering the University of Bonn in 1819, he attended the lectures of G. G. Freytag for Oriental languages and of F. K. L. Gieseler for church history, energies were principally devoted to philosophy and philology, and his earliest publication was an edition of the Arabic Moallakat of Amru'l-Qais.

In 1824 he joined the philosophical faculty of Berlin as a Privatdozent, and in 1825 he became a licentiate in theology, his theses being remarkable for their evangelical fervor and for their emphatic protest against every form of "rationalism," especially in questions of Old Testament criticism. In 1826 he became professor extraordinarius in theology; and in July 1827 appeared, under his editorship, the Evangelische Kirchenzeitung, a strictly orthodox journal, which in his hands acquired an almost unique reputation as a controversial organ.

In 1828 the first volume of Hengstenberg's Christologie des Allen Testaments passed through the press; in the autumn of that year, he became professor ordinarius in theology, and in 1829 doctor of theology. He died on the 28th of May 1869.[100]

Hengstenberg believed the millennium was represented by the church on earth and the thousand-year period was literally being fulfilled between the 9th and the 19th centuries.[101] This seems to follow a pattern similar to "Joachim of Fiore," who is referenced in the following chapter.

---

[100] *Encyclopaedia Britannica*, 11th ed. vol. 13, s.v. "Ernst Wilhelm Hengstenberg" (New York: Encyclopaedia Britannica, Inc., 1910), 269.

[101] Note: For further review on Hengstenberg's views on this subject read: Hengstenberg, Ernst Wilhelm. *The Revelation of St. John: Expounded for Those Who Search the Scriptures*. Translated by Patrick Fairbairn. Originally published as Die Offenbarung des heiligen Johannes: für solche die in der Schrift forschen. Berlin: Ludwig Oehmigke, 1849-1850.

Repr. New York: R. Carter & brothers, 1852-1853. Also reprinted in the series Clark's Foreign Theological Library in Edinburgh: Clark and London: Hamilton, Adams, 1851-1852. 2 vols. New reprint. Eugene, Oregon: Wipf & Stock Publishers, 2005. 992 pp. Source: https://www.revelation-resources.com/2008/01/09/hengstenberg-the-revelation-of-st-john/; Internet; accessed 28 April 2019.

O. T. ALLIS—A.D. 1880–1973

O. T. Allis (Ph.D., D.D.) wrote the book *Prophecy and the Church*, which is widely used today to support Amillennialism.

His book is a refutation to some theological teachings of the Plymouth Brethren movement in the early 1800s, which included in a big way dispensational theology that their doctrinal teachings supported.

Dr. Allis first served as Instructor in Semitic Philology at the Princeton Theological Seminary from 1910 to 1922 and then as Assistant Professor of Semitic Philology at the same institution, from 1922 to 1929. Reorganization of the Princeton Seminary placed modernists in control of the school and so prompted the resignations of Drs. Allis, J. Gresham Machen, Robert Dick Wilson, and Cornelius Van Til and the subsequent formation of the Westminster Theological Seminary. Dr. Allis served as Professor of Old Testament History and Exegesis at Westminster from 1929 to 1930 and as Professor of Old Testament at the same institution from 1930 to 1936. When Dr. Machen and others were forced in 1936 to leave the Presbyterian Church in the U.S.A. denomination over their involvement with the Independent Board for Presbyterian Foreign Missions, Dr. Allis chose to remain in the denomination but retired from his teaching post. Independently wealthy, he was able to devote the remainder of his life to research and writing.

Dr. Allis was the editor of *The Princeton Theological Review* from 1918 to 1929 and, beginning in 1929, maintained a position as Editorial Correspondent for *The Evangelical Quarterly* until the time of his death.[102]

ANTHONY A. HOEKEMA—A.D. 1913-1988

Anthony A. Hoekema (1913-1988) was a Christian theologian of the Dutch Reformed tradition who served as professor of Systematic Theology at Calvin Theological Seminary for twenty-one years.

Hoekema was born in the Netherlands but immigrated to the United States in 1923. He attended Calvin College (A.B.), the University of Michigan (M.A.), Calvin Theological Seminary (Th.B.) and Princeton Theological Seminary (Th.D., 1953). After pastoring several Christian Reformed churches (1944-56), he became Associate Professor of Bible at Calvin College (1956-58). From 1958 to 1979, when he retired, he was Professor of Systematic Theology at Calvin Theological Seminary in Grand Rapids, Michigan.[103]

---

[102] "Oswald Thompson Allis," Biographical Sketch, 1916-2005, Synthetic Collection MS#071, Box #261, PCA Historical Center, St. Louis, MO. [document on line]; available from http://www.pcahistory.org/findingaids/allis/index.html; Internet; accessed 1 November 2018.

[103] *Theopedia*, s.v. "Anthony Hoekema," [encyclopedia on line]; available from

Anthony Hoekema wrote *The Bible and the Future* (1979), which was a defense for Amillennialism and referenced widely in defense of Amillennialism in the twenty-first century. Hoekema was a supporter of Realized Amillennialism, holding to a similar view as B. B. Warfield on the book of Revelation, that the book represents seven parallel periods, representing the millennial period as a whole—both on earth and in heaven.

J. I. PACKER—A.D. 1926-

James Innell Packer (b. July 22, 1926) is a conservative evangelical Anglican, author, and theologian in the Calvinist tradition. He served as the Board of Governors' Professor of Theology at Regent College in Vancouver, British Columbia. He is considered to be one of the most important evangelical theologians of the late 20th century.

The son of a clerk for the Great Western Railway, Packer won a scholarship to Oxford University. It was as a student at Oxford where he first met C.S. Lewis whose teachings would become a major influence in his life. In a meeting of the Oxford Inter-Collegiate Christian Union, Packer committed his life to Christian service.

After briefly teaching Greek at Oak Hill College in London, Packer entered Wycliffe Hall to study theology and was ordained in the Anglican church. He became recognized as a leader in the

Evangelical movement in the Church of England. In 1978, he signed the Chicago Statement on Biblical Inerrancy, which affirmed the conservative position on inerrancy.

In 1979, Packer moved to Vancouver to take up a position with Regent College. A prolific writer and frequent lecturer, Packer is widely regarded in Protestant circles as one of the most important theologians and church historians of the modern era. He a frequent contributor to and an executive editor of Christianity Today. In recent years, he has become an outspoken proponent of the ecumenical movement but believes that unity should not come at the expense of orthodox Protestant doctrine. Nonetheless, his advocacy of ecumenicism has brought sharp criticism from some conservatives.[104]

Packer's view on biblical hermeneutics is expressed as a "theory of biblical interpretation." [105] He goes on to say, "Interpretation has been defined as the way of reading the old book that brings out its relevance for modern man. Biblical hermeneutics is the study of the theoretical principles involved in bringing out to this and every age the relevance of the Bible and its message." [106]

Packer holds to the same theological perspective as John Calvin and believes strongly in the authority of the Scriptures as he ties that issue to his version of the Grammatico-Historical Method, which he

https://www.theopedia.com/anthony-hoekema; Internet; accessed 9 November 2018.

[104] *Theopedia*, s.v. "James Innell Packer," [encyclopedia on line]; available from https://www.theopedia.com/j-i-packer; Internet; accessed 1 April 2019.

[105] James Packer, "Hermeneutics and Biblical Authority," *Themelios* 1, no. 1, (1975): 5. [article online]; available from http://themelios.thegospelcoalition.org/archive/
[106] Ibid.

appears to support.[107] J. I. Packer holds to an Amillennialism perspective.

DISTINGUISHING CHARACTERISTICS OF AMILLENNIALISM

HERMENEUTICS BEHIND AMILLENNIALISM

Amillennialism today takes two approaches to its hermeneutical interpretations. First, the literal approach for non-prophetic portions of Scripture; secondly, the Spiritual or Allegorical approach for the prophetic portions. This falls in line with Augustine, Thomas Aquinas, and O. T. Allis, among others.

Amillennialism is based on its own systematic approach to its theological perspective; as founded on the approach of past historical precedents set by those who chose to allegorize portions of prophetic Scripture based on the understanding and methods of the times. This can be seen in how each historical figure developed their own version of interpreting the book of Revelation as it relates to other passages— allegorically.

The result of this approach established its own interpretive pillars to build on, such as those developed by Augustine and others.

The proof of this analysis is found in the reading of the founding Fathers and all those who followed.

Example, if the original biblical writers allegorized some portion of their work to make a point, the way to understand that point would be to read the allegory within the context of their original writings. Augustine used the allegory in Matthew 12:29 to explain his interpretation of Revelation 20:1. Matthew 12 is not prophetic in nature; it holds no dual meaning. The strong man in Matthew 12 was represented as an allegorical story Jesus told to help those around him understand the faulty logic they were using for an explanation of the power behind His miracles.

To take a meaning that Jesus intended for his allegory in Matthew and misapply that meaning to John's letter to the Churches, addressed as, "The Revelation of Jesus Christ," is unrealistic.

Allegorizing John's letter using outside allegorization would change the intent or meaning, just as adding or deleting words would do. The only way the book of Revelation can be understood as intended would be to analyze it by a literal method, as expressed by Paul Lee Tan.

It's one thing to compare prophecies between each other to see if they correlate or fit a pattern or speak to an interpretive issue; but to allegorize a passage to fit another has no foundation in language or reason. It just becomes one opinion versus another. Moreover, one person's reasoning is not another person's reasoning. This is why hermeneutics is not, as J. I. Packer believes, a "theory of biblical interpretations," but should be seen as "an art and science of scriptural interpretation." A science, because its methods can be tested and proven to be valid, an art because not everyone can apply the rules with proficiency. In the end, allegory within the Scriptures is not meant to be made, but to be interpreted within the context they are made as we use, understand, and read using the customary way of a language.

Milton Terry weighs in with the following observation:

---

[107] Packer, "Hermeneutics and Biblical Authority," *Themelios* 1, no. 1, (1975): 3-12.

The allegorical method of interpretation is based upon a profound reverence for the Scriptures and a desire to exhibit their manifold depths of wisdom. But it will be noticed at once that its habit is to disregard the common signification of words and give wing to all manner of fanciful speculation. It does not draw out the legitimate meaning of an author's language, but foists into it whatever the whim or fancy of an interpreter may desire. As a system, therefore, it puts itself beyond all well-defined principles and laws.[108]

CHARACTERISTICS OF AMILLENNIALISM

Over time, allegorical interpretation has molded its own pillars in support of its theological perspective on understanding *end-time* events. The following represents these pillars:

1. There is no <u>literal</u> millennial earthly kingdom.

2. The millennial period in Revelation 20 represents the time between the First and Second Advents.

3. The binding of Satan in Revelation 20 either took place at the time of Christ's First Advent or is taking place now between the First and Second Advent.[109]

4. The Church of the New Testament has become the new spiritual Israel, or the Church has replaced Israel to fulfill God's plans moving forward.

5. The Abrahamic Covenant is <u>not</u> unconditional.[110]

6. The mysteries Paul spoke to are not new and unknown truths representing the church age or the gap between Daniel's 69 and 70th week as prophesied in Daniel 9:24-27.[111]

7. Man does not possess two natures through the salvation process as alluded to in the following passages, (Second Timothy 1:14; Second Peter 1:4; James 4:5; 5:17; Romans 7:19-23; 11:15-24; Jeremiah 31:33);[112] instead, the new man of the New Testament represents spiritual newness and growth through the sanctification process of the Holy Spirit.[113] This concept correlates to the idea in eschatology that the kingdom will grow to make things better and better over time, as the Gospel is preached to the entire world.

8. There are two schools of thought in Amillennialism:

   a. Heavenly School
   b. Earthly School

   (a) The heavenly school represents the view that the millennium is represented

[108] Terry, *Biblical Hermeneutics*, 60.
[109] Anthony A. Hoekema, *The Bible and the Future* (Grand Rapids: Willian B. Eerdmans Publishing Company, 1979), 178.
[110] Oswald T. Allis, *Prophecy and the Church*, 3 ed. (The Presbyterian and Reformed Publication Company, 1955), 58.
[111] Ibid., 90-91.
[112] Ashbaucher, *Made in the Image of God*, 2 rev ed., 127.
[113] Allis, *Prophecy and the Church*, 44.

by the rule of Christ in heaven with the saints, and takes place between the two Advents with the binding of Satan taking place during the same time.[114]

(b) The earthly school represents the view that the millennium is represented by the kingdom of Christ and the kingdom of Satan co-existing side by side here on earth until the Second Advent. This is supported through the interpretation of Matthew 13: 36-43, with the parable of the Tares, while the binding of Satan took place at the first advent.[115]

REASONS FOR THE POPULARITY OF AMILLENNIALISM AFTER THE REFORMATION

HISTORICAL BACKGROUND

Amillennialism is primarily a view held by those of Roman Catholic, Lutheran or Reformed perspectives.

The early reformers, for the most part, held to the theology of Roman Catholicism, with three primary deviations. First, the issues of justification by faith. Second, the individual right to interpret the Scriptures. Thirdly, the issue of the priesthood of the believer.

As referenced before, the historical development of hermeneutics and the principle that our knowledge and understanding is directly connected to our historical settings and experiences leads us to summarize that, even though Martin Luther revolutionized the principles behind a literal interpretive hermeneutic, this did not carry over to the elimination of spiritualizing, or the allegorical method of interpretation within the hermeneutics of that day toward prophetic Scripture.

This only makes sense if one holds a view that the progressive nature of any theological perspective is directly tied to its historical settings. One cannot add understanding to a view without new reviewed knowledge; just as science cannot move forward without a new proven or tested hypothesis proven over time.

The evidence of how human knowledge is built can be seen in the lack of modern technology in the sixteenth century. Knowledge and understanding are built over time on past knowledge and understanding. This is the reality of progressive revelation, it must come through past knowledge, understood or not, as influenced by the Holy Spirit of God in real time.

The relevance of this principle will become clearer as this study progresses.

A PHILOSOPHICAL PERSPECTIVE

The approach of Amillennialism simplifies the difficult and obscure passages, particularly those of prophecy; thus, bringing harmony to the Scriptures without the necessity of meeting the difficult standard of non-contradictions within a literal hermeneutical approach.

Nevertheless, the question remains, is Amillennialism without its own contradictions when a literal approach is applied? The standard that should prevail in all scriptural interpretations is this, there are no contradictions in Scripture, and therefore, for biblical truth to be true it must agree with all other biblical truth.

Charles Hodge writes, "and Scripture cannot contradict Scripture; for that would

---

[114] Hoekema, *The Bible and the Future*, 174.

[115] Ibid., 180.

be for God to contradict Himself." [116] Until this standard is reasonably met, biblical truth will remain elusive to its pursuers.

Another consideration of why many take the approach of Amillennialism is it can be made to fit the philosophical perspectives of both the conservative and liberal approach to one's theology.

In the end, it is just a simpler way to answer difficult questions, allowing more time to study issues that are more important in the eyes of its holders.

---

[116] Charles Hodge, *Systematic Theology*, vol. 3, (New York: Scribner, Armstrong, And Company, 1873), 871.

CHAPTER THREE

The History and Characteristics of Postmillennialism

KEY FIGURES IN THE HISTORY OF POSTMILLENNIALISM

JOACHIM OF FLORIS—A.D. 1132-1202

Joachim of Floris, Cistercian abbot and mystic, born at Celico, near Cosenza, Italy, in 1132 and died at San Giovanni in Fiore, in Calabria, 30 March 1202.[117]

The interpretation of Scriptural prophecy, with reference to the history and the future of the Church, is the main theme of his three chief works: *"Liber Concordiae Novi ac Veteris Testamenti," "Expositio in Apocalipsim,"* and *"Psalterium Decem Cordarum."* The mystical basis of his teaching is the doctrine of the "Eternal Gospel," founded on a strained interpretation of the text in the Apocalypse (14:6). There are three states of the world, corresponding to the three Persons of the Blessed Trinity. In the first age the Father ruled, representing power and inspiring fear, to which the Old Testament dispensation corresponds; then the wisdom hidden through the ages was revealed in the Son, and we have the Catholic Church of the New Testament; a third period will come, the Kingdom of the Holy Spirit, a new dispensation of universal love, which will proceed from the Gospel of Christ, but transcend the letter of it, and in which there will be no need for disciplinary institutions. Joachim held that the second period was drawing to a close, and that the third epoch (already in part anticipated by St. Benedict) would actually begin after some great cataclysm which he tentatively calculated would befall in 1260. After this Latins and Greeks would be united in the new spiritual kingdom, freed alike from the fetters of the letter; the Jews would be converted, and the "Eternal Gospel" abide until the end of the world.[118]

Joachim's development of eschatology is seen through the eyes of his philosophy of history as he develops his views on interpreting *end-time* events. The age of the Father represented the Law. The age of the Son represents the time from the first

---

[117] *The Catholic Encyclopedia*, vol. 8, s.v. "Joachim of Flora," by Gardner, Edmund (New York: Robert Appleton Company, 1910.) 26 April 2010 http://www.newadvent.org/cathen/ 08406c.htm

[118] Ibid.

advent to the year 1260 A.D. when he believed the age of the spirit would begin, ushering in the eternal kingdom.

What influenced his hermeneutical thinking? The answer is the letter/spirit antithesis!

> Far more interesting as explaining the diffusion and the religious and social importance of his doctrine is his conception of the second and third ages. The first age was the age of the Letter, the second was intermediary between the Letter and the Spirit, and the third was to be the age of the Spirit.[119]

The importance of Joachim's thinking is that he recognized the kingdom was coming in stages and saw three distinct dispensations to get him there. This is the same conceptual thinking Jesus took during his discussions with his disciples as found in Matthew 24; the past represented by Old Testament prophets, the present represented by the destruction of the Jewish temple in 70 A.D., with Jesus' prophecy of "not one stone here shall be left upon another" (Matthew 24:2), to the talk of the end of the age as found in verse three. Jesus also referenced the time of the *abomination of desolation* (Matthew 24:15) that takes place during the *Great Tribulation,* as prophesied by Daniel the prophet. This will be covered in more detail in Section 2.

DANIEL WHITBY—A.D. 1638-1726

> 1638-1726. Anglican scholar. An erudite clergyman trained at Oxford, he engaged in several controversies, including an attack on Roman

Catholicism, an attempt to gain concessions for Nonconformists so they would join the Church of England, and a refutation of Calvinism. Among his thirty-nine published works the most famous is a Paraphrase and Commentary on the New Testament (2 vols., 1703). This work continued to be used throughout the eighteenth-and nineteenth centuries. Its area of great significance was in popularizing Postmillennialism. Whitby held that the world would be converted to Christ, the Jews restored to the Holy Land, and defeat of the pope and Turks, after which the world would enjoy a time of universal peace, happiness, and righteousness for a thousand years. At the close of this millennium, Christ would personally come to earth again and the last judgment would be held. This view was adopted by most of the leading eighteenth-century ministers and commentators.[120]

Whitby wrote the *Paraphrase and Commentary on the New Testament:* in two volumes. This work includes *A-TREATISE of the True Millennium:*

From Whitby's writings, the following paragraphs reflect four methods Whitby used to expound on the topic of the millennium.

> This naturally led me to a Discourse of the *Millennium*; which being framed according to this new *Hypothesis,* I shall now offer it to the

[119] *Encyclopaedia Britannica*, 11th ed. vol. 15, s.v. "Joachim of Floris" (New York: Encyclopaedia Britannica, Inc., 1910), 418; available from The Historical Archive, [DVD], THA New Media, LLC., 2017. (http://www.TheHistoricalArchive.com)

[120] Biblicaltraining.org, "Daniel Whitby," [Free Library on line]; available from https://www.biblicaltraining.org/library/daniel-whitby; Internet; accessed 21 November 2018.

Consideration of the Learned, in the following Method.

1. I shall state the true *Millennium* of the *Ancients:* shewing how far it was received, and by whom opposed in the four first Centuries, and what were the particular Opinions which then obtained concerning the *Millennium*; and how far the *Modern Patrons* of the *Millenary* State have discarded the received Opinion of the *Ancients* who embrac'd that Doctrine.

2. I shall show what Reason I have to conceive that this *Millennium* is to begin with the Conversion of the *Jewish Nation*; and doth indeed relate to the most happy State and flourishing Condition the *Church of Christ* shall at that time enjoy.

3. I shall attempt to answer all that hath been offer'd to prove a proper and literal Resurrection of the *Martyrs*, and other *Christian Sufferers*, and *Saints to Reign on Earth a thousand years*; consider the Pretences of them who place this Reign before the Conflagration of the World as most of the Assertors of this Doctrine do; and of the *Reverend Dr. Burmet*, who makes it to begin after the Conflagration of the World. And,

4. I shall offer some Arguments against this Doctrine of the *Millennium*, or of the literal Resurrection of the Saint; and

Martyrs, to *Reign on Earth a thousand years.*[121]

Whitby, in annotation notes for chapter III, leaves this reasoning for why he believes the Christian should not believe in a literal millennium kingdom. It should be noted this is similar to Augustine's line of reasoning.

Ver. 4. Note, Hence we learn that Christians are not to expect to Reign with Christ on Earth a thousand Years, because they are not to mind or seek, (Hand written Greek word), the things upon Earth, but only those above, where Christ sitteth at the right hand of God. Whereas were this Life on Earth a Blessing and Reward which God had promised to them for their Sufferings, they might mind it, and set their Affection on it; as also from all those places where the; Reward, Inheritance of Christians, is said to be reserved in the Heavens, for them; for, as Oecumenius notes, (Hand written Greek phrase), if our Inheritance be in Heaven, the supposed Millennium on Earth must be but a Fable; Great is your Reward in Heaven, saith Christ to the Christian Sufferer, Mat. 5, 12. Luke 6. 23. Your hope is laid up for you in Heaven, Colossians. 1. 5. See 1 Peter 1. 4.[122]

We see in the end that Whitby introduces a new hypothesis, and by his own admission rejects his original views of

---

[121] Daniel Whitby, *A paraphrase and commentary on the New Testament: in two volumes,* A TREATISE of the True Millennium, Introduction (London: Printed for Amſham and John Churchill, at the Black–Swan, in Pater-Noſter-Row, 1703), 250. [digital library on-line]; available from http://www.prdl.org/author_view.php?a_id= 2422;

Internet; accessed 21 November 2018. Note: Due to the Old English spelling of words, the editor has substituted the letter that looks like an "*f*" with the letter "s," which it represents in modern English for better readability.
[122] Ibid., 368.

who he terms the Ancients, i.e. those before the fourth century. This would eliminate Justin Martyr and Irenaeus of Lyons and all those who held to a literal interpretation back to the Apostles.

CHARLES HODGE—A.D. 1797-1878

[Charles Hodge was an American Presbyterian theologian who was born in Philadelphia, PA. on Dec. 28, 1797; Hodge died in Princeton, NJ, on June 19, 1878.

Hodge's father was a surgeon in George Washington's army who died during his childhood. Hodge attended New Jersey College (Princeton) and Princeton Theological Seminary where he studied under Archibald Alexander. In 1822, Hodge was appointed professor of Oriental and Biblical literature at the seminary, where he taught until 1840. Hodge took a leave of absence between 1826 to 1828 to study at the University of Berlin under the historian John A. W. Neander.

In 1840, Hodge succeeded Alexander as professor of didactic and polemic theology, holding the position until he died. His class lectures were the basis of his *Systematic Theology*, which he published in 1872. This three-volume text became a major reference source for seminary use in the late 19th century. Hodge carried on the theological tradition of Alexander, with a philosophical mix of 17th-century Calvinist scholasticism and Scottish realism that stressed both the power of reason and a verbally inspired, inerrant Scripture. His theology was nearly universally held among Presbyterians.] [123]

Charles Hodge expressed his views on the "Final Judgment" in volume III of his *Systematic Theology*, which helps us understand his theological position on the millennium. Hodge writes,

> This judgment is to take place at the second coming of Christ and at the general resurrection. Therefore it is not a process now in progress; it does not take place at death; it is not a protracted period prior to the general resurrection. A few of the passages bearing on this point are the following: In the parable of the wheat and the tares (Matt. xiii. 37-43), already referred to, we are taught that the final separation between the righteous and the wicked is to take place at the end of the world, when the Son of Man shall send forth his angels to gather out of his kingdom all things that offend. This implies that the general resurrection, the second advent, and the last judgment, are contemporaneous events. The Bible knows nothing of three personal advents of Christ: one at the time of the incarnation; a second before the millennium; and a third to judge the world. [124]

[123] *New Catholic Encyclopedia*, s.v. "Hodge, Charles;" available from https://www.encyclopedia.com/religion/encyclopedias-almanacs-transcripts-and-maps/hodge-charles; Internet; accessed 29 November 2018.

[124] Hodge, *Systematic Theology*, vol. 3, 847.

A.H. STRONG—A.D. 1836-1921

Augustus Hopkins Strong was born in Rochester, NY on August 3, 1836. He was brought to Christ while attending Yale College, graduating in 1857. He began his theological studies at Rochester Theological Seminary and completed his D.D. in Germany.

After serving Baptist churches in Haverhill, Massachusetts, and Cleveland, Strong was elected president of Rochester Theological Seminary in 1872. He was an active promoter of Baptist missions throughout his life, and from 1907 to 1910 he served as the first president of the Northern Baptist Convention (now the American Baptist Churches in the U.S.A.).

In his forty years at Rochester Seminary, Strong taught a theology that combined traditional Reformed emphases, distinctive Baptist convictions on the ordinances and the organization of churches, and a relative openness to modern ideas. He published his multivolume Systematic Theology in 1886. This influential work was revised several times by Strong himself and continues in print to this day. Although Strong was consistently orthodox, he did use the results of modem critical scholarship more than, for example, his near Presbyterian contemporary Charles Hodge. Also, unlike Hodge, Strong

was comfortable with the idea that God may have created the world through the processes of evolution. In the 1907 edition of his theology, Strong summarized his views on modern thought: "Neither evolution nor the higher criticism has any terrors to one who regards them as part of Christ's creating an education process."

Yet late in his life Strong spoke out strongly against those who used modem thought to compromise belief in Christ's divinity or his saving work. In the 1907 revision, Strong proposed the counter to modernism that he maintained until he died: Christ as "the one and only Revealer of God, in nature, in humanity, in history, in science, in Scripture." [125]

Strong expresses his views on the millennium in his book on Systematic Theology. The end result of his interpretation is there is no rapture and Christ returns at the end of the millennium. The following is an excerpt from his Systematic Theology work.

The precursors of Christ's coming.

(a) Through the preaching of the gospel in all the world, the kingdom of Christ is steadily to enlarge its boundaries, until Jews and Gentiles alike become possessed of its blessings, and a millennial period is introduced in which Christianity generally prevails throughout the earth.

---

[125] Christian Classics Ethereal Library, s.v. "A. H. Strong," [Biography database on-line] available from https://www.ccel.org/ccel/strong; Internet; accessed 26 November 2018.

(b) There will be a corresponding development of evil, either extensive or intensive, whose true character shall be manifest not only in deceiving many professed followers of Christ and in persecuting true believers, but in constituting a personal Antichrist as its representative and object of worship. This rapid growth shall continue until the millennium, during which evil, in the person of its chief, shall be temporarily restrained.

(c) At the close of this millennial period, evil will again be permitted to exert its utmost power in a final conflict with righteousness. This spiritual struggle, moreover, will be accompanied and symbolized by political convulsions, and by fearful indications of desolation in the natural world.[126]

BENJAMIN BRECKINRIDGE WARFIELD—A.D. 1851-1921

B. B. Warfield earned his undergraduate degree from the College of New Jersey (Princeton University) in 1871, and his Masters of Divinity degree from Princeton Theological Seminary in 1876.

In 1878, Warfield took a Professorship at Western Theological Seminary in Pittsburg, teaching New Testament Literature and Exegesis. In 1880, Warfield was awarded an honorary D.D. from his alma mater College of New Jersey. In 1897, Warfield took a Professorship with Princeton Theological Seminary, following in the footsteps of Charles Hodge, who taught at Princeton for fifty-eight years and developed his own method of theology, as expressed in his three-volume *systematic theology*.[127] Warfield followed in Hodge's systematic theology, which followed in the classic Calvinist theology of the Reformation,[128] while defending the orthodoxy of the Christian faith and the battle for the inerrancy of the Scriptures of his day.

Warfield believed Augustine was wrong about the millennium as a period of time,[129] as well as his position on Revelation Chapter 20.

Warfield believed the book of Revelation was composed of seven sections, all representing one main symbol.

"The thing symbolized is obviously the complete victory of the Son of God over all the hosts of wickedness."[130] And this victory "in effect, is a picture of the whole period between the first and Second Advent, seen from the point of view of heaven." [131]

Warfield summarizes his viewpoint on the issue in this manner:

---

[126] Augustus Hopkins Strong, *Outlines of systematic theology: designed for the use of theological students* (Philadelphia: American Baptist Publication Society, 1908), 263.

[127] Barry Waugh, "Author Biography Benjamin Breckinridge Warfield (5 November 1851 - 16 February 1921)," *The Southern Presbyterian Review*, [digitized project on-line]; available from http://www.pcahistory.org/HCLibrary/periodicals /spr/bios/warfield.html; Internet; accessed 1 November 2018.

[128] Livingston, *Modern Christian Thought: The Enlightenment and the Nineteenth Century*, 2 ed., vol. 1 (Minneapolis, MN: Fortress Press, 2006), 304-308.

[129] B. B. Warfield, "The Millennium and the Apocalypse," *The Princeton Theological Review* 2, no. 4, (1904): 600.

[130] Ibid., 602.

[131] Ibid., 603.

What, then, is the eschatological outline we have gained from a study of this section? Briefly stated it is as follows. Our Lord Jesus Christ came to conquer the world to Himself, and this He does with a thoroughness and completeness which seems to go beyond even the intimations of Romans xi and 1 Cor. xv. Meanwhile, as the conquest of the world is going on below, the saints who die in the Lord are gathered in Paradise to reign with their Lord, who is also Lord of all, and who is from His throne directing the conquest of the world. When the victory is completely won there supervenes the last judgment and the final destruction of the wicked. At once there is a new heaven and a new earth and the consummation of the glory of the Church. And this Church abides forever (xxii. 5), in the perfection of holiness and blessedness.[132]

Warfield does not call this period the millennium, but the "intermediate state." [133]

Some in the theological community have seen some of Warfield's views as interchangeable with an Amillennial perspective, sometimes landing him in that classification.[134]

LORAINE BOETTNER—A.D. 1901-1990

Loraine Boettner (1901-1990) a Reformed Theologian, born on a farm in Linden, Missouri. After obtaining a Bachelor of Science degree from Tarkio College in 1925, he attended Princeton Theological Seminary where he studied Systematic Theology under Dr. Casper W. Hodge and received his Th.B. (1928) and Th.M. (1929). He taught Bible for eight years in Pikeville College, Kentucky. In 1933 he received the honorary degree of Doctor of Divinity from Tarkio College, and in 1957 the degree of Doctor of Literature. He was a member of the Orthodox Presbyterian Church.[135]

Boettner wrote a book from a Postmillennial perspective called, *The Millennium*, a 420-page work still in print through P & R Publishing, and often quoted by those defending similar positions.

ROUSAS J. RUSHDOONY — A.D. 1916-2001

Rousas John Rushdoony (1916 - 2001) was the seminal leader of the Christian Reconstructionist theology in the United States. He was the founder, in 1965, of the Chalcedon Foundation, and the editor of its monthly magazine, the Chalcedon Report, and publisher of the Journal of Christian Reconstruction.

Rushdoony was born in New York the son of Armenian immigrants. He was educated at the University of California, Berkeley, where he earned a B.A. in English in 1938, a teaching credential in 1939 and a Master of Arts in Education in

---

[132] Warfield, "The Millennium and the Apocalypse," 614-615.

[133] Ibid., 604-605.

[134] John F. Walvoord, *The Millennial Kingdom*, (Grand Rapids: Zondervan Publishing House, 1959), 71. (See footnote 12.)

[135] *Theopedia*, "Loraine Boettner," [on-line encyclopedia of Biblical Christianity]; available from https://www.theopedia.com/loraine-boettner; Internet; accessed 26 November 2018.

1940. He also attended the Pacific School of Religion. He later received an honorary Doctorate from Valley Christian University for his book, *The Philosophy of the Christian Curriculum*.[136]

Rushdoony wrote a book called, *Thy Kingdom Come: Studies in Daniel and Revelation*, published by Ross House Books, a 284-page work reflecting his Postmillennial position.

We find the prize importance of Rushdoony's views in his support for Christian Reconstructionist theology and his influence in the Christian Education and Home School movements.

TYPES OF POSTMILLENNIALISM

THE CONSERVATIVE APPROACH

The conservative approach reflects on the power of the Gospel preached and would be best represented by the teachings of Charles Hodge.

THE LIBERAL APPROACH

Daniel Whitby and his emphases of the "Happy State" of the millennium best represents the liberal approach. Some refer to this period as the *Golden Age*. The idea that things will gradually get better and better as the gospel is proclaimed, bringing about a better world.

DISTINGUISHING CHARACTERISTICS

OPTIMISTIC

The most marked characteristic is its optimism of either world conversions or world improvement.

IMMINENT PERSPECTIVE

Postmillennialists do not hold to an imminent return of Christ. This stands in contrast to Amillennialists such as O. T. Allis, as he writes, "All Amillennialists of today, whether they hold with Augustine or with Kliefoth, are in a position to maintain that the coming of the Lord is 'imminent.'"[137]

A DECLINING VIEW

By summarizing John Walvoord's (Th.D.) analysis of Postmillennialism, we can learn the following. [The inherent problems with postmillennial theology lie with its hermeneutical approach of spiritualization of Scripture, leaving the interpreter to solve issues with an earthly millennium on their own with weak arguments that are acceptable to Calvinist, Arminian, and Unitarians.

This view lends itself to liberalism, with a few adjustments in the nature of its hermeneutics. If one can spiritualize the prophecies, then why not other doctrines within the Scriptures?

It is a system that fails in the facts of world events. Especially within the events of WWI and WWII, reflective of a world that does not seem to be getting better but more chaotic in nature.

It is a system that found a lack of converts in the twentieth century, all due to

---

[136] *Theopedia*, "Rousas John Rushdoony," [online encyclopedia of Biblical Christianity]; available

from https://www.theopedia.com/rousas-john-rushdoony; Internet; accessed 26 November 2018.
[137] Allis, *Prophecy and the Church*, ed. 3, 6.

the shift in liberal theology and philosophy; it was found to be too impractical, with a need to become more biblically grounded.

Many that held this view have since moved to Amillennialism, with Loraine Boettner being one of the last twentieth-century scholars defending this view.] [138] Walvoord states:

> Amillennialism seemed to be the answer for many. This viewpoint gave some freedom. They could believe the coming of the Lord indefinitely postponed, or they could believe it was imminent. They could believe the present age was a millennium if they chose, or they could relegate it to heaven. They would be in the comfortable fellowship of most of the Reformers, the Roman Church, and modern liberal theologians.[139]

---

[138] John F. Walvoord, *The Millennial Kingdom*, 34-36.

[139] Ibid., 36.

CHAPTER FOUR

The History and Characteristics of Premillennialism

HISTORY BY PERIODS

PRE-APOSTOLIC PERIOD

The evidence of a premillennial position held by those who promised such a literal kingdom is provided by Nathaniel West (D.D.) in his book, *The Thousand Years in Both Testaments*—a work close to 500 pages.

Rev. West tells us some of the reasoning behind his work as he writes,

> These pages re-assert, upon the ground of God's word along— redundant with its justifying proof,—that Doctrine of the *Pre-Millennial Coming of Christ*, which, in the apostolic and old-Catholic Church, was for 300 years, "the test of orthodoxy," and formed a chief article of faith and hope. They profess to demonstrate the revelation and the designation of "the 1000 years," in the Old as well as in the New Testament, and repeatedly in the former than in the latter. Hence the title of the book: *"The Thousand Years in both Testaments."* [140]

Rev. West opens his work with this observation.

> It is a very common opinion, widely spread throughout Christendom, and in most cases believed to be true, that "the thousand years" of which John speaks in the Apocalypse. Rev. xx: 1-7, are mentioned nowhere else in the sacred Scriptures. The doctrine of a millennial kingdom on earth, introduced by the advent of Christ in His glory, is a Jewish fable without support from the word of God. A deeper study of the sacred volume dissipates this false prejudice and reveals the fact that, not only are "the thousand years" of which John speaks found everywhere in both Testaments, but that next to the eternal state, the millennial blessedness of God's people on earth, and of the nations, is the one high point in all prophecy, from Moses to John, the bright, broad tableland of all eschatology. The prejudice against the study of a theme so sublime and far-reaching, and occupying so much space in the

---

[140] Rev. Nathaniel West, D.D., *The Thousand Years in both Testaments* (New York: Fleming H. Revell, 1880), vii.

revelation God has been pleased to give us, is as remarkable in our age, as it is inexcusable, although by no means surprising.[141]

Within this remarkable work, Rev. West (D.D.) reveals some history of how the Jewish sect understood the millennial kingdom and Christ as the Messiah.

> They saw clearly enough that the messianic days, the kingdom of the 1,000 years, the Millennium of their prophets, *followed* the great tribulation. Attaching the 70th week, however, to the 69th in immediate sequence, and history failing to bring the fulfillment, they concluded that Jesus of Nazareth was not the Messiah foretold by the prophets. The relation of the 70th week, however, to the advent of Messiah as a victorious no judging Prince, sent to restore the kingdom of Israel, they understood. The Jewish literature is crowded with evidence of this.[142]

Rev. West expounds on the evidence of the millennial kingdom as found in both the Old and New Testaments and is a work well worth the study.

As to the hermeneutical position of Rev. West, he expresses his method this way:

> Should anyone, reading these pages, dream that the writer, by adhering to the literal and realistic interpretation, i.e. the grammatical and historical, as opposed to the false systems just named, has robbed the "*Church*" of her inheritance in the promise of God, it is enough to answer, *Man! Thine hour is not yet come!* "Salvation is *from* the Jews."[143]

The evidence of the Millennium taking place here on earth as promised to the Jewish Nation is expressed throughout the Old Testament prophecies. Rev. West expresses how these prophecies should be understood and interpreted,

> The *Time-Designations* in Hosea, Isaiah, Ezekiel, the Psalms, and the implications in the Pentateuch, for the *Millennial Age*, are the archaeology of eschatology. The end is contemplated from the Beginning. The Intervals represented by them, and of the *Eschata* that bound them, rest not on any mere external accident, or similarity in prophecy, but upon the inner connection, and inter-connection, of the parts of prophecy, and the advancing organism of the whole along its fixed, original, and pre-determined lines.... Either the *whole* prophetic word is false, or the 1,000 years in John are a literal historic time. Either the pre-formative expressions in Hosea, Isaiah, and Ezekiel, forecast the 1,000 years in John, *as chronological*, or the prophetic word in both Testaments is not a unit, nor an organism, but a mass of isolated sentences, a sheaf of incoherent oracles, ambiguous as Sibyl's utterances. This cannot be. The proofs are "Legion" that the Bible is *One Word which "cannot be broken," One Organic Whole*, to be studied as a whole, dealt with as a whole, expounded as a whole, each part an index to the whole, a complex, end-developing and one-aimed whole, continually expanding and unfolding from narrower to wider, and

---

[141] West, *The Thousand Years in both Testaments*, 1.
[142] Ibid., 359.

[143] Ibid., vii.

obscurer to clearer, until, at last, its hidden ages and ends, stand out in bold relief, displayed in all their brightness.[144]

Within the twenty-first century, two arguments are used to oppose such history.

This opposition hinges on a two-pillar argument held by those outside Premillennialism. First, that the promises to Israel no longer stand because of Israel's idolatry toward God. Therefore, God has permanently divorced Israel and taken on a new bride called the Church. And the second, that the New Covenant has replaced all other covenants made throughout the Old Testament, leaving no Old Testament prophetic covenants as unconditional, with the exception of the New Covenant.

These views interpret the original language of the Abrahamic and Davidic Covenant of *everlasting* and *forever* in a different light, rendering them as less than unconditional.

God declares to Abraham in Genesis 17:7: "And I will establish My covenant between Me and you and your descendants after you throughout their generations for an everlasting covenant, to be God to you and to your descendants after you." God then declares to David in Second Samuel 7:12-17:

> When your days are complete and you lie down with your fathers, I will raise up your descendant after you, who will come forth from you, and I will establish his kingdom. He shall build a house for My name, and I will establish the throne of his kingdom forever. I will be a father to him and he will be a son to Me; when

he commits iniquity, I will correct him with the rod of men and the strokes of the sons of men, but My lovingkindness shall not depart from him, as I took it away from Saul, whom I removed from before you. And your house and your kingdom shall endure before Me forever; your throne shall be established forever. In accordance with all these words and all this vision, so Nathan spoke to David.

Despite the sin of a nation, God will forgive Israel and preserve his covenant with them forever. This is accomplished through the New Covenant made with Israel in Jeremiah 31:33-34.

> But this is the covenant which I will make with the house of Israel after those days, declares the Lord, I will put My law within them, and on their heart I will write it; and I will be their God, and they shall be My people. And they shall not teach again, each man his neighbor and each man his brother, saying, 'Know the Lord,' for they shall all know Me, from the least of them to the greatest of them, declares the Lord, for I will forgive their iniquity, and their sin I will remember no more.

As Jesus arrives on earth to consummate the New Covenant, the angel Gabriel makes this arriving pronouncement:

> And the angel said to her, 'Do not be afraid, Mary; for you have found favor with God. And behold, you will conceive in your womb, and bear a son, and you shall name Him

---

[144] West, *The Thousand Years in both Testaments*, 259-260.

Jesus. He will be great, and will be called the Son of the Most High; and the Lord God will give Him the throne of His father David; and He will reign over the house of Jacob forever; and His kingdom will have no end.' (Luke 1:30-33)

This pronouncement represents the fulfillment of all unconditional covenants of the Old Testament, that is, the Abrahamic Covenant, Davidic Covenant, and the New Covenant.

As to the issue of God divorcing his chosen people Israel, God states the following: "And I saw that for all the adulteries of faithless Israel, I had sent her away and given her a writ of divorce, yet her treacherous sister Judah did not fear; but she went and was a harlot also." (Jeremiah 3:8)

Then God tells the prophet, "Go, and proclaim these words toward the north and say, 'Return, faithless Israel,' declares the Lord; 'I will not look upon you in anger. For I am gracious,' declares the Lord; 'I will not be angry forever." Jeremiah goes on to state, upon Israel's repentance, God will restore them in the last days to their land. (Jeremiah 3:9-18)

Yes, it is true that Israel has been set aside for a time (Romans 11), but the Apostle Paul reassures Israel in Romans 11:25-27 of the following:

> For I do not want you, brethren, to be uninformed of this mystery, lest you be wise in your own estimation, that a partial hardening has happened to Israel until the fulness of the Gentiles has come in;

and thus all Israel will be saved; just as it is written,

> *The Deliverer will come from Zion,*
> *He will remove ungodliness from Jacob.*
> *And this is My covenant with them,*
> *When I take away their sins.*

Accordingly, if we follow Rev. West's lead and see the Scriptures and its prophecies as a whole and not in part, this would bring better comprehension to the conclusion of the passages just shared, that the Abrahamic and Davidic Covenants are all consummated through the New Covenant and Christ its consummator.

APOSTLES TO AUGUSTINE

The history of Premillennial thinking can be traced through the Church Fathers up through the fourth century. The following individuals represent those recorded in that history.

Papias

Papias lived during the lifetime of the Apostles (A.D. 61-67), was the Bishop of Hierapolis (close to Laodicea and Colossæ in the valley of the Lycus in Phrygia) and an Apostolic Father. Papias is known to have written a work of five books called, *logion kyriakon exegesis*, most of which has been lost—but for a few fragments.[145]

St. Irenaeus writes,

> Now testimony is borne to these things in writing by Papias, an ancient man, who was a hearer of John, and a friend of Polycarp, in the fourth of his books; for five books were composed by him.[146]

---

[145] *The Catholic Encyclopedia*, vol. 11, s.v. "St. Papias," by John Chapman (New York: Robert Appleton Company, 1911.) 26 Apr. 2010. http://www.newadvent.org/cathen/11457c.htm.

[146] Papias Fragments I. *Ante-Nicene Fathers*, vol. 1, ed. Alexander Roberts, James Donaldson, A. Cleveland Coxe, trans. Alexander Roberts, James Donaldson (Buffalo, NY: Christian Literature Publishing Co., 1885.) Revised and edited for New

The most notable part of Papias' life were the sources of his information. He tells us that he did not know the Apostles personally but did know those who had direct contact with them while they were all alive collectively. Papias writes,

But I shall not be unwilling to put down, along with my interpretations, whatsoever instructions I received with care at any time from the elders, and stored up with care in my memory, assuring you at the same time of their truth. For I did not, like the multitude, take pleasure in those who spoke much, but in those who taught the truth; nor in those who related strange commandments, but in those who rehearsed the commandments given by the Lord to faith, and proceeding from truth itself. If, then, anyone who had attended on the elders came, I asked minutely after their sayings—what Andrew or Peter said, or what was said by Philip, or by Thomas, or by James, or by John, or by Matthew, or by any other of the Lord's disciples: which things Aristion and the presbyter John, the disciples of the Lord, say. For I imagined that what was to be got from books was not so profitable to me as what came from the living and abiding voice.[147]

The records of history reflect Papias' experiences as follows:

The residence of the Apostle Philip with his daughters in Hierapolis has been mentioned above. We must now point out how

Papias, who lived at the same time, relates that he had received a wonderful narrative from the daughters of Philip. For he relates that a dead man was raised to life in his day. He also mentions another miracle relating to Justus, surnamed Barsabas, how he swallowed a deadly poison, and received no harm, on account of the grace of the Lord. The same person, moreover, has set down other things as coming to him from unwritten tradition, among these some strange parables and instructions of the Saviour, and some other things of a more fabulous nature. Amongst these, he says that there will be a millennium after the resurrection from the dead, when the personal reign of Christ will be established on this earth.[148]

It is said that Papias wrote his books in the latter part of his life, sometime between 115 and 140 A.D.[149] According to the writings of Papias, it was the Apostle Philip's daughters that relayed the understanding of a millennial kingdom to him, providing us with a better understanding of how the Apostles understood Christ's teachings. For assuredly the daughters learned their understanding of the coming kingdom through their father, the Apostle Philip.

Justin Martyr (A.D. 100-165)

Justin Martyr was an apologist and self-taught philosopher, who studied several systems of philosophy to include that of the Old Testament prophets.[150]

Advent by Kevin Knight.
http://www.newadvent.org/fathers/0125.htm.
[147] Papias Fragments I.
[148] Papias Fragments VI.

[149] *The Catholic Encyclopedia*, vol. 11, s.v. "St. Papias," by John Chapman.
[150] Justin Martyr Dialogue with Trypho 1-8.

Converted to Christianity around 130 A.D., Justin makes a major contribution to Christian theology by separating Christian revelation from human speculation. He sums up this view by showing that God spoke directly to the Prophets, who then made Him known to us.[151]

Within Justin's arguments over the reliability of translations of the Old Testament Scriptures, he sees the Old Testament prophecies as being literally fulfilled in the life of Christ. This was the beginning of Justin Martyr's hermeneutical approach of interpretation.[152]

Justin also argues for two advents, with an understanding of a literal kingdom.[153] He goes on to state there will be a thousand-year kingdom after the resurrection of the dead, based on the prophets of Ezekiel and Isaiah.[154] Justin then explains the interpretation of his views through his explanation of Isaiah 65:17-24 in relationship to an analogy on Adam, Revelation 20, and Luke 20:35f.[155]

On the opinion of Justin regarding the reign of a thousand years, he writes,

> I admitted to you, that I and many others are of this opinion, and (believe) that such will take place, as you assuredly are aware; but, on the other hand, I signified to you that many who belong to the pure and pious faith, and are true Christians, think otherwise. Moreover, I pointed out to you that some who are called Christians, but are godless, impious heretics, teach doctrines that are in every way blasphemous, atheistical, and foolish. But that you

may know that I do not say this before you alone, I shall draw up a statement, so far as I can, of all the arguments which have passed between us; in which I shall record myself as admitting the very same things which I admit to you. For I choose to follow not men or men's doctrines, but God and the doctrines (delivered) by Him.[156]

IRENAEUS OF LYONS (A.D. 140-202)

Irenaeus of Lyon was born around 130 A.D. in Proconsular Asia, and died around 201 A.D.

Irenaeus served as bishop of Lugdunum (Lyon), and as a young man he had some contact with Bishop Polycarp who was seen as a disciple of the Apostle John.

Irenaeus wrote extensively in Greek, which secured his place in Christian literature, of which only a few full versions of his work that were translated into Latin survived.[157]

Irenaeus' view on the millennial kingdom is expressed in these terms. "For after the times of the kingdom, he says, 'I saw a great white throne, and Him who sat upon it, from whose face the earth fled away, and the heavens; and there was no more place for them.'" (Revelation 20:11)[158]

Irenaeus also interpreted the Abrahamic Covenant as being part of the earthly kingdom as he writes,

> But when this Antichrist shall have devastated all things in this world, he will reign for three years

[151] *The Catholic Encyclopedia*, vol. 8, s.v. "St. Justin Martyr," by Jules Lebreton (New York: Robert Appleton Company, 1910.) 26 Apr. 2010 http://www.newadvent.org/cathen/08580c.htm.
[152] Justin Martyr Dialogue with Trypho 7.
[153] Ibid., 31-47, 31, 32.
[154] Ibid., 69-88, 80.
[155] Ibid., 69-88, 81.
[156] Ibid., 69-88, 80
[157] *The Catholic Encyclopedia*, vol. 8, s.v. "St. Irenaeus," by Albert Poncelet.
[158] Irenaeus Against Heresies 5, 35.2.

and six months, and sit in the temple at Jerusalem; and then the Lord will come from heaven in the clouds, in the glory of the Father, sending this man and those who follow him into the lake of fire; but bringing in for the righteous the times of the kingdom, that is, the rest, the hallowed seventh day; and restoring to Abraham the promised inheritance, in which kingdom the Lord declared, that "many coming from the east and from the west should sit down with Abraham, Isaac, and Jacob." (Matthew 8:11)[159]

Through his writings, it can be seen that Irenaeus believed a literal kingdom comes after a time of great tribulation and before the New Heaven and New Earth, tying these events to the fulfillment of the Abrahamic Covenant.

HIPPOLYTUS OF ROME (A.D. 170-236)

Not until 1851 with the publication of *Philosophumena*, written by Hippolytus, could Hippolytus' life be validated. From what has been verified through this discovery follows.

Hippolytus was a presbyter of the Church of Rome at the beginning of the third century.

There is no difficulty in admitting that he could have been a disciple of St. Irenæus either in Rome or Lyons. It is equally possible that Origen heard a homily by Hippolytus when he went to Rome about the year 212.[160]

It could also be said, "Hippolytus was the most important theologian and the most prolific religious writer of the Roman Church in the pre-Constantinian era." [161]

Within his written discourse on the *end of the world*, Hippolytus explained in detail his interpretation of several Old Testament prophecies in relationship to John's Revelation. His view expounds on the belief of a seven-year tribulation period[162] which the Church will be part of,[163] followed by the judgment seat of Christ, a description of the Great White Throne Judgment, then followed by the eternal kingdom.[164]

---

[159] Irenaeus Against Heresies 5, 30.4

[160] *The Catholic Encyclopedia*, vol. 7, s.v. "St. Hippolytus of Rome," by Johann Peter Kirsch (New York: Robert Appleton Company, 1910.) 26 Apr. 2010 http://www.newadvent.org/cathen/07360c.htm.

[161] Ibid.

[162] Hippolytus On the End of the World 21. *Ante-Nicene Fathers*, vol. 5, ed. Alexander Roberts,

James Donaldson, and A. Cleveland Coxe, trans. J.H. MacMahon (Buffalo, NY: Christian Literature Publishing Co., 1886.) Revised and edited for New Advent by Kevin Knight. http://www.newadvent.org/fathers/0504.htm.

[163] Ibid., 34.

[164] Ibid., 38-49.

LACTANTIUS (A.D. 250-AFTER 317)

[Lactantius was an African-born fourth-century Christian apologist. Lactantius' early days were spent as a pagan and a teacher of rhetoric. His life was lived out in poverty until his talents were discovered. "At the request of Emperor Diocletian, he became an official professor of rhetoric in Nicomedia." After losing this position sometime in 303 A.D., he became a convert to Christianity.

Approximately around 312 A.D., through his friendship with Emperor Constantine, he was appointed as a Latin tutor to the Emperor's son Crispus, a position he held for the remainder of his life. Crispus died in 326 A.D.

Through further research of Lactantius, we learn that:

> Among the works of his pen extant, the earliest is the "De Opificio Dei," written in 303 or 304 during the Diocletian persecution, and dedicated to a former pupil, a rich Christian named Demetrianus. The apologetic principles underlying all the works of Lactantius are well set forth in this treatise, which may be considered as an introduction to his great work "The Divine Institutions" (Divinarum Institutionum Libri VII), written

between 303 and 311. This the most important of all the writings of Lactantius is systematic as well as apologetic and was intended to point out the futility of pagan beliefs and to establish the reasonableness and truth of Christianity. It was the first attempt at a systematic exposition of Christian theology in Latin, and though aimed at certain pamphleteers who were aiding the persecutors by literary assaults on the Church, the work was planned on a scale sufficiently broad enough to silence all opponents.[165]

We are also told that Lactantius was lacking in theological training.] [166] However, despite this seeming shortcoming, it is interesting to note his interpretation of the book of Revelation within the context of providing a philosophical defense supporting the argument that there is life after death.

With relationship to eschatology, Lactantius describes the events of the tribulation period,[167] followed by the coming of Christ, followed by the binding of Satan,[168] followed by a resurrection and judgment for Christians,[169] followed by the resurrection and judgement of other souls,[170] followed by a 1,000-year kingdom,[171] followed by the loosening of Satan and the final judgement.[172]

The emphasis within his discourse is on the philosophical issue of life after death, defending the view that there will be life,

---

[165] *The Catholic Encyclopedia*, vol. 8, s.v. "Lucius Caecilius Firmianus Lactantius," by Albert Poncelet.
[166] Ibid.
[167] Lactantius The Divine Institutes vii, 15-18. *Ante-Nicene Fathers*, vol. 7, ed. Alexander Roberts, James Donaldson, and A. Cleveland Coxe, trans. William Fletcher (Buffalo, NY: Christian Literature Publishing Co., 1886.) Revised and edited for New

Advent by Kevin Knight.
http://www.newadvent.org/fathers/07017.htm.
[168] Ibid., vii, 19.
[169] Ibid., vii, 20.
[170] Ibid., vii, 21-23.
[171] Ibid., vii, 24.
[172] Ibid., vii, 26.

through a resurrection and final judgment for all.

For someone with supposedly so little theological training and understanding of the Scriptures, Lactantius, surprisingly to some, captured the true essence of the book of John's Apocalypse.

VICTORINUS OF PETTAU (A.D. 250-303)

Victorinus was "an ecclesiastical writer who flourished about 270 and suffered martyrdom, probably in 303 under Diocletian."[173] Through additional research we learn he was bishop of the City of Pettau (Petabium, Poetovio), on the Drave in Styria (Austria); hence his surname of Petravionensis or sometimes Pictaviensis, e.g. in the Roman Martyrology,... According to St. Jerome, who gives him an honorable place in his catalogue of ecclesiastical writers, Victorinus composed commentaries on various books of Holy Scripture such as Genesis, Exodus, Leviticus, Isaiah, Ezekiel, Habakkuk, Ecclesiastes, the Canticle of Canticles, St. Matthew, and the Apocalypse, besides treatises against the heresies of his time. All his works have disappeared save extracts from his commentaries on Genesis and the Apocalypse.[174]

Victorinus' commentary on John's Apocalypse writings is set forth in the same format as the twenty-one chapters of the book of Revelation of today, making it easy to follow. Victorinus' views are that of a Premillennialist. He reads the Scriptures and takes them literally, holding to a tribulation period, the binding of Satan and then the 1,000-year millennial rule of Christ.[175]

In Summary

J. Dwight Pentecost (Th.D.) explains, "It is generally agreed that the view of the church for the centuries immediately following the Apostolic era was the premillennial view of the return of Christ."[176] He goes on to quote O. T. Allis on the subject of Premillennialism, which reads,

(Premillennialism) was extensively held in the Early church, how extensively is not definitely known. But the stress which many of its advocates place on earthly rewards and carnal delights aroused widespread opposition to it, and it was largely replaced by the "spiritual" view of Augustine. It reappeared in extravagant forms at the time of the Reformation, notably among the Anabaptists. Bengel and Mede were among the first modern scholars of distinction to advocate it. But it was not until early in the last century that it became at all widely influential in modern times. Since

[173] *The Catholic Encyclopedia*, vol. 15, s.v. "St. Victorinus," by Léon Clugnet (New York: Robert Appleton Company, 1912.) 26 Apr. 2010 http://www.newadvent.org/cathen/15414a.htm.
[174] Ibid.
[175] Victorinus Commentary on the Apocalypse 1-21. *Ante-Nicene Fathers*, vol. 7, ed. Alexander Roberts, James Donaldson, and A. Cleveland Coxe,

trans. Robert Ernest Wallis (Buffalo, NY: Christian Literature Publishing Co., 1886.) Revised and edited for New Advent by Kevin Knight. http://www.newadvent.org/fathers/ 0712.htm.
[176] J. Dwight Pentecost, *Things to Come* (Grand Rapids: Zondervan Publishing House, 1964), 373.

then it has become increasingly popular; and the claim is frequently made that most of the leaders in the Church today, who are evangelical, are Premillennialists.[177]

Pentecost continues this line of reasoning as he quotes Whitby, a postmillennialist who states,

> The doctrine of the Millennium, or the reign of saints on earth for a thousand years, is now rejected by all Roman Catholics, and by the greatest part of Protestants; and yet it passed among the best Christians, for two hundred and fifty years, for a tradition epostolical; and, as such, is delivered by many Fathers of the second and third century, who speak of it as the tradition of the Lord and His apostles, and of all the ancients who lived before them; who tell us the very words in which it was delivered, the Scriptures which were then so interpreted; and say that it was held by all Christians that were exactly orthodox.[178]

Pentecost then sums up these statements by writing, "That such concessions should be made by anti-premillenarians is only because history records the fact that such a premillennial belief was the universal belief of the church for two hundred and fifty years after the death of Christ." [179]

AUGUSTINE TO THE REFORMATION

Matthew Allen (J.D.) in 2004 wrote an article and submitted it to Bible.org for online publication. The article was based on his personal research that provided reasonable and historical factors to the theological community, explaining why premillennialism may have been abandoned by early Church Fathers by the fourth century. The following information is a summary of his article as republished on March 10, 2012 with Bible.org.

[Matthew Allen explains to us there were three major factors that contributed to a shift in theological thought in the second and third centuries, which provided a *paradigm shift* from a position of premillennialism of the ancient church Fathers to an Amillennialism or postmillennialism position advocated for during the Medieval times and beyond. This shift would dominate eschatological thinking, starting in the fourth century in church history through a good part of the nineteenth century.

The first factor came in the second century when the early church Fathers failed to maintain a clear scriptural distinction between Israel and the Church. The evidence of this comes through the writings of Clement of Rome in his first letter to the church of Corinth, which reads in part:

> Let us then draw near to Him with holiness of spirit, lifting up pure and undefiled hands unto Him, loving our gracious and merciful

---

[177] Oswald T. Allis, *Prophecy and the Church* (Philadelphia: Presbyterian and Reformed Publishing Company, 1945), 238, quoted in J. Dwight Pentecost, *Things to Come* (Grand Rapids: Zondervan Publishing House, 1964), 373.

[178] G. N. H. Peters, *Theocratic Kingdom*, vol. 3 (Grand Rapids, MI: Kregel Publications, 1952), 482-83, quoted in J. Dwight Pentecost, *Things to Come* (Grand Rapids: Zondervan Publishing House, 1964), 373-4.

[179] Pentecost, *Things to Come*, 374.

Father, who has made us partakers in the blessings of His elect. For thus it is written, When the Most High divided the nations, when He scattered the sons of Adam, He fixed the bounds of the nations according to the number of the angels of God. His people Jacob became the portion of the Lord, and Israel, the lot of His inheritance. Deuteronomy 32:8-9 And in another place (the Scripture) says, "*Behold, the Lord takes unto Himself a nation out of the midst of the nations, as a man takes the first-fruits of his threshing-floor; and from that nation shall come forth the Most Holy.*" [180]

These statements could be interpreted to mean the church is included in Israel's promised inheritance. The vagueness of these statements is better understood through the writings of Justin Martyr in *Dialogue with Trypho* as he writes:

What larger measure of grace, then, did Christ bestow on Abraham? This, namely, that He called him with His voice by the like calling, telling him to quit the land wherein he dwelt. And He has called all of us by that voice, and we have left already the way of living in which we used to spend our days, passing our time in evil after the fashions of the other inhabitants of the earth; and along with Abraham we shall inherit the holy land, when we shall receive the inheritance for an endless eternity, being children of Abraham through the like faith. For as he believed the voice of God, and it was imputed to him for righteousness, in

like manner we having believed God's voice spoken by the apostles of Christ, and promulgated to us by the prophets, have renounced even to death all the things of the world. Accordingly, He promises to him a nation of similar faith, God-fearing, righteous, and delighting the Father; but it is not you, 'in whom is no faith.'[181]

Trypho: What, then? Are you Israel? And speaks He such things of you?

Justin: If, indeed, we had not entered into a lengthy discussion on these topics, I might have doubted whether you ask this question in ignorance; but since we have brought the matter to a conclusion by demonstration and with your assent, I do not believe that you are ignorant of what I have just said, or desire again mere contention, but that you are urging me to exhibit the same proof to these men.

And in compliance with the assent expressed in his eyes, I continued:

Justin: Again in Isaiah, if you have ears to hear it, God, speaking of Christ in parable, calls Him Jacob and Israel. He speaks thus: 'Jacob is my servant, I will uphold Him; Israel is my elect, I will put my Spirit upon Him, and He shall bring forth judgment to the Gentiles. He shall not strive, nor cry, neither shall anyone hear His voice in the street: a bruised reed He shall not break, and smoking flax He shall not quench; but He shall bring forth judgment to

---

[180] Clement of Rome First Epistle 29. *Ante-Nicene Fathers*, vol. 9, ed. Allan Menzies, trans. John Keith (Buffalo, NY: Christian Literature Publishing Co., 1896.) Revised and edited for New Advent by

Kevin Knight http://www.newadvent.org/fathers/1010.htm.
[181] Martyr Dialogue with Trypho 119.

truth: He shall shine, and shall not be broken till He have set judgment on the earth. And in His name shall the Gentiles trust.' (Isaiah 42:1-4) As therefore from the one man Jacob, who was surnamed Israel, all your nation has been called Jacob and Israel; so we from Christ, who begot us unto God, like Jacob, and Israel, and Judah, and Joseph, and David, are called and are the true sons of God, and keep the commandments of Christ.[182]

Through the conversation between Justin and a Jewish man named Trypho, it becomes clear that Justin's interpretation is that the church should be part of Israel's inheritance through the Abrahamic Covenant of promise. Hence, a clear distinction between the two entities is becoming blurred.] [183]

It should be noted here that the interpretation of these two early Fathers is not of one entity replacing the other, but the two becoming one. This is the same hope the Apostle Paul spoke to in Ephesians 2:11-16:

> Therefore remember, that formerly you, the Gentiles in the flesh, who are called 'Uncircumcision' by the so-called 'Circumcision,' which is performed in the flesh by human hands— remember that you were at that time separate from Christ, excluded from the commonwealth of Israel, and strangers to the covenants of promise, having no hope and

without God in the world. But now in Christ Jesus you who formerly were far off have been brought near by the blood of Christ. For He Himself is our peace, who made both groups into one, and broke down the barrier of the dividing wall, by abolishing in His flesh the enmity, which is the Law of commandments contained in ordinances, that in Himself He might make the two into one new man, thus establishing peace, and might reconcile them both in one body to God through the cross, by it having put to death the enmity.

When Paul writes, "For He Himself is our peace, who made both groups into one, and broke down the barrier of the dividing wall, by abolishing in His flesh the enmity, which is the Law of commandments contained in ordinances, that in Himself He might make the two into one new man...," he is making a reference to two groups, represented by the Jews (Israel) and the newly founded sect called Christians founded in Christ.

Holding to the view that Scripture should be understood as a whole and not in part,[184] the truth of Paul's writings in Ephesians Chapter 2 must be placed in context to the mystery explained in the first eight verses in Chapter 3. Paul's first mention of this mystery comes to us in Colossians 1:25-27 which reads,

> Of this church I was made a minister according to the stewardship from God bestowed on

---

[182] Martyr Dialogue with Trypho 123.

[183] Matthew Allen, "Theology Adrift: The Early Church Fathers and Their Views of Eschatology," [article online]; available from https://bible.org/article/theology-adrift-early-church-fathers-and-their-views-eschatology-0; accessed; 15 December

2018. Note: The referenced source for the *Ante-Nicene Fathers* provided in the original article was substituted with the author's references to the same material.

[184] Terry, *Biblical Hermeneutics*, 18-19.

me for your benefit, that I might fully carry out the preaching of the word of God, that is, the mystery which has been hidden from the past ages and generations; but has now been manifested to His saints, to whom God willed to make known what is the riches of the glory of this mystery among the Gentiles, which is Christ in you, the hope of glory.

With all this said, the mystery of Christ must be understood in the relationship of Paul's teaching found in Romans 11:11 and 11:25-32, with the major points expressed this way: "I say then, they did not stumble so as to fall, did they? May it never be! But by their transgression salvation has come to the Gentiles, to make them jealous (Romans 11:11)." Paul goes on to say in 11:25-27:

> For I do not want you, brethren, to be uninformed of this mystery, lest you be wise in your own estimation, that a partial hardening has happened to Israel until the fulness of the Gentiles has come in; and thus all Israel will be saved; just as it is written,

> *The Deliverer will come from Zion,*
> *He will remove ungodliness from Jacob.*
> *And this is My covenant with them,*
> *When I take away their sins.*

This is a reflection that the New Covenant was made with Israel, not the Church; through the "mystery of Christ" as revealed by the Apostle Paul. God is now offering salvation to the Gentiles (non-Jews) at the same time he is offering salvation to the Jews; not to replace them, but as a temporary bypass, as expressed in Romans 11:11. The Apostle goes on to express this concept as a *grafting in* process (Romans 11:17-24).

How does this tie into the Abrahamic Covenant? The Covenant made with Abraham had three components to it, which will be discussed at greater length in other chapters. This covenant is represented as the promise for land, the promise to be a great nation, and the promise to be a blessing to the world, which came through the Gospel of Christ as represented in the New Covenant. This is what the Apostle Paul meant when he said, "And the Scripture, foreseeing that God would justify the Gentiles by faith, preached the gospel beforehand to Abraham, saying, 'All the nations shall be blessed in you'" (Galatians 3:8), referring back to the statement made in Genesis 12:3 which reads, "And I will bless those who bless you, And the one who curses you I will curse. And in you, all the families of the earth shall be blessed."

To further support this argument, one must also take into account two additional mysteries, the mystery of the church as expressed in Romans 11:25, represented in the phrase, "until the fullness of the Gentiles has come in," interpreted to mean the *Church Age,* and is more clearly referenced in Ephesians 3:4-13, which reads in part:

> To me, the very least of all saints, this grace was given, to preach to the Gentiles the unfathomable riches of Christ, and to bring to light what is the administration of the mystery which for ages has been hidden in God, who created all things; in order that the manifold wisdom of God might now be made known through the church to the rulers and the authorities in the heavenly places. This was in accordance with the

eternal purpose which He carried out in Christ Jesus our Lord, in whom we have boldness and confident access through faith in Him.

The question becomes, was the interpretation of the early Fathers correct, or did they miss something in the wider context of the subject matter? In light of the immediate context, the Fathers seem to get it right, but in the context of the scriptures as a whole, they missed some steps along the way.

Within the context of society at the time, the Fathers could have been distracted on this point on several levels. Matthew Allen continues to explain his argument by providing four factors at this point in history that could have made it much easier for the Christian community as a whole to understand the scriptures in the manner the Fathers missed in their understanding.

[The first historic factor is based on the *Enmity* between the Jewish and Christian sects in the first century, as demonstrated within the examples of the following scriptures: Acts 4:1ff; 5:17ff; 6:12ff; 9:1; 1 Thess. 2:14-16 and Rev. 2:9.

Historically, this played out with the Christian sect abandoning the Jews in 70 A.D. when the Romans destroyed the temple in Jerusalem. Then in 90 A.D., the Jewish proclamation at the *Council of Jamnia* [185] went out, stating that all who departed from the standard Jewish faith were cursed.

The second historic factor is based on the Jewish wars in 70 A.D. and 132-135 A.D. With these Jewish defeats, the Christian community may have become swayed by the idea that God was moving away from the Jewish people as a whole.

The third historic factor is based on the Jews still refusing to accept Christ as their Messiah as time moved on into the second century.

The fourth historic factor was more subtle in nature, reflecting itself in the growing composition of the Christian sect to becoming more Gentile vs. Jewish in nature by the second century. This would allow for the Christian community as a whole to move on in their current theological developments, leaving the Jewish sect out of the picture.

With all these factors at play, the newly found Church would find it easy to believe God had abandoned his original chosen people and placed themselves in that role to become the new Israel.

The second major factor Allen presents is the move from a literal textual hermeneutic to a functional hermeneutic. As an example, Allen speaks about how some early Fathers would take the Apostle Paul's writings and use them in their own writings, applying them out of context to support their own situations. This made it easier for others to later move from a literal hermeneutic to allegorization, which is what took place with Origen, who played the first major role in making allegorization acceptable within the structure of the Christian church.

The third and last major factor that influenced the moving away from Premillennialism by the fourth century, is expressed by Allen as he writes,

> The crushing blow for premillennialism came with the

---

[185] Dr. Eli Lizorkin-Eyzenberg, "Council of Jamnia," [article on line]; available from https://blog.israelbiblicalstudies.com/jewish-studies/jamnia/; Internet; accessed 23 January 2019.

Note: This footnote is provided as an additional resource of information to the historical setting of the Council of Jamnia.

Edict of Milan in AD 313, by which Constantine reversed the Roman Empire's policy of hostility toward Christianity and accorded it full legal recognition and even favor. Historian Paul Johnson calls the issuance of this edict 'one of the decisive events in world history.'[186]

With it, no longer was the blood of the martyrs the seed of the church. Rather, Christianity would be, in many ways, a mirror image of the empire itself. 'It was Catholic, universal, ecumenical, orderly, international, multi-racial and increasingly legalistic.'[187] 'It was a huge force for stability.'[188] Hence, Christianity after 313 would become worldly, rather than other-worldly.

Jerome complained that 'one who was yesterday a catechumen is today a bishop; another moves overnight from the amphitheater to the church; a man who spent the evening in the circus stands next morning at the altar, and another who was recently a patron of the stage is now the dedicator of virgins.'[189] He wrote that 'our walls glitter with gold, and gold gleams upon our ceilings and the capitals of our pillars; yet Christ is dying at our doors in the person of his poor, naked and hungry.'[190]

With persecution gone, the need for hope of a new kingdom begins to fade away, providing a new avenue to doing away with such thought toward a new perspective called Amillennialism, which came through Augustine to the Reformation without any real opposition.][191]

REFORMATION TO TODAY

J. Dwight Pentecost (Th.D.) brings to our attention that, despite the ascendancy of Roman Amillenarianism, there always remained a small remnant who held to the premillennial position, such as the Waldensians, Paulicians, and the Cathari.[192]

Within this mix, Anabaptists could also be included, as we are told,

> The Anabaptists were great readers of Revelation and of the Epistle of James, the latter perhaps by way of counteracting Luther's one-sided teaching of justification by faith alone. Luther feebly rejected this scripture as 'a right strawy epistle.' English Anabaptists often knew it by heart. Excessive reading of Revelation seems to have been the chief cause of the aberrations of

---

186 Paul Johnson, *A History of Christianity* (New York: Athenium, 1976), 67, quoted in Matthew Allen, "Theology Adrift: The Early Church Fathers and Their Views of Eschatology," [article on-line]; available from https://bible.org/article/theology-adrift-early-hurch-fathers-and-their-views-eschatology-0; Internet; accessed 15 December 2018.

187 Paul Johnson, *A History of Christianity*, 76.

188 Ibid.

189 Paul Johnson, *A History of Christianity*, quoted Ibid., 78.

190 Jerome Letters 128, 4. *Nicene and Post-Nicene Fathers*, Second Series, vol. 6, ed. Philip Schaff and Henry Wace, trans. W.H. Fremantle, G. Lewis and W.G. Martley, (Buffalo, NY: Christian Literature Publishing Co., 1893.) Revised and edited for New Advent by Kevin Knight. http://www.newadvent.org/fathers/3001128.htm; quoted in Johnson, *A History of Christianity*, 79. Note: Footnote reference expanded through additional research.

191 Matthew Allen, "Theology Adrift: The Early Church Fathers and Their Views of Eschatology," [article on-line]; available from https://bible.org/article/theology-adrift-early-church-fathers-and-their-views-eschatology-0; Internet; accessed 15 December 2018.

192 Pentecost, *Things to Come*, 383.

the Münster fanatics. Those who yielded to stress of persecution fell back into Papalism and went to swell the tide of the Catholic reaction.[193]

Michael D. Stallard (Ph.D.) provides some additional history of the post-Reformation Anabaptists.

> The eschatology of the sixteenth-century Anabaptists was largely premillennial. However, it is hard to generalize about a movement with so many diverse strands, especially if identification is made of Anabaptism in general with the Radical Reformation.
>
> … What is clear by this survey of the varied strands of Anabaptist chiliasm is that there is not yet development along the lines of dispensational premillennialism as found in John Nelson Darby in the early nineteenth century. The Anabaptists were historicists, not futurists in their understanding of most key prophetic passages. The exact nature of the earthly kingdom once Christ returned is also not as clear as in Darby's system. In fact there is no clear delineation of the roles of the Jews, the nation of Israel, and the Church as they related to the final destiny brought about by God. However, there can be little doubt that the primary direction of Anabaptist eschatology was premillennial.[194]

TYPES OF PREMILLENNIALISM

COVENANT HISTORICAL

To provide a historical perspective to historical Premillennialism, let us look at two views expressed by two sources from two separate periods.

Post-millennialist Charles Hodge, in his three-volume *Systematic Theology* work published in 1873, expresses his understanding of Premillennialism and its history in the following manner:

> *The Theory of the Pre-millennial Advent.*
>
> The common doctrine of the Church stated above, is that the conversion of the world, the restoration of the Jews, and the destruction of Antichrist are to precede the second coming of Christ, which event will be attended by the general resurrection of the dead, the final judgment, the end of the world, and the consummation of the Church.
>
> In opposition to this view, the doctrine of a pre-millennial advent of Christ has been extensively held from the days of the Apostles to the present time. According to this view, (1.) The nations are not to be converted, nor are the Jews to be restored to their standing in the Church, until the second coming of Christ. (2.) His advent is to be personal and glorious. (3.) He will establish Himself in Jerusalem as the

---

[193] *Encyclopaedia Britannica*, 11th ed. vol. 1, s.v. "Anabaptist of sixteenth century" (New York: Encyclopaedia Britannica, Inc., 1910), 905; available from The Historical Archive, [DVD], THA New Media, LLC., 2017.

[194] Michael D. Stallard, "Anabaptists, Eschatology," [article on line]; available from https://www.tyndale.edu/wp-content/uploads/files/HIST5317-Stallard/HIST5317%20History%20of%20Eschatology%20Stallard%20Anabaptists.doc; Internet; accessed 28 November 2018.

head of a visible, external kingdom. (4.) When He comes, the martyrs, as some say, or, as others believe, all who sleep in Jesus, shall be raised from the dead and associated with Him in this earthly kingdom. (5.) The Jews are to be converted, restored to their own land, invested with special honors and prerogatives, and made the instruments of the conversion of the world. (6.) This kingdom is to be one of great splendor, prosperity, and blessedness, and is to continue a thousand years; which, however, as stated above, is understood in different senses. (7.) After the expiration of the millennium, the general resurrection of the dead, the end of the world, and the final consummation of the Church are to occur. Such are the general features of the scheme which, with many modifications as to details, is known as the pre-millennial advent theory.[195]

Paul Lee Tan (Th.D.) defines Covenant Premillennialism as "a system of eschatology which attempts to reconcile premillennialism with covenantism while avoiding dispensationalism and pretribulationism." [196] Ultimately, this is accomplished through how covenant theologians view Israel and the Church. Tan writes,

> Covenant theologians teach that the Old Testament Israel and the New Testament church are one people, one being the continuation and successor of the other. While

some covenant theologians begin this line of people with Abraham (leaving out saints who lived before Abraham), most covenant theologians would backtrack the line to Adam. It has moreover been affirmed that the church is not to be linked with the entire ancient nation Israel but only with the *true* Israelites of that nation.[197]

This becomes a dilemma for those holding to such a view. Tan states, "Covenant theologians themselves do not see eye to eye on how the promises to Israel are fulfilled in the church."[198]

Tan goes on to provide one reason for the rejection of the Nation of Israel as part of the church is because of Israel's rejection of the Messiah through their act of Christ's crucifixion.[199] How do they come to such conclusions? It is all about how one hermeneutically interprets the Scriptures.

Tan explains just what this really means from a hermeneutical perspective.

[Covenant Premillennialism is less consistent in its approach to a literal hermeneutic. On one hand they see the 144,000 witnesses in Revelation 7 to represent the church through their spiritualization of the Scriptures and see the 1,000 years of Revelation 20 literally as an earthly Kingdom. This is what we call selective inconsistency, picking and choosing what we should see as literal or what we should be spiritualizing. Tan expresses his concern with this method of interpretation as he writes,

> The danger in selective inconsistency is that, based neither entirely on the literal method nor

---

[195] Hodge, *Systematic Theology*, vol. 3, 861-862.
[196] Tan, *The Interpretation of Prophecy*, 364.
[197] Ibid., 247

[198] Ibid., 248
[199] Ibid.

entirely on the non-literal, the interpreter finds himself constantly struggling with the question of how far he should go spiritualizing or when he should stop literalizing. This is especially troublesome for those who wish to face eschatological issues squarely and extensively. Daniel P. Fuller, after attacking consistent literality and the dispensational system, candidly admits that[200] 'the whole problem of how far a literal interpretation of the Old Testament prophets is to be carried is still very perplexing to the present writer.' [201]

Tan goes on to say that the reason for this inconsistency is to avoid the issue of pretribulational dispensationalism.

Berkhof, an amillennialist, treats the issue of premillennialism and dispensationalism as interconnected as a matter of consistency. "The main pillars on which it (premillennialism) rests are undoubtedly the so-called literal or natural interpretation of the prophets, and the dispensational interpretation of the Bible. If this foundation is removed, the building falls flat." [202] Tan goes on to state, "Consistent premillennialism leads to pretribulationism. The latter is the logical product of the former."[203]] [204]

Historical Development of Dispensationalism

J. N. Darby Early Years 1825-1900	Scofield/Chafer Later Years 1909-1948	McClain/Pentecost Walvoord/Ryrie 1950-1990	Bock/Blaising Progressive Years 1991-Present Time
Classical Period	Modern Period	Fundamental Period	Revisionary Period

Table 4.1 [205]

---

[200] Tan, *The Interpretation of Prophecy*, 268.

[201] Daniel Peyton Fuller, *The Hermeneutics of Dispensationalism* (Doctor's dissertation, Northern Baptist Theol. Seminary, Chicago, 1957), 374, quoted in Tan, *The Interpretation of Prophecy*, 269.

[202] Louis Berkhof, *The Kingdom of God* (Grand Rapids: Wm. B. Eerdmans Pub. Co., 1951), 160, quoted in Tan, *The Interpretation of Prophecy*, 270.

[203] Tan, *The Interpretation of Prophecy*, 270.

[204] Ibid., 268-270.

[205] Charles C. Ryrie, *Dispensationalism* (Chicago: Moody Publishers, 2007), 190. Note: Table 4.1 was formulated as a result of the discussion on the "Origins of the Movement" in chapter 9 of *Dispensationalism* by Charles Ryrie.

DISPENSATIONAL

Dispensational Theology is based on six essential principles as expressed in chapter one. To maintain the continuity of this chapter, we will list them again.

1. The hermeneutical principle of a literal interpretation of the Scriptures.

2. The literal fulfillment of Old Testament prophecies.

3. A clear recognized distinction between the Nation of Israel and the New Testament Church.

4. This view supports a pre-tribulation rapture.

5. This view supports a literal millennial Kingdom.

6. Salvation is always by grace through faith and that the dispensations are rules of life, never the basis or cause of salvation.

Dispensationalism in the U. K.

This history starts with John Nelson Darby and the Plymouth Brethren movement.

JOHN NELSON DARBY—A.D. 1800-1882

John Nelson Darby has been assigned the title, Father of early Dispensationalism by historians, with his views supported by many of the early church fathers in the first three centuries after Christ's ascension.

Even Christ referenced differing time periods where God would be doing things differently, such as Old Testament times, the present age and the age to come.[206]

Who was John Darby and what were his views?

John Nelson Darby was born in Westminster, London, and christened at St. Margaret's on 3 March 1801. He was the youngest of the six sons of John Darby and Anne Vaughan. The Darbys were an Anglo-Irish landowning family seated at Leap Castle, King's County, Ireland, (present-day County Offaly). He was the nephew of Admiral Henry D'Esterre Darby and his middle name was given in recognition of his godfather and family friend, Lord Nelson.

Darby was educated at Westminster School and Trinity College, Dublin where he graduated Classical Gold Medallist in 1819. Darby embraced Christianity during his studies, although there is no evidence that he formally studied theology. He joined an inn of court, but felt that being a lawyer was inconsistent with his religious belief. He, therefore, chose ordination as an Anglican clergyman in Ireland, "lest he should sell his talents to defeat justice." In 1825, Darby was ordained deacon of the established Church of Ireland and the following year as priest....

John Nelson Darby was an Anglo-Irish Bible teacher, one of the influential figures among the original Plymouth Brethren and the founder of the Exclusive Brethren. ... He

---

[206] Matt. 24:3-29.

produced translations of the Bible in German "Elberfelder Bibel," French "Pau" Bible, Dutch New Testament, and English (finished posthumously) based on the Hebrew and Greek texts called The Holy Scriptures: A New Translation from the Original Languages by J. N. Darby. It has furthermore been translated into other languages in whole or part.[207]

What John Nelson Darby believed about eschatology is best understood from his own lectures, published in 1868.

According to 33 pages of published lecture notes, these lectures took place in his home country—England—in the cities of London, Glasgow, Dublin, and Guernsey. We find that in lecture 2 entitled, "Lectures on the Second Coming of Christ," John Darby was able to articulate his views as he pulled together, in a very systematic way, a literal interpretation of the Scriptures, starting with Ephesians Chapter One and tying the concept of the Christian's promised inheritance in Christ, as joint-heirs, with all future activities of Christ, effecting the Church directly, as demonstrated through the Old Testament prophecies with their connection to the New Testament Messiah.[208]

Darby ties the whole of Scripture to this topic and opens his lecture with the following dialogue:

At the last lecture I mentioned that the two Epistles in which the second coming of the Lord is not

spoken of are the Galatians and the Ephesians. It may seem strange that, this being the case, I should have selected on this occasion the chapter we have just read. But I have done so, (and shall refer to other passages with the same intention, desiring to found all I say upon Scripture) because that chapter gives us a general view of the whole scheme and plan that will be fully accomplished at the second coming of our Lord. It does not speak of the fact of Christ's coming, but it does tell of the purpose which God has, and that will then be accomplished. And not only that, but it shows us the way in which the church of God (I mean all true saints gathered to Christ by the Holy Ghost sent down from heaven) at the coming of Christ have a portion or part in it— what their place in this great plan of God is, that plan having necessarily for its centre the exaltation of the Son, "the brightness of God's glory." He was humbled to be exalted.[209]

Darby expresses his views on the current attitude of the church at large by saying,

And there is not a greater proof of the extent to which the church has lost its conscious identity with Christ, than its giving up its expectation of the coming of Christ. And why is that but because there

[207] *Wikipedia*, s.v. "John Nelson Darby," [encyclopedia on line]; available from https://en.wikipedia.org/wiki/John_Nelson_Darb; Internet; accessed 13 January 2019.

[208] J. N. Darby., "Lectures on the Second Coming of Christ," Lecture II, Based on Ephesians 1, given at (London: George Morrish, 24 Warwick Lane, Paternoster Row, E.C.; Glasgow: R.L. Allan,

75 Sauchiehall Street; Dublin: F. Cavenagh, The Tract Depot, 32 Wicklow Street; Guernsey: J. Tunley, 104 Victoria Road, 1868); available from https://www.brethrenarchive.org/people/john-nelson-darby/pamphlets/lectures-on-second-coming-lecture-ii/; Internet; accessed 1 January 2019.

[209] Ibid., 3.

are so many whose hearts do not enter into this thought, that God has brought them so near to Himself that they are considered as having been taken into His family? "Sons and daughters," the expression is, and sons and daughters too of full age. That was not their position under the law.[210]

The Abrahamic Covenant

Darby ties the Abrahamic Covenant to promises made to the saints that are not directly associated with Abraham.

> The Lord says, "Shall I hide from Abraham that thing which I do" And what He then told Him was not merely that he personally was in His favour—that He told him long before. He does not merely show him the promises which belonged to him and his seed. But He told him too what concerned the world, and did not immediately concern himself. This was the special mark of friendship.[211]

God's Overall Plan for His People

Darby expresses his view on what God's plan is for the saints, then goes on to explain how God will accomplish that plan.

> We are not waiting to be sons— we are all the children of God through faith in Christ Jesus; but we are waiting to get what belongs to the sons. Poor earthen vessels that we are here, in the wilderness, we are waiting for that. He has given us "the Holy Spirit of promise, which is the earnest of our inheritance, until the redemption of the purchased

possession, unto the praise of His glory." That is, the glory of His grace we have got, the redemption; but the glory we have not got—this we are waiting for.

> "That in the dispensation of the fulness of times He might gather together in one all things in Christ, both which are in heaven and which are on earth"—under Christ as the Head. But when Christ takes this place as man—of course as God He is over all always—but when He takes this place as man, we take the inheritance along with Him. We are joint-heirs—"in whom also we have obtained an inheritance." And, again in Romans, "if children, then heirs, heirs of God, and joint-heirs with Christ."

> Now the principle of that is what many Christians are sadly unmindful of, having lost the consciousness of the way in which they have been brought by God into the Same place as Christ, who became a man on purpose to bring us into the same place with Himself. "The glory which thou gavest me I have given them." If He is a Son, so are we. He is our life, our righteousness; and we share His glory, the fruit of righteousness. When He was transfigured, Moses and Elias appeared in the same glory, talking familiarly with Him. And we should consider that the Lord has come down in lowliness and humiliation amongst us, that our hearts might get near enough to Him to understand that.

---

[210] Darby, "Lectures on the Second Coming of Christ," Lecture II, 4.

[211] Ibid.

Having got the plan then, we shall now go through some passages of Scripture to show how the Lord brings it about.[212]

Darby points out that the promises made to the New Testament saints have not been realized yet, opening the door to the need of the second coming of Christ. "But the point is this, that what He created as God, He takes for an inheritance as man, in order that we might take it with Him; but that time is not come yet."[213]

The Binding of Satan

You will find this remarkably brought out, if you turn to Colossians 1. I wish to dwell a little on this, that we may get to as full an understanding as possible of the thoughts and scope and plan of God, which seem to me to be very plainly set forth in Scripture. Begin at the 12th verse, which shows where we, (I mean all believers) are "Giving thanks unto the Father, which hath made us meet." *He hath* made us meet—that is all settled. You will always find this in Scripture; you will not find anything there about growing to be meet; it speaks about growing up to Christ in everything, but this is a different thing. "Which hath made us meet to be partakers of the inheritance of the saints in light, who hath delivered us from the power of darkness, and hath translated us into the kingdom of his dear Son; who is the image of the invisible God, the first born of every creature; for by him"—this is the reason why He is set over all things—"by him were all things

created that are in heaven, and that are on earth, visible and invisible, whether they be thrones, or dominions, or principalities, or powers; all things were created by him. and for him." He is to take them all under subjection, but not in this state of wickedness in which they are now. "We see not yet all things put under Him."

And how does He take them? He takes them as a man—"whom he hath appointed heir of all things," (Hebrew i. 2), and we are appointed joint heirs with Him, as the Scripture tells us. You will see, therefore, how the second part comes in. "And he before all things, and by him all things consist"—that is, because He is a divine person—"And he is the head of the body, the church; who is the beginning, the first born from the dead; that in all things he might have the pre-eminence." He has this double headship, which is also brought together in the chapter of Ephesians I was reading—head over all things, and head to the church. "By him to reconcile all things unto himself; by him, I say, whether they be things, in earth or things in heaven. And you that were sometime alienated and enemies in your mind by wicked works, yet now hath he reconciled, in the body of his flesh through death." "Hath reconciled,"—it is always *hath*, as regards the saints. It is not said "He will reconcile," but "hath reconciled."

---

[212] Darby, "Lectures on the Second Coming of Christ," Lecture II, 7-8.

[213] Ibid., 12.

But the reconciliation of all things in heaven and earth is future, because Satan is not yet bound.[214]

The Church and Israel as Separate Entities

What I have been seeking to show you, is, that the Church of God (all the saints whom in this present time God is gathering by His grace in the Gospel) are being associated with Christ, as the centre of blessing, that they get the central place with Himself, under whom all possible existences are to be placed. But the time for this which the Scripture speaks of is when Christ receives the kingdom and returns, when the dispensation of the fulness of times comes. Then everything will be brought into order and blessedness under the authority of Christ. When God the Father has put everything under His feet, He will bring everything into order, and will then deliver up His kingdom. But the central thing during the dispensation of the fulness of times in the heavenly places will be the Church, and the central thing in earthly places will be the Jews.

This brings in what are the two great subjects of Holy Scripture, after personal redemption. The Church is that in which He displays sovereign grace, bringing its numbers to share the glory of Christ. The Jews are those in whom He reveals as a centre, the government of this world. These are the two great subjects in Scripture, after personal salvation. The Scripture speaks of the Church of God, as those who are associated with Christ, who are the heirs of Christ's glory.[215]

Resurrection and Rapture of the Saints

If you turn again to the Corinthians xv., you will see this same truth brought out in its relation to the resurrection. The point I am now to impress upon you is, that Scripture shows us these two things—that we are to be like Him, completely like Him, save that He is a divine person; and that the time we shall be like Him is when we shall be raised from the dead. It is then we shall appear with Him.—We are not of the world now, but it is said that the world will only know that we have been loved as Christ was loved, when they see us in the same place of glory with Him, when the Lord takes us up to be with Him and to put us in this glory; so that when He appears to the world we shall appear along with Him in the same glory.[216]

… In like manner, we get what may be called the public announcement of this in the fourth chapter of 1st Thessalonians— "Them also which sleep in Jesus will God bring with him. For this we say unto you by the word of the Lord, that which are alive and remain unto the coming of the Lord." See how the apostle constantly expected the coming of the Lord. Some people have boldly dared to say that Paul made a mistake in expecting the coming of the Lord in his day. It is they who are making an awful miss-

---

214 Darby, "Lectures on the Second Coming of Christ," Lecture II, 15-16.

215 Ibid., 17-18.
216 Ibid., 21-22.

mistake. It was never revealed when Christ would come, and Paul did not pretend to know it.[217]

… Here, then, we have the details of it. The Lord hath declared that he will come and receive us unto Himself; and now the apostle, by the revelation given unto him, explains how it will be. He will come and call us up to meet the Lord in the air. The passage in 1 Corinthians, which I have already read, refers to the same thing, when it says, "afterward they that are Christ's at His coming." "But every man in his own order, Christ the first fruits." The specific thing here is that it is not a resurrection of the dead, but a resurrection from among the dead. The raising of Christ was not a resurrection "of the dead," simply, but a resurrection "from among the dead." This was its whole character, a taking up from among the dead, and why? Because the Father's delight was in Him. And why are we in like manner taken up from among the dead? Because His delight is in us.[218]

The Second Advent

And, if you turn to Colossians iii. you will see that, when Christ appears, we shall appear in this glory along with Himself and like Him. He will have already come and taken us up to Himself; and then He comes manifesting Himself to the world, and we appear with Him. You will remember what I have before quoted, that the glory which was given Him, He hath given to us, that the world might know, & C'. Now turning to Colossians iii., and you will see how thoroughly the apostle identifies us with Christ. Look first at chapter ii. 20, "If ye be dead with Christ." Then, at the beginning of the third chapter, "If ye then be risen with Christ, seek those things which are above, where Christ sitteth on the right hand of God. Set your affection on things above, not on things on the earth. For ye are dead and your life is hid with Christ in God." He is hid in God; He is your life, and your life therefore is hid there. "When Christ, who is our life, shall appear, then shall ye also appear with Him in glory." When He appears, we shall appear with Him. There can be no separation. If He is hid in God, our life is hid in God. If he appears, we appear. If He appears in glory, we must appear in glory with Him. We are heirs of God, and joint heirs with Christ.[219]

Second Advent tied to Revelation 20

Further, as to this appearing with Him, I shall now refer to the Book of Revelation; but, before doing that, you may turn for a moment to Zechariah xiv., where it is said the Lord shall come and all His saints with Him, and his feet shall stand in that day upon the Mount of Olives. This is referred to by the angel, when, after Christ's ascension from Mount Olivet, he said to the disciples, "Why stand ye gazing up into heaven? this same Jesus, which is taken up from you into heaven, shall so come in like manner as ye

---

[217] Darby, "Lectures on the Second Coming of Christ," Lecture II, 23.

[218] Ibid., 25.
[219] Ibid., 26-27.

have seen him go into heaven." Again in verse 14 of the epistle of Jude, you find— "And Enoch also, the seventh from Adam, prophesied of these, sayings, Behold, the Lord cometh with myriads of his saints, to execute judgment upon all." Here they are associated with Christ in the executing of judgments. "The Lord cometh with ten thousands"— properly myriads, that is, an immense number,— "of his saints to execute judgment." This shows how entirely we are associated with Christ. And what a place does not that put us in! Yet Scripture is so simple and plain upon the point that it cannot he misinterpreted.[220]

Darby Summarizes

Darby closes out his lecture with the final judgment of Satan and the rest of the world as he reemphasizes God's plan to keep his promises to his Church—the bride of Christ.

Then to-night we have found that the Lord reveals to us with wisdom and prudence His plan, namely, "that he might gather together in one all things in Christ, both which are in heaven, and which are on earth"—reconciling them all in Christ—not merely for their own selfish good, but as a plan for Christ's glory; and with this view He has associated us with Christ in the place He takes as head over all, so that being associated with Him as heirs of God, joint heirs with Christ, we have the inheritance with Him; that when He takes it, we shall have it with Him; that, when He comes, we shall come with Him; that, whereas he was presented to the earth among the Jews, according to the promise of God, and they would not have Him, He then took another place, that of Son of Man, that place He will take in his resurrection and in His glory, and will raise us up to have it with Him when the time comes; and not we alone, but all saints will have it with Him; that we see not yet all things put under Him, but we do see Jesus crowned with glory and honour, and are waiting, as lie is, till His enemies are made His footstool; that when that time comes—when it will be, nobody knows; God has not revealed it—the first thing He will do will be to have His body; He is not to be head without the body, but will catch us up to meet Him in the air; that, if dead, He will raise us, if alive He will change us, and take us up to meet the Lord in the air; that He will-come and take us to His Father's house; that this is our place, and that he will have everything there in order for us—only He must have His heirs with Him; that He cannot take a step in entering on the possession of His inheritance, without having His heirs, His body, His bride with Him.[221]

For John Nelson Darby, eschatology was not about how to interpret the Scriptures. He seems to handle his exegetic explanations proficiently. However, as one reads through his lecture notes, what is emphasized throughout, is hope, not only through the resurrection of Christ, but the hope of the promised inheritance that ties

---

[220] Darby, "Lectures on the Second Coming of Christ," Lecture II, 27-28.

[221] Ibid., 30.

the saints to all that Christ does in the future.

Here lies the purpose of Dispensational Theology, its message of "Christ in you, the hope of glory," [222] in which we "were sealed in Him with the Holy Spirit of promise, who is given as a pledge of our inheritance, with a view to the redemption of God's own possession, to the praise of His glory." [223]

Dispensationalism in the U.S.

This new teaching {U.K. Dispensationalism} spread in America through prophecy conferences such as the Niagara Bible Conferences (1883-1897). James H. Brookes (1830-1898), a pastor in St. Louis and prominent figure in the Niagara Conferences, disseminated dispensationalist ideas through his ministry and publications. Most importantly, Dwight L. Moody was sympathetic to the broad outlines of dispensationalism and had as his closest lieutenants dispensationalist leaders such as Reuben A. Torrey (1856-1928), James M. Gray (1851-1925), Cyrus I. Scofield (1843-1921), William J. Eerdman (1833-1923), A. C. Dixon (1854-1925), and A. J. Gordon (1836-1895). These men were activist evangelists who promoted a host of Bible conferences and other missionary and evangelistic efforts. They also gave the dispensationalist movement institutional permanence by assuming leadership of the new independent Bible institutes such as the Moody Bible Institute (1886),

the Bible Institute of Los Angeles (1907), and the Philadelphia College of the Bible (1914). The network of related institutes that soon sprang up became the nucleus for the spread of American dispensationalism.[224]

It cannot be left unsaid that Cyrus I. Scofield played a significant role in the propagation of dispensational theology to the faithful saints who studied their Bibles all across the country, using the Scofield Reference Bible.

Dispensational teaching was later found allied with Lewis Sperry Chafer, who founded Dallas Theological Seminary in 1924 and wrote *Chafer's Systematic Theology* in 1948.

The Seminary then drew or produced scholars that fine-tuned and promoted Dispensational Theology in their writings and teachings for the next era, now referenced here as the *fundamental* period or, as the Progressive Dispensationalists label it, the *essentialist* period (1950-1990). This period included scholars like: J. Dwight Pentecost, who wrote, *Things to Come*; John Walvoord, *The Millennial Kingdom* and *The Rapture Question*; Charles Ryrie, *Dispensationalism Today* and its revised and expanded version *Dispensationalism*; and Paul Lee Tan, who wrote *The Interpretation of Prophecy*.

Another important individual who played a role in this period was Alva J. McClain who founded Grace Theological Seminary of Winona Lake, Indiana in 1937, and authored, *The Greatness of the Kingdom: An Inductive Study of the Kingdom of God.*

---

[222] Col. 1:27.
[223] Eph. 1: 13-14.
[224] *Theopedia*, s.v. "Dispensationalism," [encyclopedia on line]; available from

https://www.theopedia.com/dispensationalism; Internet; accessed 16 January 2019.

PROGRESSIVE OR REVISED DISPENSATIONALISM

Robert L. Thomas (Th.D.) was a Professor of New Testament at Master's Seminary and a member of the Evangelical Theological Society from 1961 until his passing in 2017.[225]

Charles Ryrie informs us that Progressive Dispensationalism was introduced publicly to the Theological community at the annual meeting of The Evangelical Society in Atlanta, Georgia on November 26, 1986.[226] So it is fitting that Dr. Thomas, a long-time member of that Society provided the introduction to this new view.

> Progressive Dispensationalism differs from Dispensationalism in a number of ways, one of them being in not viewing the time of the rapture to be as crucial. Progressive dispensationalists view themselves as a continuation of the dispensational tradition, but realize they are moving toward a nondispensational systems. The movement's desire for rapprochement with other theological systems has involved a hermeneutical shift in its understanding of Scripture. It has replaced grammatical-historical interpretation with a system of hermeneutics called historical-grammatical-literary-theological.
>
> Several comparisons that illustrate the differences between the two hermeneutical systems relate to the function of the interpreter, the historical dimension, the "single-meaning" principle, the issue of sensus plenior, and the importance of thoroughness. The bottom line is that a choice between Dispensationalism and Progressive Dispensationalism amounts to a choice of which system of hermeneutics an interpreter chooses to follow. ... The leaders in the movement view themselves and their supporters as taking a further step in the continuing development of dispensational theology. For example, Bock sees himself as combining two elements, one from what he calls Scofieldian dispensationalism and the other from so-called essentialist dispensationalism, into his system. Advocates of PD, in other words, see themselves in the lineage of dispensational theology.
>
> ...With PD's desire for rapprochement, however, has come a hermeneutical shift away from literal interpretation—also call the grammatical-historical method— that has been one of the ongoing hallmarks of dispensationalism. In late twentieth-century writings, advocates of this developing theological perspective have shifted in the direction of nondispensational systems by adopting some of the same hermeneutical practices as found in these other systems. For whatever reason, proponents of PD sometimes call their hermeneutics by the name "grammatical-historical,"

---

[225] Resource of information through, https://dispensationalpublishing.com/reflections-on-the-life-of-robert-l-thomas-th-d/; Internet; accessed 16 January 2019.

[226] Charles C. Ryrie, *Dispensationalism* (Chicago: Moody Publishers, 2007), 189.

but they mean something quite different by the phrase.[227]

Mal Couch (Th.D.) founder of Tyndale Theological Seminary, in Ft. Worth, TX, adds the following evaluation as he writes,

> Recently, some who claim to be interpreting Scripture literally have introduced what they call "complementary hermeneutics." Those who use this approach classify themselves as progressive dispensationalists. They also still wish to be numbered among premillennial pretribulation dispensationalists. Darrell Bock, who seems to have been the one who introduced the term "progressive dispensationalism," defines it (complimentary hermeneutic) this way: "The New Testament does introduce change and advance; it does not merely repeat Old Testament revelation. In making complementary additions, however, it does not jettison old promises."[228]

The method at the present time does not seem to be applied to all of Scripture, but is applied to the promise of the Davidic covenant of 2 Samuel 7. It is admitted that when the covenant was originally given, it was made exclusively with Israel. However, in Acts 2 on the Day of Pentecost, Peter brought in the church as recipients of the covenant as well. This is defended by Peter's use of Psalm 110. In this way it is "inferred" or "implied" that the kingdom promises to Israel are now being fulfilled in part by Christ's position at the right hand of the Father. This means the Davidic kingdom is "now but not yet" in all its fullness. What the New Testament is said to have done is "complement" here what was given in the Old Testament.

What this means, if applied unilaterally to all of Scripture, is that the original recipients of the revelation could never know precisely what the text meant until the promise was fulfilled or the canon of Scripture was closed. After all, later "complements" might introduce drastic changes in the original promise.[229]

HYPER OR ULTRA-DISPENSATIONALISM

Ethelbert William Bullinger (December 15, 1837 - June 6, 1913) was a Vicar of the Church of England, Biblical scholar, and dispensationalist theologian.

---

[227] Robert L. Thomas, "The Hermeneutics of Progressive Dispensationalism," *Master's Seminary Journal*, (1995): 6(1), 78; available from Theological Journal Library, Vol. 1-5, (Faithlife Corporation product available from Logos.com.)

[228] Craig Blaising and Darrell L. Bock, "Dispensationalism, Israel and the Church: Assessment and Dialogue," in *Dispensationalism, Israel and the Church* (Grand Rapids: Zondervan, 1992), 392–93, quoted in Mal Couch, "Progressive Dispensationalism: What Really Is It?," *Conservative Theological Journal* (1999), Volume 3, 3(9), 258–260; available from Theological Journal Library, Vol. 1-5, (Faithlife Corporation product available from Logos.com.)

[229] Mal Couch, "Progressive Dispensationalism: What Really Is It?," *Conservative Theological Journal* (1999): 3(9), 258–260; available from Theological Journal Library, Vol. 1-5, (Faithlife Corporation product available from Logos.com.)

Born in Canterbury, England, his family traced its lineage back to the noted Swiss reformer Heinrich Bullinger (1504-1557). He was educated at King's College, London, and gained recognition in the field of Biblical languages.

E. W. Bullinger was noted broadly for three works: A Critical Lexicon and Concordance to the English and Greek New Testament (1877); for his ground-breaking and exhaustive work on Figures of Speech Used in the Bible (1898); and as the primary editor of The Companion Bible (published in 6 parts, beginning in 1909; the entire annotated Bible was published posthumously in 1922). These works and many others remain in print (2004).

Bullinger's theology was extreme dispensationalism on which he wrote numerous articles which appeared in his Monthly Journal *Things to Come*. His name has become virtually synonymous with Hyper-dispensationalism.[230]

Bullinger is seen as the Father of extreme dispensationalism, but over the years a more moderate view has emerged and is held by American groups such as, Grace Missions, Grace Gospel Fellowship, and Berean Bible Society.

Names associated with this view are: Cornelium R. Stam, J. C. O'Hair and Charles F. Baker.[231]

Charles Ryrie tells us that *"Berean Searchlight* and *Truth* are representative magazines,"* and that Grace Bible College out of Grand Rapids, Michigan supports this more moderate perspective.[232]

CHARACTERISTICS OF PREMILLENNIALISM

COVENANT TYPE

Covenant premillennial theology is best understood through the eyes of one who rarely preached or taught on the subject, but studied the subject a great deal and over the course of his life, periodically spoke and wrote on the issue.[233] The following characteristics of Covenant or Historical Premillennialism comes from the studies of C. H. Spurgeon.

> *The second coming of Christ.* The feature that Spurgeon identified as a foundational eschatological issue was "The Second Advent of Christ." That Spurgeon believed in the personal and literal return of Christ to the earth is an indisputable fact.[234]
>
> *The millennial reign of Christ.* On the theme of a millennial reign of Christ, Spurgeon was far from silent. Though he did not give a great deal of attention to it, when he did, his view was consistent. In 1865 he stated, Some think that this descent of the Lord will be post-millennial— that is, after the thousand years of his reign. I cannot think so. I conceive that the advent will be pre-millennial; that he will come first; and then will come the millennium

---

[230] *Theopedia*, s.v. "E. W. Bullinger," [encyclopedia on line]; available from https://www.theopedia.com/e-w-bullinger; Internet; accessed 6 February 2019.

[231] Ryrie, *Dispensationalism*, 231-232.

[232] Ibid., 232.

[233] Dennis M. Swanson, "The Millennial Position of Spurgeon," *Master's Seminary Journal* (1996): 7(2), 191; available from Theological Journal Library, Vol. 1-5, (Faithlife Corporation product available from Logos.com.)

[234] Ibid.

as the result of his personal reign upon earth.[235]

The resurrection of the dead. A third area of Spurgeon's eschatological interest lay in the resurrections of the just and the wicked. Throughout his ministry he taught separate resurrections of the just and unjust. The discussion above has cited his distinction between "the first and second resurrection." That he believed in a literal and physical resurrection is undeniable:

Yet this Paul believed, and this he preached—that there would be a resurrection of the dead, both the just and the unjust, not that the just and the unjust would merely live as to their souls, but that their bodies should be restored from the grave, and that a resurrection, as well as an immortality, should be the entail of every man of woman born, whatever his character might be. In the same sermon Spurgeon declared the resurrections would be distinct, separated by a period of time: "Notice that this reaping comes first, and I think it comes first in order of time. If I read the Scriptures aright, there are to be two resurrections, and the first will be the resurrection of the righteous."[236]

{*The Millennium*} Despite this, he firmly declared his belief that the thousand-year millennial reign would separate the two resurrections. In 1861 he told his congregation this:

I think that the Word of God teaches, and teaches indisputably, that the saints shall rise first. And be

the interval of time whatever it may, whether the thousand years are literal years, or a very long period of time, I am not now about to determine; I have nothing to do except with the fact that there are two resurrections, a resurrection of the just, and afterwards of the unjust,—a time when the saints of God shall rise, and after time when the wicked shall rise to the resurrection of damnation.

In the same sermon he expressed his belief that both resurrections are literal and physical. He attacked the position of the famous American Presbyterian, Albert Barnes (1798–1870), an amillennialist, who rejected the literal resurrection spoken of in Revelation 20:4–6, 12. He charged Barnes with holding a position that spiritualized the resurrection. In concluding his argument against Barnes, he said,

Now I appeal to you, would you, in reading that passage, think this to be the meaning? Would any man believe that to be its meaning, if he had not some thesis to defend? The fact is, we sometimes read Scripture, thinking of what it ought to say, rather that what it does say....It is—we have no doubt whatever—a literal resurrection of the saints of God, and not of principles nor of doctrines.[237]

First of all, he believed that the Jews would physically and literally return to inhabit and have political control over their ancient land. He explained, There will be a native government again; there will again

---

[235] Swanson, "The Millennial Position of Spurgeon," 191–192.

[236] Ibid., 194.
[237] Ibid., 195–196.

be the form of a body politic; a state shall be incorporated, and a king shall reign. Israel has now become alienated from her own land....If there be anything clear and plain, the literal sense and meaning of this passage (Ezekiel 37:1–10)—a meaning not to be spirited or spiritualized away—must be evident that both the two and the ten tribes of Israel are to be restored to their own land, and that a king is to rule over them.

He also believed that the conversion of the Jews would come through Christian preaching by means of the church and other societies and mission agencies that God would raise up for that task.[238]

{*Israel and the Church*} The primary one was his monumental work on the Psalms, *The Treasury of David.* Spurgeon spent nearly fifteen years completing the seven volumes which he and his closest associates considered his magnum opus. It was his only thoroughly expository work and has remained in print without interruption since his death. In the Treasury, as in most of Spurgeon's works, he sees references to Israel in the Psalms as being the church.[239]

{*A literal Millennium*} Spurgeon sees specifically a personal reign of Christ over nations on earth. Commenting further on this Psalm, he discussed the political nature of Christ's reign on earth. He believed that nations would exist in the millennium with their own kings and leaders, but that all would be subject to Christ and His government in Jerusalem. He also saw Christ's personal reign as a certain, but future event: "But since we see Jesus crowned with glory and honour in heaven, we are altogether without doubt as to his universal monarchy on earth."[240]

Other Characteristics

(1) Its belief on a literal kingdom is mostly based on a literal interpretation of Revelation 20:1-6

(2) This view does not necessarily support Old Testament prophecies being fulfilled by Israel.

(3) This view makes no clear distinction between Israel and the church.

(4) This view strongly opposes Dispensationalism.

(5) This view most often holds to a post-tribulation rapture.

(6) This view tends to be more optimistic than Amillennialism or Post-millennialism.

DISPENSATION TYPE

Charles Ryrie (Th.D.) provides us with five major features of dispensational eschatology as summarized here.

(1) [The Hermeneutical Principle—Dispensationalism is the only eschatological system that uses a literal hermeneutic 100% of the time toward biblical interpretations.

(2) Fulfillment of Old Testament Prophecies—Dispensationalism requires a literal fulfillment of Old Testament prophecies, particularly

---

[238] Swanson, "The Millennial Position of Spurgeon," 196–197.

[239] Ibid., 197.
[240] Ibid., 198.

those dealing with the Abrahamic, Davidic and New Covenants. Literal interpretation requires a literal time and place for the prophecies and the covenant promises to be fulfilled.

(3) A Clear and Consistent Distinction Between Israel and the Church— Dispensationalism is the only system that maintains Israel, and not the Church, will fulfill Old Testament prophecies concerning the nation of Israel. All other systems see the Church as the fulfilling entity of the promises and prophecies made to Israel in the Old Testament.

(4) Pretribulation Rapture—The Rapture is a highlight of the dispensational system since the classical period and is not just tied to the intimate return of Christ issue, but is tied to the uniqueness and nature of the New Testament Church separate from the plan God has for Israel.

(5) The Millennial Kingdom—The Millennium is an integral part of dispensationalism as it is tied to the fulfillment of the Abrahamic and Davidic Covenants to Israel. With regard to the historic premillennial view, the millennial kingdom only becomes necessary to fulfill Revelation 20:1-7 literally. Without Revelation 20 all other systems would most likely dismiss the millennium altogether.] [241]

PROGRESSIVE TYPE

Stephen J. Nichols (Ph.D.), president of Reformation Bible College, provides the following review of Progressive Dispensationalism (PD).

(1) Dispensationalism teaches that the Davidic kingdom was offered to and rejected by Israel, and that as a result of this rejection the kingdom has been postponed until after the Church Age. These things (the offer, rejection, and postponement of the Davidic Kingdom) are absent from PD.

(2) Dispensationalism teaches that Jesus will be seated on David's throne at the start of the Millennium. PD teaches that Jesus has been seated on David's throne since His ascension.

(3) Dispensationalism teaches that Jesus will not begin His rule as the Davidic King until after the Tribulation. PD teaches that on the one hand Jesus already rules as the Davidic King, in a spiritual sense, today, but on another hand, He is not yet physically ruling over that Kingdom.

(4) As a consequence of the previous points, Nichols finds "absent (from PD) the view that the church is distinct from (the Davidic) kingdom" (p. 235). "The distinguishing feature of dispensationalism, i.e., the consistent distinction between Israel and the church, is all but absent" (p. 239).[242]

Charles Ryrie (Th.D.) provides seven basic tenets to progressive dispensationalism, summarized here.

[241] Ryrie, *Dispensationalism*, 171-173.
[242] Wilkin, R. N. "Review of The Dispensational View of the Davidic Kingdom: A Response to Progressive Dispensationalism" by Stephen J.

Nichols, *Journal of the Grace Evangelical Society* (1997): 10, 10(18), 93; available from Theological Journal Library, Vol. 1-5, (Faithlife Corporation product available from Logos.com.)

- [The unifying theme in biblical history is the kingdom of God.

- There are four dispensational periods representing biblical history from beginning to the end.

- The Davidic reign of Christ comes in two states. First, Christ is reigning as he sits on the right hand of the Father now, and second, he will reign as king on earth during the millennium based on Acts 2 and Psalm 110. This is not unique to this system.

- The New Covenant is seen as initiated but not fully implemented until the millennium.

- The distinction between Israel and the Church as two separate plans for God become blurred, and the doctrine of the mysteries of the church has become blurred as well.

- This system uses two separate hermeneutical approaches to its prophetic interpretations; the grammatical-historical and the complementary hermeneutic.

- The system promotes holistic redemption, which means they promote social justice norms as part of biblical living. This ideal will only be fully realized in the millennial kingdom but should be practiced in the here and now.] [243]

HYPER OR ULTRA TYPE

The major difference between this view and the traditional view can be seen in the interpretation of when the Church began.

The traditional view holds that the Church began at Pentecost, while the Hyper viewpoint believes that the Church began with the Apostle Paul, with a split within their own perspective as to when this actually occurred.

This view also adds a dispensation, starting sometime in the book of Acts.

Dr. Roy L. Aldrich writes,

This school makes a separate dispensation out of part or all of the book of Acts. There are two types of ultradispensationalism: (1) The extreme believe that the mystery church began after Acts 28, i.e., after Paul's imprisonment. (2) The moderate believe the mystery church began sometime (they are vague about the starting point) after Paul's conversion, or between Acts 9 and 13.

Both the extreme and moderate types of ultradispensationalism agree on the following: (1) The great commissions in Matthew and Mark are Jewish. (2) The ministry of the Twelve was only a continuation of the ministry of Christ. (3) The church (mystery or body church) did not begin at Pentecost. (4) The sign gifts were Jewish and related to the kingdom period only. (5) Water baptism is not for this age. (6) That there is a distinction between Paul's early and later ministries. (7) That the mystery church began with Paul. (8) That Acts 2:38, Mark 16:16, Luke

---

[243] Ryrie, *Dispensationalism*, 193-207.

7:30, etc., teach a legalistic plan of salvation different from the grace plan for this age.[244]

Charles Ryrie adds to this list that ultra-dispensationalists believe the bride of Christ is represented by Israel not the Church.[245]

Point of View Differences Between the two Groups [246]

Differences	Extreme	Moderate
When the Church Begins	Acts Chapter 28	Before Acts Chapter 28
Time Frame for Transition of Acts	Until Acts Chapter 28	Until Acts Chapter 9 or 13.
Application of the Lord's Supper	No application	Appropriate to observe.
Scriptures that apply to the Church	Prison epistles only.	Prison and other epistles.

Table 4.2

[244] R. L. Aldrich, "An Outline Study on Dispensationalism," *Bibliotheca Sacra* (1961): 118, 134–135; available from Theological Journal Library, Vol. 1-5, (Faithlife Corporation product available from Logos.com.)

[245] Ryrie, *Dispensationalism*, 232.
[246] Ibid., 232-233.

CHAPTER FIVE

Understanding the Kingdom of God

INTRODUCTION

Jesus' words recorded in the synoptic gospels have brought about a great debate concerning the subject of *the kingdom of God*. Questions arise like, has the kingdom of God come, is the kingdom still allusive, or is the kingdom coming in a progressive manner?

There are many approaches taken in trying to come to a consensus on the proper view of the kingdom of God. Frederick Borsch states his approach in this manner:

> As most scholars have now come to recognize, the parables of Jesus seem treated best when they are viewed within the twin coordinates of history and literature and when these two focuses come together as hermeneutics.[247]

Paul Lee Tan states:

> Most people know something about the teachings of prophecy, but a comparative few are acquainted with the hermeneutical principles and procedures on which prophecy is based. This is unfortunate, for hermeneutics is foundational and should be studied first.[248]

So, how shall we proceed? T. W. Manson makes this observation about the timing of self-interpretation of the believer:

> Only toward the end of the eighteenth century was the right of Scripture to say something on its own account, and not merely to be called in to ratify the decisions of Ecumenical Councils or Assemblies of Protestant Divines, openly proclaimed by Gabler.[249]

With this in mind, we will let the Scriptures speak for themselves while following two presuppositions. First,

> We observe, accordingly, that the writer of Biblical Introduction examines the historical foundations and canonical authority of the books of Scripture. The textual critic detects interpolations, emends false readings, and aims to give us the very words which the sacred writers used. The exegete takes up these words, and by means of the principles of hermeneutics, defines their meaning, elucidates the scope and plan of each writer, and brings forth the Grammatico-historical sense of what each book contains.[250]

---

[247] Frederick Hauk Borsch, *Many Things in Parables* (Philadelphia: Fortress Press, 1988), 7.
[248] Tan, *The Interpretation of Prophecy*, 21.

[249] T. W. Manson, *The Teaching of Jesus* (Cambridge: The University Press, 1931), 4.
[250] Terry, *Biblical Hermeneutics*, 19.

Second, we will stand on the principle of the following Scripture:

> But evil men and impostors will proceed from bad to worse, deceiving and being deceived. You, however, continue in the things you have learned and become convinced of, knowing from whom you have learned them; and that from childhood you have known the sacred writings which are able to give you the wisdom that leads to salvation through faith which is in Christ Jesus. All Scripture is inspired by God and profitable for teaching, for reproof, for correction, for training in righteousness; that the man of God may be adequate, equipped for every good work.[251]

From the synoptic gospels, let us examine the statements Jesus made concerning the kingdom of God and then attempt to answer the opening questions that have eluded many.

THE PROBLEM DEFINED

"The key to the meaning of the Kingdom is Christology. Jesus not only utters the message of the Kingdom of God, He is Himself the message."[252] As we look at some Gospel texts, we will find this view to the overall truth.

The record of Jesus' statement in Mark, coupled with His statements recorded in Luke, will give us some insight into the historical timeline of the kingdom of God.

> And after John had been taken into custody, Jesus came into Galilee, preaching the gospel of God, and saying, "The time is fulfilled, and the kingdom of God is at hand; repent and believe in the gospel."[253]

> The Law and the Prophets were proclaimed until John; since then the gospel of the kingdom of God is preached, and everyone is forcing his way into it. But it is easier for heaven and earth to pass away than for one stroke of a letter of the Law to fail.[254]

Jesus proclaims a clear distinction in God's economy at this point in history. The proclamations of the Law and the Prophets have come to fulfillment in the presence of Jesus, as reflected in Jesus' earlier comments: "Do not think that I came to abolish the Law or the Prophets; I did not come to abolish, but to fulfill."[255] This supports amillennialist Geerhardus Vos' position that the kingdom is an extension of Old Testament prophecy and Jesus expected everyone to understand that.[256] Jesus states, "and Jerusalem will be trampled under foot by the Gentiles until the times of the Gentiles be fulfilled."[257] This continues to show that Jesus recognized economies or God working in stages to bring the kingdom of God to us in history. This would support historic premillennialist George Ladd's position that "God's reign expresses itself in

---

[251] 2 Tim. 3:12-17.

[252] George E. Ladd, *Jesus and the Kingdom* (New York: Harper and Row, 1964); reprint, *The Presence of the Future* (Grand Rapids: William B. Eerdmans Publishing Company, 1974), 27.

[253] Mark 1:14-15.

[254] Luke 16:16-17.

[255] Matt. 5:17.

[256] Geerhardus Vos, *The Teaching of Jesus Concerning the kingdom of God and the Church* (New York: American Tract Society, 1903), 12.

[257] Luke 24:21.

different stages through redemptive history." [258]

Through several of Jesus' statements, we can see how Jesus presented the kingdom of God in the present.

Jesus makes the statement in Mark 9:1, "And He was saying to them, 'Truly I say to you, there are some of those who are standing here who shall not taste death until they see the kingdom of God after it has come with power.'" [259]

The Scriptures continue in that context and states that a week later Jesus was transfigured in a glorious form, along with Moses and Elijah.

If we follow Grammatical-historical hermeneutics, we would see this as a fulfillment of what Jesus had just spoken of a week before. If this is the correct interpretation, then one aspect of the kingdom of God could be seen as being another dimension of our present world, one not accessible in our present form. Another aspect of the kingdom can be seen in Mark 12 which says,

> And one of the scribes came and heard them arguing, and recognizing that He had answered them well, asked Him, 'What commandment is the foremost of all?' Jesus answered, 'The foremost is, Hear, O Israel! The Lord our God is one Lord; and you shall love the Lord your God with all your heart, and with all your soul, and with all your mind, and with all your strength.' The second is this, 'You shall love your neighbor as yourself.' There is no other commandment greater than these. And the scribe said to Him, 'Right, Teacher, You have truly stated that

He is One; and there is no one else besides Him; and to love Him with all the heart and with all the understanding and with all the strength, and to love one's neighbor as himself, is much more than all burnt offerings and sacrifices.' And when Jesus saw that he had answered intelligently, He said to him, 'You are not far from the kingdom of God.' And after that, no one would venture to ask Him any more questions.[260]

If by taking on a correct attitude and viewpoint concerning God and the kingdom results in bringing us closer to the kingdom, this may suggest that another aspect of the kingdom is spiritual. Mark recorded Jesus' parable as he writes,

> And He was saying, The kingdom of God is like a man who casts seed upon the soil; and goes to bed at night and gets up by day, and the seed sprouts up and grows— how, he himself does not know. The soil produces crops by itself; first the blade, then the head, then the mature grain in the head. But when the crop permits, he immediately puts in the sickle, because the harvest has come.[261]

This illustrates another aspect of the present Kingdom is its progressive nature. It grows and spreads in a mysterious manner. They expected the kingdom of God to come in a physical presence, but instead Jesus spoke in terms of its nature and its mysteries, of its birth, and growth, and finally its appearance in the future. How should we understand this?

---

[258] George Eldon Ladd, *The Gospel of the Kingdom* (Grand Rapids: WM. B. Eerdmans Publishing Company, 1959), 22.

[259] Mark 9:1.
[260] Mark 12:28-34.
[261] Mark 4:26-29.

THE MYSTERIES EXPLAINED

And He answered and said to them, To you it has been granted to know the mysteries of the kingdom of heaven, but to them it has not been granted. For whoever has, to him shall more be given, and he shall have an abundance; but whoever does not have, even what he has shall be taken away from him. Therefore I speak to them in parables; because while seeing they do not see, and while hearing they do not hear, nor do they understand. And in their case the prophecy of Isaiah is being fulfilled, which says,

You will keep on hearing, but will not understand; And you will keep on seeing, but will not perceive; For the heart of this people has become dull, And with their ears they scarcely hear, And they have closed their eyes Lest they should see with their eyes, And hear with their ears, And understand with their heart and return, And I should heal them.[262]

What did Jesus mean by the mysteries of the kingdom? Simply put, he was referring to things about the kingdom that were not revealed in times past. How do we know this? Consider the words of the Apostle Paul,

For this reason I, Paul, the prisoner of Christ Jesus for the sake of you Gentiles—if indeed you have heard of the stewardship of God's grace which was given to me for you; that by revelation there was made known to me the mystery, as I wrote before in brief. And by referring to this, when you read you can understand my insight into the mystery of Christ, which in other generations was not made known to the sons of men, as it has now been revealed to His holy apostles and prophets in the Spirit; to be specific, that the Gentiles are fellow heirs and fellow members of the body, and fellow partakers of the promise in Christ Jesus through the gospel, of which I was made a minister, according to the gift of God's grace which was given to me according to the working of His power. To me, the very least of all saints, this grace was given, to preach to the Gentiles the unfathomable riches of Christ, and to bring to light what is the administration of the mystery which for ages has been hidden in God, who created all things; in order that the manifold wisdom of God might now be made known through the church to the rulers and the authorities in the heavenly places.[263]

According to these two texts, Isaiah prophesied Israel's rejection of the messiah, postponing the earthly kingdom to Israel at this point in history; instead, the mystery revealed is a new economy or a new stage of the progressive kingdom.

In simpler terms, the Kingdom of God was going to be offered to the Gentiles through the mystery of *Christ in you*, "that is, the mystery which has been hidden from the past ages and generations; but has now been manifested to His saints, to whom God willed to make known what is the riches of the glory of this mystery among the Gentiles, which is Christ in you, the hope of glory." [264]

---

[262] Matt. 13:10-15.
[263] Eph. 3:1-10.

[264] Col. 1:26-27.

Consequently, the Church becomes the next stage in the kingdom revealed.

It is clear from the Scriptures stated so far that the historical Jesus and the Gospel writers, of which three were Apostles and the other a physician, were in complete harmony concerning the mysteries of the kingdom.

IN WHAT FORM IS THE PRESENT KINGDOM?

As we have seen demonstrated in the Scriptures, the kingdom at this point in history is not fully of this world, and it seems to be of a spiritual nature. Let us consider some additional statements Jesus makes in Matthew.

At that time the disciples came to Jesus, saying, 'Who then is greatest in the kingdom of heaven?' And He called a child to Himself and set him before them, and said, 'Truly I say to you, unless you are converted and become like children, you shall not enter the kingdom of heaven.' [265]

Does this sound similar to other words Jesus spoke? "Jesus answered and said to him, 'Truly, truly, I say to you, unless one is born again, he cannot see the kingdom of God.'"[266] The kingdom is coming through the new birth, which cannot be realized before Jesus' death, burial and resurrection. Does this mean that Israel has been bypassed forever? No! The Apostle Paul states:

I say then, God has not rejected His people, has He? May it never be! For I too am an Israelite, a descendant of Abraham, of the tribe of Benjamin. God has not rejected His people whom He foreknew. Or

do you not know what the Scripture says in the passage about Elijah, how he pleads with God against Israel? 'Lord, they have killed Thy prophets, they have torn down Thine altars, and I alone am left, and they are seeking my life.' But what is the divine response to him? 'I have kept for Myself seven thousand men who have not bowed the knee to Baal.' In the same way then, there has also come to be at the present time a remnant according to God's gracious choice. But if it is by grace, it is no longer on the basis of works, otherwise grace is no longer grace. What then? That which Israel is seeking for, it has not obtained, but those who were chosen obtained it, and the rest were hardened; just as it is written,

God gave them a spirit of stupor, Eyes to see not and ears to hear not, Down to this very day.

And David says,

Let their table become a snare and a trap, And a stumbling block and a retribution to them. Let their eyes be darkened to see not, And bend their backs forever.

I say then, they did not stumble so as to fall, did they? May it never be! But by their transgression salvation has come to the Gentiles, to make them jealous.[267]

The kingdom has bypassed Israel so God could fulfill the covenant He made to Abraham back in Genesis Chapter 12, which reads: "And I will bless those who bless you, And the one who curses you I will curse. And in you all the families of the

[265] Matt. 18:1-3.
[266] John 3:3.

[267] Rom. 11:1-11.

earth shall be blessed." [268] God collaborates this proclamation through the Apostle Paul as he writes,

> And the Scripture, foreseeing that God would justify the Gentiles by faith, preached the gospel beforehand to Abraham, saying, 'All the nations shall be blessed in you.' So then those who are of faith are blessed with Abraham, the believer. (Galatians 3:8-9)

God's plan all along was to be the Savior of the world, as stated in John 1:29, 3:16-17, 12:47, 2 Cor. 5:19, 1 John 4:14.

If Israel was bypassed, then what happens to Israel next? Alternatively, will they be bypassed forever? The Apostle Paul states,

> For I do not want you, brethren, to be uninformed of this mystery, lest you be wise in your own estimation, that a partial hardening has happened to Israel until the fullness of the Gentiles has come in; and thus all Israel will be saved; just as it is written,
> *The Deliverer will come from Zion, He will remove ungodliness from Jacob. And this is My covenant with them, When I take away their sins.*
> From the standpoint of the gospel they are enemies for your sake, but from the standpoint of God's choice they are beloved for the sake of the fathers; for the gifts and the calling of God are irrevocable.[269]

According to this passage, Israel will have a place in the Kingdom of God. Therefore, there must be a future aspect of

the Kingdom. Nevertheless, for now, the church seems to be the form the kingdom has taken in the present. Vos states it this way: "That form which the kingdom assumes in the church shows it to be inseparably associated with the person and work of Jesus himself." [270]

It appears two separate entities make up the kingdom of God. How can this be reconciled? Jesus provides the answer to this dilemma in John 10:15-16 when he states, "even as the Father knows Me and I know the Father, and I lay down My life for the sheep. And I have other sheep, which are not of this fold; I must bring them also, and they shall hear My voice, and they shall become one flock with one shepherd." What is Jesus referring to when he says he has "other sheep" and he must unite them together into one fold? It is my view that in order to harmonize the Scriptures as a whole, the two flocks of sheep represent the Jews (Israel) and the Gentile Christians. This interpretation makes perfect sense within a dispensational perspective and fits the narrative teachings of the "scriptural mysteries."

THE CULMINATION OF THE KINGDOM

The Scriptures that confuse us the most on the future kingdom are found in Matthew 24. However, if we look closely and apply a few hermeneutical principles, an answer may be obtainable. Let us consider the following passage.

> And as He was sitting on the Mount of Olives, the disciples came to Him privately, saying, Tell us, when will these things be, and what

[268] Gen. 12:3.
[269] Rom. 11:25-29.
[270] Vos, *The Teaching of Jesus*, 193.

will be the sign of Your coming, and of the end of the age? [271]

If we look closely, the disciples are asking three separate questions, and at this point, Jesus the prophet answers by making three statements grouped together in one passage. "Do you not see all these things? Truly I say to you, not one stone here shall be left upon another, which will not be torn down." [272] This was the statement that brought about their first question, and Jesus answers it in verses 4-6.

> See to it that no one misleads you. For many will come in My name, saying, 'I am the Christ,' and will mislead many. And you will be hearing of wars and rumors of wars; see that you are not frightened, for those things must take place, but that is not yet the end.[273]

Notice the phrase, "but that is not yet the end." This is a transitional phrase to the next answer of the second question. Jesus answers question two in verses 7-14 and transitions that answer to the third question with this phrase, "and then the end shall come." [274] Jesus concludes His response and answers question three in verses 15-31. With all this said, it is evident that the future kingdom is coming in stages as Ladd suggests.[275] The question that comes to us is, are we interpreting this correctly?

Paul Lee Tan (Th.D.) gives us some hermeneutical perspective,

> The perspective of prophecy (also known as "the law of time relationship") means that two or more future events, widely separated

in time, may be seen by the prophet in a single profile of side-by-side.[276]

It was common for Old Testament Prophets to give a near prophecy and a far prophecy to prove they were true prophets of God in their generational period. So, the first answer Jesus gave was in reference to the destruction of Jerusalem in 70 A.D., an event which would have been witnessed by that present generation, certifying Jesus as a prophet of God during his time in history. The remaining statements are prophecies still outstanding and remain yet to be fulfilled, for Jesus relegates these events to the historical period called the "end of the age." [277]

IN SUMMARY

From the time of Abraham and the everlasting covenant made with him to the everlasting New Covenant given to Jeremiah, to the time of Jesus, to the establishment of the church, which is the body of Christ, God has been directing historical events towards the eventual culmination of his Kingdom. This is evident in the progressive revelation of God through the Holy Scriptures.

The kingdom was proclaimed in the past, revealed, and partially fulfilled in the present, and will culminate in the future.

How should we ultimately define the kingdom of God? It is the realm of a holy God where He is the ruling King and sovereign over all time and space.

By this definition we can find the kingdom in the present, in the realm of the temple of the Holy Spirit residing in the believer, and in the future in the realm of his earthly Kingdom, and in the new age,

---

[271] Matt. 24:3.

[272] Matt. 24:2.

[273] Matt. 24:4-6.

[274] Matt. 24:7-14.

[275] Ladd, *The Gospel of the Kingdom*, 22.

[276] Tan, *The Interpretation of Prophecy*, 91.

[277] Matt. 24:14.

the age of the new heaven and the new
earth.

CHAPTER SIX

The Hermeneutics of Prophecy

INTRODUCTION

DEFINING THE TERM

Milton S. Terry states:

> HERMENEUTICS is the science of interpretation. The word is usually applied to the explanation of written documents, and may therefore be more specifically defined as the science of interpreting an author's language. This science assumes that there are divers modes of thought and ambiguities of expression among men, and, accordingly, it aims to remove the supposable differences between a writer and his readers, so that the meaning of the one may be truly and accurately apprehended by the others.[278]

Bernard Ramm states:

> HERMENEUTICS is the science and art of Biblical interpretation. It is a science because it is guided by rules within a system; and it is an art because the application of the rules is by skill, and not by mechanical imitation. As such, it forms one of the most important members of the theological sciences.[279]

Paul Lee Tan provides additional insight to the meaning behind *interpret* by saying, "To 'interpret' means to explain the original sense of a speaker or writer. To interpret 'literally' means to explain the original sense of the speaker of the writer according to the normal, customary, and proper usages of words and language." [280]

THE IMPORTANCE OF HERMENEUTICS IN THE STUDY OF PROPHECY

Paul Lee Tan explains [there are many motivations behind prophetic interpretations, along with the many approaches individuals or groups take.

These approaches include liberal and neo-orthodox interpreters who reject the supernatural and anything that contradicts their reasoning. The pietistic interpreters who rely on some inter-light where feelings come first over rules of language. Then there are the interpreters who require or rely on extra-Biblical sources, such as the Apocrypha, the Book of Mormon, Science and Health with Key to the Scriptures, or revelations provided by religious cult founders.] [281] Then "in Covenant Theology,

---

[278] Terry, *Biblical Hermeneutics*, 17.
[279] Bernard Ramm, *Protestant Biblical Interpretation*, 3 rev ed. (Grand Rapids: Baker Book House, 1970), 1.

[280] Tan, *The Interpretation of Prophecy*, 29.
[281] Ibid., 25-26.

there is the tendency to impute to passages a meaning which would not be gained merely from their historical and grammatical associations. This phase of interpretations is called the 'theological' interpretation." [282]

Tan goes on to explain:

> The only dependable approach to prophecy, however, is the *literal method of interpretation*. This method assumes that Bible prophecy, written in regular human language, should be interpreted according to laws governing written communication. It is a trustworthy and God-honoring method of interpretation which takes the Bible at its word.[283]

Without an agreement on which hermeneutical method or principle one will use, there can be no basis for discussion between entities or studies within eschatology. For the covenant theologian says this, and the dispensationalist says that, while others may say something entirely different.

Until one can agree on the method of hermeneutics, the study of eschatology will carry no reliable meaning between those who differ.

This is why it is important to remember that there are no contradictions in Scripture. For biblical truth to be true, it must agree with all other biblical truth.

TWO METHODS OF INTERPRETATION THAT AFFECT PROPHECY

THE ALLEGORICAL METHOD

While the discipline of hermeneutics had its historical developing stages, the allegorical method of interpretation has gone through its own process of development as well.

Bernard Ramm (Ph.D.) completed some research that provides us information, as summarized here.

[Through the centuries there have developed four Allegorical Schools of thought.

The first falls under *Greek Allegorism* that followed two traditions. One flowed through a religious tradition of Homer and Hesiod. The second flowed through a philosophical and historical tradition that developed principles of logic, science, ethics, and religion. These two traditions were at odds with each other and was resolved through the allegorizing religious heritage, in short, "The stories of the gods, and the writings of the poets, were not to be taken *literally*." [284]

The point that Ramm wants to make here is that these traditions spread to Alexandria where there was a great Jewish population, and later a great Christian population to be influenced. This history naturally led into the development of the next school of thought.

The next school falls under *Jewish Allegorism* that flowed out of Alexandria. Here, the Jews dealing with Moses, the law and divine revelation, had issues with interpretation just as the Greeks had within their own system. Some Jews found part of

---

[282] Daniel Payton Fuller, "The Hermeneutics of Dispensationalism," (Doctor's dissertation, Northern Baptist Theol. Seminary, Chicago, 1957), 147, quoted in footnote 1 of Paul Lee Tan, *The Interpretations of Prophecy*, 26.

[283] Tan, *The Interpretation of Prophecy*, 26.

[284] Ramm, *Protestant Biblical Interpretation*, 25.

their solution in Greek philosophy, particularly in Plato. Ramm writes,

> The Greek faced the tension of a religious-poetic-myth tradition and a historical-philosophical tradition. The Jew face the tension of his own national Sacred Scriptures and the Greek philosophical tradition (especially Plato). How could a Jew cling to both? The solution was identical to the Greek's solution to the problem.[285]

The answer for both laid in allegorization. All of this was later passed on to the Christian church, which leads us to our next school of thought.

The third school to come on the scene was the *Christian and Patristic Allegorism*.

From the Greeks to the Jews to now, the Christians, this system was adopted by the Christian church with the exception of the Syrian school of Antioch and the Vitrines of the Middle ages.[286] This method was practiced by Clement of Alexandria, Origen, Jerome, and Augustine. Although Jerome was an allegorist, he was greatly influenced by the literal views of the school of Antioch.

All this history led Augustine to write his handbook on hermeneutics and homiletics called *De Doctrina Christiana*, in which Allegorism was very much a part of his system of interpretation.

This brings us to the fourth school called *Catholic Allegorism*. From the time of Augustine and beyond, biblical hermeneutics was divided into two sections

the literal and the spiritual, which required allegorization to aid in its interpretation.

The spiritual or mystical was seen as the more important of the two and further divided into three divisions. (i) The allegorical which included typology. (ii) Moral interpretations (tropological). (iii) Anagogical, as related to the church eschatologically.[287]

Within the recognition of some early church Father's abuse of allegorization methods, the Alexandrians were repudiated.[288] [289]

Today, the Catholic view on Scriptural interpretation can be best understood from a document called, *"Dogmatic Constitution on Divine Revelation,"* generated from the Second Vatican Council, Nov. 18, 1965.

The reasoning behind this document is established in the preface.

> Therefore, following in the footsteps of the Council of Trent and of the First Vatican Council, this present Council wishes to set forth authentic doctrine on divine revelation and how it is handed on, so that by hearing the message of salvation the whole world may believe, by believing it may hope, and by hoping it may love.[290]

As expressed in this Constitution, the following ten points are extracted and represents the official position on Catholic thought.

---

[285] Ramm, *Protestant Biblical Interpretation*, 26.
[286] Ibid., 28.
[287] Ibid., 38.
[288] Ibid., 39.
[289] Ibid., 23-38.
[290] "Dogmatic Constitution on Divine Revelation," Second Vatican Council - Nov. 18, 1965, 1. [document on line]; available from https://www.vatican.va/archive/hist_councils/ii_vatican_council/documents/vat-ii_const_19651118_dei-verbum_en.html; Internet; accessed 19 January 2019.

(1) The Cannon of Scriptures are closed.

The Christian dispensation, therefore, as the new and definitive covenant, will never pass away and we now await no further new public revelation before the glorious manifestation of our Lord Jesus Christ (see 1 Tim. 6:14 and Tit. 2:13).[291]

(2) The Scriptures can be understood by human reason (Romans 1:20), as the Holy Spirit presents it.

As a sacred synod has affirmed, 'God, the beginning and end of all things, can be known with certainty from created reality by the light of human reason' (See Rom. 1:20); but it teaches that it is through His revelation 'that those religious truths which are by their nature accessible to human reason can be known by all men with ease, with solid certitude and with no trace of error, even in this present state of the human race.' [292]

(3) Church tradition and its succession is defined.

This commission was faithfully fulfilled by the Apostles who, by their oral preaching, by example, and by observances handed on what they had received from the lips of Christ, from living with Him, and from what He did, or what they had learned through the prompting of the Holy Spirit. The commission was fulfilled, too, by those Apostles and apostolic men who under the inspiration of the same Holy Spirit committed the message of salvation to writing.

But in order to keep the Gospel forever whole and alive within the Church, the Apostles left bishops as their successors, 'handing over' to them 'the authority to teach in their own place.' This sacred tradition, therefore, and Sacred Scripture of both the Old and New Testaments are like a mirror in which the pilgrim Church on earth looks at God, from whom she has received everything, until she is brought finally to see Him as He is, face to face (see 1 John 3:2).[293]

And so the apostolic preaching, which is expressed in a special way in the inspired books, was to be preserved by an unending succession of preachers until the end of time. Therefore the Apostles, handing on what they themselves had received, warn the faithful to hold fast to the traditions which they have learned either by word of mouth or by letter (see 2 Thess. 2:15), and to fight in defense of the faith handed on once and for all (see Jud. 3).[294]

(4) Tradition and Scripture are directly connected to the Apostle's authority.

Hence there exists a close connection and communication between sacred tradition and sacred Scripture. For both of them, flowing from the same divine wellspring, in a certain way merge into a unity and

---

[291] "Dogmatic Constitution on Divine Revelation," Second Vatican Council - Nov. 18, 1965, 4.

[292] Ibid., 6.
[293] Ibid., 7.
[294] Ibid., 8.

tend toward the same end. For sacred Scripture is the Word of God inasmuch as it is consigned to writing under the inspiration of the divine Spirit, while sacred tradition takes the Word of God entrusted by Christ the Lord and the Holy Spirit to the Apostles, and hands it on to their successors in its full purity, so that led by the light of the Spirit of truth, they may in proclaiming it preserve this Word of God faithfully, explain it, and make it more widely known.[295]

(5) The Church is the final authority on Scripture interpretations.

But the task of authentically interpreting the Word of God, whether written or handed on, has been entrusted exclusively to the living teaching office of the Church, whose authority is exercised in the name of Jesus Christ. This teaching office is not above the Word of God, but serves it, teaching only what has been handed on, listening to it devoutly, guarding it scrupulously and explaining it faithfully in accord with a divine commission and with the help of the Holy Spirit; it draws from this one deposit of faith everything which it presents for belief as divinely revealed.[296]

(6) The Scriptures are holy inspired.

Those divinely revealed realities which are contained and presented in sacred Scripture have been committed to writing under the inspiration of the Holy Spirit. For holy mother Church, relying on the belief of the Apostles (see John 20:31; 2 Tim. 3:16; 2 Peter 1:19-21; 3:15-16), holds that the books of both the Old and New Testaments in their entirety, with all their parts, are sacred and canonical because written under the inspiration of the Holy Spirit, they have God as their author and have been handed on as such to the Church herself.[297]

(7) The interpretation of Scriptures comes through the Grammatico-historical-traditional method and finalized through the authority of the Church.

To search out the intention of the sacred writers, attention should be given, among other things, to 'literary norms.' For truth is set forth and expressed differently in texts which are variously historical, prophetic, poetic, or of other forms of discourse. The interpreter must investigate what meaning the sacred writer intended to express and actually expressed in particular circumstances by using contemporary literary forms in accordance with the situation of his own time and culture. For the correct understanding of what the sacred author wanted to assert, due attention must be paid to the customary and characteristic styles of feeling, speaking and narrating which prevailed at the time of the sacred writer, and to the patterns men normally employed at the period in their everyday dealings with one another.

---

[295] "Dogmatic Constitution on Divine Revelation," Second Vatican Council - Nov. 18, 1965, 9.

[296] Ibid., 10.
[297] Ibid., 11.

But, since holy Scripture must be read and interpreted in the same spirit in which it was written, no less serious attention must be given to the content and unity of the whole Scripture if the meaning of the sacred texts is to be correctly worked out. The living tradition of the whole Church must be taken into account along with the harmony which exists between elements of the faith. It is the task of exegetes to work according to these rules toward a better understanding and explanation of the meaning of sacred Scripture so that through preparatory study the judgement of the Church may mature. For all of what has been said about the way of interpreting Scripture is subject finally to the judgement of the Church, which carries out the divine commission and ministry of guarding and interpreting the Word of God.[298]

(8) *The Kingdom of God has been established.*

Christ established the Kingdom of God on earth, manifested His Father and Himself by deeds and words, and completed His work by His death, resurrection and glorious Ascension and by the sending of the Holy Spirit. Having been lifted up from the earth, He draws all men to Himself (see John 12:32, Greek text), He who alone has the words of eternal life (see John 6:68).[299]

(9) *A commitment to making the Scripture available to Christians that are committed to the faith.*

Easy access to sacred Scripture should be provided for all the Christian faithful. That is why the Church from the very beginning accepted as her own that very ancient Greek translation of the Old Testament which is called the Septuagint; and she has always given a place of honor to other Eastern translations and Latin ones, especially the Latin translation known as the Vulgate. But since the Word of God should be accessible at all times, the Church by her authority and with maternal concern sees to it that suitable and correct translations are made into different languages, especially from the original texts of the sacred books.[300]

(10) *The terms of Catholic exegetics is defined.*

Catholic exegetes then and other students of sacred theology, working diligently together and using appropriate means, should devote their energies, under the watchful care of the sacred teaching office of the Church, to an exploration and exposition of the divine writings.[301]

The term "sacred theology" is defined as follows: "Sacred theology rests on the written Word of God, together with sacred tradition, as its primary and perpetual foundation.[302]

Based on these statements, it would appear that the Catholic position on an

---

[298] "Dogmatic Constitution on Divine Revelation," Second Vatican Council - Nov. 18, 1965, 12.
[299] Ibid., 17.

[300] Ibid., 22.
[301] Ibid., 23.
[302] Ibid., 24.

allegorical hermeneutic is grounded in the Grammatico-historical method but treats past allegorical interpretations of church Fathers as part of church tradition and must be considered in any current or future interpretations.

This would imply that the traditional allegorical interpretations of Augustine still stand as an official interpretation based on church tradition.

This was the Reformation difference between the Roman Catholic Church and the Protestant movement, the issue of the individual priesthood of true believers and the right to self-determination concerning the Scriptures.

As many can see, over the years allegorical interpretations have changed, and been modified to current practices of the day.

Much of allegorical interpretation has a past history, and many theologians stand on these past allegorical interpretations to build their theological systems, just as the Catholic tradition has. All this in spite of, or without regard for, current reasonable hermeneutical practices of a literal approach that produces as its goal a non-contradictory approach to the Scriptures as a whole.

Defining the Allegorical Method

"Allegorization—A method of interpretation based on the assumption that the Scriptures contains multiple sense."[303]

The Dangers of the Allegorical Method

The dangers of an allegorical approach to Scripture was facilitated by two events in church history. (i) The move towards ecclesiasticism and the establishment of Church authority in all matters of Christian doctrinal interpretations is the first.

Farrar claims Augustine was the first to place Scriptural interpretation under the sole authority of the Church. "He laid down the rule that the Bible must be interpreted with reference to Church Orthodoxy, and that no Scriptural expression can be out of accordance with any other." [304]

If the second part of this demand was held to its highest standard, then the first part would not be an issue. But it is evident, when allegory is the norm of the day, the requirements that all Scripture must agree with itself could never be achieved with any real consistency or agreement within the Church as a whole.

It is clear from this view that Augustine would be in agreement with the ultimate premise of this work, that there are no contradictions within the Scriptures, therefore, for biblical truth to be true, it must agree with all other biblical truth.

(ii) The second event that brought about dangerous interpretive policy within church history was Greek Allegorism that came out of Alexandria.

Tan writes, "The allegorical method introduced by the Alexandrian Jews left deep and lasting scars on the study of the Scriptures. It lingered for more than fifteen hundred years on up to the time of the Reformation, vestiges of it continuing to the present." [305] J. Dwight Pentecost supports this line of thinking with this assessment: "The previous study should make it obvious that the allegorical method was not born out of the study of the Scriptures, but rather from a desire to unite Greek philosophy and the Word of God....

---

[303] Tan, *The Interpretation of Prophecy*, 363.
[304] Frederic W. Farrar, *History of Interpretation* (London: Macmillan and Co., 1886), 236.

[305] Tan, *The Interpretation of Prophecy*, 47.

It was not the child of orthodoxy, but of heterodoxy."[306]

The dangers of the methodology itself are as follows:

(1) Allegorists put an emphasis on the spiritual meaning of the text, looking for hidden spiritual meaning in every verse. This tends to ignore the literal that brings the context to the true meaning,[307] which then invalidates the original intent, making the Scriptures null and void.

(2) The allegorist becomes the sole authority in his or her interpretation, which then produces chaos within the local church. This is especially true in the area of prophetic interpretations.[308] This method would forfeit the doctrinal norm of *Sola Scriptura* that many of the Reformers held to, as well as being one of eight theological positions of Baptist doctrine. Simply stated, the Scriptures are the sole authority in faith and practice.

(3) This method leaves no means to test its interpretation for truth or accuracy, other than to compare their views with others who agree with them.[309]

W. A. Criswell (Ph.D.) was a longtime pastor of the First Baptist Church of Dallas, Texas, with membership in his later years reaching over 26,000.[310] Criswell supported a literal method of interpretation. His reasoning behind this was a practical one.

If we preach the Bible literally, it is like telling the truth. You do not have to remember what you said. But if you spiritualize,… what you said about a passage yesterday may be diametrically opposed to what you make it mean today… A man will find himself contradicting himself over and over again as he preaches through the years.[311]

Arguments Supporting Allegorical Methodology

Firstly, it is argued that the Apostle Paul used an allegorical method in Galatians 4:21-31.

The answer to this is, Paul is dealing with an historical narrative which is never allegorized. Paul is simply making an allegory out of a historical event, making the point that one woman represents the law and its enslavement to the flesh and the other represents the promise of God that ultimately provides freedom from the law and the way of eternal life.

This is not interpreting the Scriptures using an allegorical method of interpretation, but instead making a spiritual point using allegory.

A second argument made is that the Scriptures use types, therefore, this usage represents allegorical or spiritual methods of interpretation.

Types are not the same as allegory. Types are historical parallelisms that represent a biblical truth. The first man Adam is a type for Christ (Romans 5:14). Adam was a real person in history just as

---

[306] Pentecost, *Things To Come*, 23-24.
[307] Tan, *The Interpretation of Prophecy*, 37.
[308] Ibid., 73.
[309] Ibid., 74.
[310] *Wikipedia*, v.s. "W. A. Criswell" [encyclopedia on line]; available from

https://en.wikipedia.org/wiki/W._A._Criswell; Internet; accessed 20 January 2019.
[311] W. A. Criswell, *Why I Preach that the Bible is Literally True* (Nashville, Tenn.: Broadman Press, 1969), 145, quoted in Tan, *The Interpretation of Prophecy*, 74.

Christ was, with parallel meanings to their lives that represent a biblical truth.

Jonah's historical event spending three days in the belly of a great fish, was a type representing an event in the life of Christ, who historically spent three days in the heart of the earth after his crucifixion (Matthew 12:40)

J. N. D. Kelly expands on this subject of Typological Exegesis by saying,

> Essentially it was a technique for bringing out the correspondence between the two Testaments, and took as its guiding principle the idea that the events and personages of the Old were 'types' of, i.e. prefigured and anticipated, the events and personages of the New. The typologist took history seriously; it was the scene of the progressive unfolding of God's consistent redemptive purpose.[312]

Allegory, as used in scripture, is used to make a spiritual point that is true, usually through telling a story that helps the hearer understand the point being made.

Jesus' illustration concerning the strong man in Matthew 12:28-29 could be seen as an allegory (defined as the expression by means of symbolic fictional figures and actions of truths or generalizations about human existence),[313] illustrating the point that he did not represent the kingdom of Satan but the Kingdom of God. This allegory was necessary because he was being accused of using the power of Satan's kingdom to heal. Jesus' point was, how could this be true. For this to be true he would have to beat the strong man Satan first, which would ultimately collapse Satan's kingdom. But instead he was casting out demons not as a servant of Satan, but through the authority of God's kingdom who has all such power and authority. So, then he asks them, "by whom do your sons cast them out?" (Matthew 12:27)

The point is, this is an allegory and should not be allegorized to prove some point in another part of the Scriptures as Augustine did.[314] To allegorize an allegory misses the point of the original intent of the writer.

So the question is, Are we interested in understanding the truth proclaimed in the Scripture, or as students of the Word, more interested in propping up passages that we may not fully understand yet, like Revelation 20:1-7?

The third argument made is the Bible is filled with figures of speech which obviously should not be taken literally.

The answer to that argument is four-fold. (i) Figures of speech are legitimate means to express a literal truth. (ii) To interpret a figure of speech is one thing, but to spiritualize a normal statement is entirely different. (iii) Some things given in figurative language have been literally fulfilled. (iv) And lastly, if the truth be known, Premillennialism, as a system, can stand on its own without the use of any figures of speech, with figurative language defined as, "The legitimate expression of an original literal idea in a figure of speech or figurative act."[315]

THE LITERAL METHOD

As this study continues, we learn from Bernard Ramm's (Ph.D.) research, five historical schools that represent the history

---

[312] J. N. D. Kelly, *Early Christian Doctrines*, 71.

[313] *Merriam-Webster's 11th Collegiate Dictionary*, s.v. "Allegory," [dictionary online]; available from https://www.merriam-webster.com/dictionary/allegory; Internet; accessed 24 January 2019.

[314] Augustine The City of God 20. 8.

[315] Tan, *The Interpretation of Prophecy*, 365.

behind the literal method of interpretation as summarized here.

[*Jewish Literalism* begins with the prophet Ezra during the Babylonian captivity (586-538 B.C.).

During this time the Jewish people lost their connection to their own language—Hebrew, which required Ezra to be their interpreter between themselves and the Hebrew Scriptures. Ezra was seen to be the founder of the Jewish interpretive school, becoming an interpreter between Aramaic and Hebrew.

"Out of the captivities came Judaism with its synagogues, rabbis, scribes, lawyers, and traditions."[316]

Over time the system produced reasonable hermeneutical rules, but many times they were not followed. Rabbinic exegesis was based on sound principles but was also known to be sometimes inconsistent by those who used it. It is said the major weakness in the system was the development of hyperliteralism or *letterism*. This grew from a philosophy that every word in Scripture was important and needed to be considered, this, on top of the Scripture's authorship of God, meant there must be multiple meanings behind its writings.

The system eventually developed the Cabbalist system, using a letterism and allegorism form of interpretation. The end result of this rabbinical exegesis was the destructiveness of letterism, as it zeroed in on the less important, leaving the true sense of the message lost to its readers and interpreters.

The second school mentioned is the *Syrian School of Antioch*, which had been accused by the orthodox of being heretical through their supposed connection with the Nestorians. This Christian community was influenced by the Jewish School while avoiding the letterism of the Jews and the allegorism that came out of Alexandria. This school was represented by individuals such as Lucian, Dorotheus, Diodorus, Chrysostom and Theodore of Mopsuestia.

This school opposed the methods of Origen and supported methods of literal and historical interpretation. They held to a plain literal and a figurative literal. This school also avoided dogmatic exegesis, which became representative of the Roman Catholic exegesis.

Their strong point was their insistence on the historical aspect of the Old Testament versus allegorizing away the importance of the historic narrative of the same.

The reputation of the exegesis used by this school was reflected by "The commentary of Theodore (of Mopsuestia) on the minor epistles of Paul is the first and almost the last exegetical work produced in the ancient Church which will bear any comparison with modern commentaries."[317]

The third school was known as *The Victorines*.

Medieval scholars have established the existence of a school located in the Abbey of St. Victor in Paris. This school represented the historical/literal approach to biblical interpretation and was influenced by Jewish scholars of the medieval period.

The Victorines held that the liberal arts, history and geography were necessary to the pursuit of exegesis. They held to a literal interpretation and insisted that until the literal was fully explored, the spiritual sense could not be known.

The fourth school in the timeline—*The Reformers*. The Syrian school was reflected in

---

316 Ramm, *Protestant Biblical Interpretation*, 46.

317 Ibid., 50. (See footnote 33.)

the Victorines, which ultimately became the hermeneutical thought of the Reformers.

This was a time of not just the Reformation, but also the time of a hermeneutical reformation.

Two major factors prepared the way for this hermeneutical reformation, with the first being led by Martin Luther, who was greatly influenced by Occam the philosopher. Luther was ultimately able to find the balance between divine revelation and human reason without the influence of church tradition, but he relied more so on the authority of the Scriptures and God's direct enlightenment.

Along this same timeline came the second major factor of this hermeneutical reformation, the renewal of studying the original languages of the Scriptures— Hebrew and Greek.

This came about due to the work of "Reuchlin, a humanist and lawyer, who translated Kimchi's Hebrew grammar into Latin." [318] This allowed anyone with the time to decipher elements of the Hebrew language to do so.

Within the same timeline, there was a renewed interest in Greek which produced the first Greek New Testament published by Erasmus in 1516.[319]

Within this environment, Martin Luther developed six principles to his literal approach of hermeneutics.

(1) *The psychological principle.* The interpreter must seek the illumination of the Holy Spirit and depend on that leading.

(2) *The authority principle.* The Scriptures are the final authority in all matters of theology. This would include authority presented by ecclesiastical or other documents by others.

(3) *The literal principle.* Martin Luther believed that the literal method of interpretation took precedent over the current four-fold system of scholastics. This was defined as the literal and the Spiritual, with the spiritual sub-divided into the allegorical, anagogical and the tropological. Luther's literal contained three concepts. (i) The rejection of Allegory, (ii) the primacy of the original languages, and (iii) attention must be paid to the historical and grammatical aspects of the writings.

(4) *The sufficiency principle.* Any Christian considered competent could interpret the Scriptures on their own, and the Scriptures are clear enough to be understood by its reader. The Scriptures interpret themselves.

(5) *The Christological principle.* Literal interpretation was not an end in itself but a means to reveal Christ, which the Scriptures are all about collectively.

(6) *The Law-Gospel principle.* The Law and the Gospel work together, not as a system of salvation, but working together in the light of the Law reveals our sin and the need for the Gospel, which tells us about the Christ who saves us through his grace.

John Calvin also contributed to this school after Martin Luther. His views are reflected in five positions he took.

(1) He insisted on the concept of the illumination of the Spirit.

(2) He rejected the method of allegorical interpretation.

---

[318] Ramm, *Protestant Biblical Interpretation*, 52.

[319] Ibid., 53.

(3) He believed as a basic conviction that Scripture interprets Scripture.

(4) He believed in his independence of exegesis.

(5) He believed study should include the historical settings to all prophetic and Messianic Scriptures.

The fifth school of literalism was *Post-reformation.* This school is best represented by Ernesti who in 1761 published—*Institutio Interpretis.*

Ernesti was a classical scholar who believed that grammatical exegesis took priority over dogmatic exegesis, and the literal form of interpretation took persistence over allegorical. His main principle was to emphasize the importance of sound philology in exegesis.] [320]

Defining the Literal Method

"Literal Interpretation—The art of explaining the original meaning of Scripture according to the normal and customary usages of its language." [321]

Evidence for the Literal Method

God is the creator of all language. From the time of creation to the Tower of Babel; God has been the author of it all. Adam could speak and communicate directly with God and his mate, Eve, instantly. God also chose that same language to communicate his words in writing. In Luke 10:25-26, Jesus responded to a question from a lawyer by telling him to read the law in the Scriptures and then explain to him how he understood them. The underlining principle to understand is this, God

intended for us to communicate plainly, which should be understood as the norm. [322]

Moses states in Deuteronomy 29:29, "The secret things belong to the Lord our God, but the things revealed belong to us and to our sons forever, that we may observe all the words of this law." This concept, that anything God reveals is meant to be understood, is a second evidence for a literal approach to understanding the Scriptures. [323]

A third evidence comes through the historical beginning of interpretation of the Scriptures during the time of Christ. The Jews of the day interpreted the Scriptures literally, as did Christ's Apostles, as they followed the lead of Jesus in his approach to the Scriptures. This can be seen in Matthew 4:1-7, as Jesus holds a conversation with Satan where both quoted and understood the Scriptures from a literal perspective.

The last evidence in this line of thought is found in the literal fulfillment of Old Testament prophecies. Tan states that at the time of Christ's first advent over 300 Old Testament prophecies were fulfilled literally. [324]

Isaiah 7:14 speaks about the virgin birth of Christ more than 700 years before it happened as recorded in Matthew 1:23. Isaiah 53:9-12 speaks of Christ being buried with the rich. Matthew 27:57-60 confirms that. Psalm 22:18 describes Christ's clothes being gambled over, or lots cast to see who would get them. Luke 23:34 confirms this taking place. Psalm 69:21 prophesied that gall and vinegar (wine) would be offered Christ as he hung on the

---

[320] Ramm, *Protestant Biblical Interpretation*, 45-59.
[321] Tan, *The Interpretation of Prophecy*, 367.
[322] Ibid., 59-61.

[323] Ibid., 61.
[324] Ibid., 63.

Cross, and Matthew 27:34 confirms it. Psalm 22:1 quotes Jesus' dying words on the cross which Matthew 27:46 confirms. Psalm 34:20 predicts that the coming Christ would not have any of his bones broken in his death, and John 19:36 testifies that no bones were broken. Zechariah 12:10 refers to the pierced side of Christ during his crucifixion. John 19:34 confirms that this took place. Psalm 16:10 prophesied that Christ would be raised from the dead; a fact confirmed by Mark 16:6-7. There are many more details like these and, as a matter of interest, the Psalms listed here were written between 1011 and 971 B.C., nearly 1,000 years before their fulfillment.[325]

The Literal Method and Figurative Language

A literal method does not rule out figurative language, but instead incorporates rules inside its hermeneutical system to provide proper interpretations from a literal perspective. Terry expresses it this way.

> Biblical Hermeneutics is a department of General Hermeneutics, and, as we have seen, calls in the main for the application of the general principles required in the interpretation of all literature. But as so large a portion of the Bible is composed of poetry and prophecy, and contains so many examples of parable, allegory, type, and symbol, it is proper in treating the science of biblical interpretation to devote more space to Special than

to General Hermeneutics. Parables, allegories, types, and symbols, have their peculiar laws, and Grammatico-historical interpretation must give attention to rhetorical form and prophetic symbolism, as well as to the laws of grammar and the facts of history.

> The principles of Special Hermeneutics must be gathered from a faithful study of the Bible itself. We must observe the methods which the sacred writers followed. Naked propositions or formulated rules will be of little value unless supported and illustrated by self-verifying examples. It is worthy of note that the Scriptures furnish numerous instances of the interpretation of dreams, visions, types, symbols, and parables. In such examples we are to find our principles and laws of exposition. The Holy Scripture is no Delphic oracle, to bewilder the heart by utterances of double meaning. Taken as a whole, and allowed to speak for itself, the Bible will be found to be its own best interpreter.[326]

Tan holds to the same view but does not speak in terms of a special hermeneutic, instead incorporating all the same concepts under one hermeneutical umbrella called the Grammatical-Historical Method. Tan writes,

> Consistent literal interpretation however means that the interpreter consistently acknowledge and accepts the *customary* usage of Bible

---

[325] Reid A. Ashbaucher, *The Christian Faith: A Quick Guide to Understanding its Inter-Workings*, 2 ed. (Toledo: Reid Ashbaucher, 2017), 44.

[326] Terry, *Biblical Hermeneutics*, 143.

language. And customary usage certainly involves both nonfigurative and figurative languages. In interpreting figurative language, one must not base his interpretation on the literal words forming the figure and symbol but on the literal sense which the figure and symbol are intended to convey.[327]

J. Dwight Pentecost adds,

It will thus be observed that the literalist does not deny the existence of figurative language. The literalist does, however, deny that such figures must be interpreted so as to destroy the literal truth intended through the employment of the figures. Literal truth is to be learned through the symbols.[328]

GENERAL PRINCIPLES TO GUIDE IN USING THE LITERAL METHOD[329]

INTERPRET THE WORDS OF THE TEXT

(1) Study usage of the word to find its normal meaning in various contexts.

(2) Select the meaning of the word that best fits the near and remote context. The simplest most apparent meaning is normally correct.

(3) Realize the word has only one meaning in any given context—not all possible meanings of the word.

(4) Watch carefully for distinction of operantly synonymous words.

(5) Interpret the word in view of the general teaching of scripture.

(6) Beware of grammatical construction that determines meaning of words.

INTERPRET IN CONTEXT

(1) Context may be a verse; a few verses; a chapter; a book or the whole Bible.

(2) No explanation should be given that does not fit the context.

(3) Learn to watch for transitional words and phrased in context.

INTERPRET IN HISTORICAL CONTEXT

A passage to be fully understood normally is placed in its historical setting. Tan writes,

The proper concept of the historical in Bible interpretation is to view the Scriptures as written during given ages and cultures. Applications may then be drawn which are relevant to our times. For instance, the subject of meat offered to idols can only be interpreted from the historical and cultural setting of New Testament times. Principles to be drawn are relevant to us today. Besides those Scriptures which relate to the historical situations of Bible times, a large portion of God's Word contains doctrinal teaching and spiritual truths which are ageless or directly applicable in any age. In these instances, historical and

---

[327] Tan, *The Interpretation of Prophecy*, 264.
[328] Pentecost, *Things to Come*, 13.

[329] Note: The majority of the principles listed under this section are derived from *The Interpretation of Prophecy* by Paul Lee Tan.

cultural factors would not assume as large a consideration.[330]

INTERPRET GRAMMATICALLY

Scriptural passages should be interpreted according to the normal rules of Grammar. This is best done from the original language. But at least observe the rules of English grammar. Tan states, "Scriptural revelation must therefore be interpreted according to regular rules of earthly grammar and rhetoric. Being divinely intended for human comprehension, the Bible should be interpreted according to the normal mode of Communication used among men." [331]

INTERPRET BY THE ANALOGY OF SCRIPTURE

The simplest way to understand this concept comes to us through Tan's explanation, in which he writes,

> The principle of the "analogy of faith" was first brought to the attention of Christians by the Protestants reformers. The principle in based on the observation that there is no better interpreter of Scriptures than the Scriptures itself. As the apostle Paul puts it, "Compare spiritual things with spiritual" (1 Cor. 2:13; see Romans 12:6). The justification for comparing Scripture with Scripture lies in the fact that Scriptures do not contradict each other.
>
> When applied to interpretation, the principle of analogy of faith demands that every interpretation be in harmony with the uniform teaching of Scripture. No interpretation is allowable which

does not harmonize with the uniform teaching of the Bible on that given subject. Passages are to be explained, not on the basis of individual texts, but on the whole tenor of Scripture.[332]

INTERPRET FIGURATIVE LANGUAGE

(1) Reasons for Figures of Speech.

Figure of speech is a legitimate grammatical device used to more vividly convey the original idea.

Within prophecy, the future things described are sometimes beyond the realm of human experience, accordingly they could only be described in human terms by using figurative language.

Within prophecy, figures of speech are sometimes both revealed to the believer and concealed from the unbeliever. If a prophecy was completely open, evil individuals would be tempted to try to tamper with its fulfillment.

(2) When is language to be regarded as figurative?

David L. Cooper (Ph.D.) says, "When the plain sense of Scripture makes common sense, seek no other sense; therefore, take every word at its primary, ordinary, usual, literal meaning unless the facts of the immediate context, studied in the light of related passages and

---

[330] Tan, *The Interpretation of Prophecy*, 103-104.
[331] Ibid., 32-33.

[332] Ibid., 109-110.

axiomatic and fundamental truths, indicate clearly otherwise."[333]

(3) How to Interpret Figurative Language.

- "The identification and interpretation of Bible figures by the Bible itself is a rule not an exception." [334]

- Consult the context. The writer often explains his figure of speech.

- Consult parallel passages in which the same thing is given in non-figurative language or in a more command figure of language.

- Do not push figurative language too far.

GENERAL CHARACTERISTICS OF PROPHECY

THE TIME ELEMENT IN PROPHECY

Prophecy in the Bible often lacks time perspective. Although certain areas of the future are definitely cloaked as to a time sequence and extent, we find no absolute continuous and unbroken chronology of the future. The prophets themselves were aware of this problem (1 Peter 1:9-12), which can only be overcome by a careful comparison of Scripture with Scripture.[335]

This could better be called the telescopic character of prophecy. Some prophecy may have all the characteristics of literary unity, yet refer to some event in the near future in connection with the historical situation of the prophet, and also to some distant event connected with the Messiah and the Kingdom. When the first event arrives, it becomes the earnest and divine forecast of the more distant and final event.[336]

A word of warning should be given. This is not as common as some people think. We should not force such a double reference into the text. It should arise from the literal interpretation of the text.[337]

The following is a summary of these concepts.

(1) Prophecy often speaks of future events as if it were in the present.

(2) Prophecy often speaks of the future events as past. (Isa. 53:5)

(3) Prophetic events may be grouped together when given while not actually together in time, this is known as the *mountain peak* view.[338]

(4) Prophecy may be given in reverse time sequence. (Isa. 61:2; Isa. 9:6-7)

(5) Prophecy may have a so-called double reference. (Duet. 18; Acts 3:22-23) [339]

SOME PROPHECIES ARE CONDITIONAL EVEN WHEN NO CONDITIONS ARE STATED [340]

If this is the case, how can we know when a prophecy is conditional and when it is not?

---

[333] David L. Cooper, "The Golden Rule of Interpretation," The Biblical Research Society [article on line]; available from http://www.biblicalresearch.info/index.html; Internet; accessed 25 January 2019.

[334] Tan, *The Interpretation of Prophecy*, 143.

[335] Ibid., 91-94.
[336] Ibid., 91-95.
[337] Ibid., 94.
[338] Ibid., 92.
[339] Ibid., 178.
[340] Ibid., 187-189.

Prophecies that depends upon human activity or upon the response of those to whom it was given may be conditional, even when the conditions are not stated. But a prophecy that depends only on God cannot be conditional unless conditions are clearly stated.

CHAPTER SEVEN

Dispensations

INTRODUCTION

Paul J. Scharf (M.Div.) provides the following observation on this topic as he writes,

> As both a founding father of the modern Biblical creationism movement and a highly respected teacher of Bible prophecy—and theology in general—Dr. Whitcomb showed me firsthand that dispensationalism was not an obscurantist position relegated to contemplating "mysterious periods of sevens" (as one opponent of dispensationalism once characterized it in my hearing). Rather, he explained how it went to the very heart of the teaching of the Bible, covering all of history—from a literal creation week at the beginning to a literal 1,000-year kingdom at the end.[341]

Those who hold to a dispensational view may differ in their assessment of the number of dispensations. There are those who believe in three, four, five, seven, eight or even more. However, the number of dispensations is not the pillar of this theological system, providing one maintains the following concepts. (i) Israel and the Church are separate entities. (ii) The prophetic unconditional covenants have not been replaced by the New Covenant. (iii) And that God will fulfill his Abrahamic and Davidic Covenant promises to Israel through a literal millennial Kingdom.

It is clear from Christ's perspective there are at least three separate economies represented in the mind of Jesus; the Old Testament period, the existing age in which Christ was living on earth, and the age to come, representing the millennial Kingdom—read Matthew 24.

WHAT IS A DISPENSATION?

SIMPLE DEFINITIONS

"Bible history does not run in an uninterrupted fashion. It comes under distinct stages, periods, and dispensations."[342]

The word οἰκονομία (dispensation) comes from the Greek term οἶκος (house) + νόμος (to manage a governing principle or law), denoting a stewardship, management, or rule of life. A dispensation is simply "a distinguishable economy in the outworking of God's purpose."[343]

---

[341] Paul J. Scharf, "Five Dispensationalists Who Changed My Direction," [article on line]; available from https://dispensationalpublishing.com/five-dispensationalists-who-changed-my-direction/; Internet; accessed 31 January 2019.

[342] Tan, *The Interpretation of Prophecy*, 243.

[343] Charles C. Ryrie, *Dispensationalism Today* (Chicago, ILL: Moody Press, 1965), 29, quoted in *Tan, Interpretation of Prophecy*, 243n.

Dispensations are the divine administrations of human affairs from Adam through the end of time. Though time is not a primary consideration, each divine administration, or Dispensation, relates to a definite period of human history....

Dispensations are not different ways of forgiveness and eternal life, but different administrations of God as He superintends the way mankind lives on earth. Eternal salvation was, is, and always will be a gift by grace alone through faith alone in Jesus Christ alone (Ephesians 2:9–10).[344]

NEW TESTAMENT USE OF THE TERM DISPENSATION

The Apostle Paul speaks to three dispensations, similar to how Christ saw human history when he spoke to his disciples in Matthew 24.

(1) Ephesians 1:10 — "... with a view to an administration suitable to the fulness of the times, that is, the summing up of all things in Christ, things in the heavens and things upon the earth."

Jamieson, Fausset and Brown Commentary on the Old and New Testaments provide the following insight on Ephesians 1:10, as they reflect on the many examples within Scripture of a dispensational concept. It would appear the concept in verse 10 of *the fullness of time* is future in nature.

"The ends of the ages" (Greek,1 Corinthians 10.11); "the times (same Greek as here, 'the seasons,' or 'fitly appointed times') of the Gentiles" (Luke 21.24); "the seasons which the Father hath put in His own power" (Acts 1.7); "the times of restitution of all things which God hath spoken by the prophets since the world began" (Acts 3:20, 21). The coming of Jesus at the first advent, "in the fulness of time," was one of these "times." The descent of the Holy Ghost, "when Pentecost was fully come" (Acts 2:1), was another. The testimony given by the apostles to Him "in due time" ("in its own seasons," Greek) (1 Timothy 2:6) was another. The conversion of the Jews "when the times of the Gentiles are fulfilled," the second coming of Christ, the "restitution of all things," the millennial kingdom, the new heaven and earth, shall be severally instances of "the dispensation of the fulness of the times," that is, "the dispensation of" the Gospel events and benefits belonging to their respective "times," when severally filled up or completed. God the Father, according to His own good pleasure and purpose, is the Dispenser both of the Gospel benefits and of their several fitting times (Acts 1:7).[345]

(2) Ephesians 3:1-2— "For this cause I Paul, the prisoner of Jesus Christ for you Gentiles, If ye have heard of the

[344] Chafer Theological Seminary, "Dispensations," [article on line]; available from https://www.chafer.edu/dispensations; Internet; accessed 28 January 2019.
[345] *A commentary, critical and explanatory, on the Old and New Testaments*, vol. 2, "Ephesians 1:10," by Rev.

Robert Jamieson, Rev. A. R. Fausset and Rev. David Brown (New York: S.S. Scranton and company, 1873), 342; available from http://hdl.handle.net/2027/miun.ajg3934.0002.001; Internet; accessed 29 January 2019.

dispensation of the grace of God which is given me to youward:" (KJV)

Jamieson, Fausset and Brown Commentary provides the following insight on Ephesians 3:2, as this concept seems to be in the present. "The dispensation—'The office of dispensing, as a steward, the grace of God which was (not 'is') given me to you-ward,' viz., to dispense to you."[346]

(3) Colossians 1:25-26— "Whereof I am made a minister, according to the dispensation of God which is given to me for you, to fulfill the word of God; Even the mystery which hath been hid from ages and from generations, but now is made manifest to his saints:" (KJV)

Jamieson, Fausset and Brown Commentary, provides the following insight on the term *dispensation* found in Colossians 1:25.

Dispensation—the *stewardship* committed to me to dispense in the house of God, the Church, to the whole family of believers, the goods of my Master (Luke 12.42; 1 Corinthians 4.1-2; 9.17; Ephesians 3.2). Which is given—*Greek*, "which *was* given." for you—with a view to you, Gentiles (v.27; Romans 15.16). To fulfil—to bring it fully to all: the end of his stewardship: "fully preached" (Romans 15.19). "The *fulness* of Christ (v. 19), and of the times (Ephesians 1.10) required him so to do."[347]

The dispensation expressed here, seems to be in the past, and Paul's usage reflects the same sense as dispensationalists use the term today.

THE CHARACTERISTICS OF DISPENSATIONS

(1) Primary Characteristics

Dispensations or economies can be distinguished between one another through a change in a governing relationship between God and humanity, resulting in a change in humanity's responsibilities and reflected by a change in God's revelation to the world as recorded in the Scriptures.[348]

Examples: Adam and Eve's relationship with God came with the responsibility to walk with God and care for the garden. After the fall, this changed.

A second economy can be seen coming through the Mosaic Law. God is now governing through the Law, with Israel's responsibility to be obedient to the Law which they found themselves under.

After Christ's ministry was complete, a new change in the economy took place, God's people are no longer under the law, but under grace. Humanity's responsibility is now repentance and faith in Christ, as God is now ruling in the hearts of his people.[349]

(2) Secondary Characteristics

[As a secondary nature to dispensations, three elements reflect the changes God has made in his dealing with the world. (i) A test which reflects on the total nature of God's new pronouncements to humanity in the

---

[346] *A commentary, critical and explanatory, on the Old and New Testaments*, vol. 2, "Ephesians 3:2," 347.

[347] *A commentary, critical and explanatory, on the Old and New Testaments*, vol. 2, "Colossians 1:25," 374.

[348] Charles C. Ryrie, *Dispensationalism* (Chicago: Moody Publishers, 2007), 39-40.

[349] Ibid.

area of God's relationship with his creation, which ultimately measures humanity's responsibility success rate. (ii) A visible failure on humanity's part toward their responsibility in honoring God within this new economy in which they are living. (iii) A judgment that generally ends the dispensation, transitioning the world into a new one.

These are not set in stone, there could be some variations to this by some of these things having no visual appearance or practical effect on the world at the time. But in the end, these secondary attributes are not the determining factor in determining dispensations. Some examples of this can be seen in the end of the Mosaic Law with the death and resurrection of Christ, which reflected on Israel's failure that culminated in their rebellion towards God. Subsequently this age will end with the world-wide rebellion against God, ushering in the millennial Kingdom. Then that age will end with the world's rebellion against God, ushering in the end of the Age and a New Heaven and New Earth. Test, failure, followed by Judgment. In most cases all three will be reflected in all dispensations.] 350

ATTRIBUTES REFLECTING A CHANGE IN DISPENSATIONS

"A new period always begins only when from the side of God a change is introduced in the composition of the principles valid up to that time; that is, when from the side of God three things concur: (i) A continuance of certain ordinances remain valid until then; (ii) An annulment of other regulations that are currently valid; (iii) A fresh introduction of new principles not before valid."351

Some people err by failing to recognize that a change in dispensations takes place when God institutes the change, not when man fully understands what God has done.

NAMES AND CHARACTERISTICS OF DISPENSATIONS MOST COMMONLY IDENTIFIED 352

Dispensations are determined through studying the Scriptures and applying the principles already discussed. There are differing opinions on how many dispensations there are. The following information will list the most commonly identified dispensations today, while providing a table reflecting the views of differing opinions at the end of this section.

THE DISPENSATION OF INNOCENCE OR FREEDOM

- Biblical reference: Genesis 1:28- 3:6

- The responsibility in this dispensation was for Adam to care for the garden and not eat the fruit of the tree of the Knowledge of Good and Evil. As a result, in Adam's perfect state, he walked with God. This was considered Adam's stewardship to maintain.

- Adam failed by eating the fruit that was forbidden.

---

350 Ryrie, *Dispensationalism*, 40-42.
351 Eric Sauer, *Dawn of World Redemption: A Survey of the History of Salvation in the Old Testament*

(Grand Rapids, Wm. B. Eerdmans Publishing Company, 1964), 194.
352 Ryrie, *Dispensationalism*, 59-65.

- Hence, God's judgement of casting Adam and Eve out of the garden and pronouncing death as their ultimate end, both physically and spiritually.

THE DISPENSATION OF CONSCIENCE OR SELF-DETERMINATION

- Scripture reference: Genesis 4:1-8:14

- Man was responsible to God through human conscience. The title for this dispensation came from Romans 2:15: "… in that they show the work of the Law written in their hearts, their conscience bearing witness, and their thoughts alternately accusing or else defending them,…."

- Three individuals are mentioned as people of faith during this time, Abel, Enoch and Noah. The end result of this period was a pervasive evil among the world population, with no conscience of God's holiness in their minds.

- God's pronounced judgment on humanity through the worldwide flood of Genesis 6:17.

THE DISPENSATION OF HUMAN OR CIVIL GOVERNMENT

- Scripture reference: Genesis 8:15-11:9.

- Noah was the central person of interest during this time, with God pronouncing new revelation as he states that all living things outside the human realm will fear humanity and humanity would be in charge over them. Humanity was commanded to be fruitful and multiply, inhabiting all the earth. Humanity was also given all other moving creatures for food, with the exception of consuming their blood. God also pronounced capital punishment as a means to control the acts of murdering one another. This ultimately provided law or governance of the people.

- Humanity failed through their rebellion of not multiplying and moving out to inhabit the earth.

- God pronounced judgement at the tower of Babel and created multiple languages, then scattered them throughout the world. The languages created a barrier, preventing them from coming back together as one people again.

DISPENSATION OF PROMISE OR PATRIARCHAL RULE

- Scripture reference: Genesis 11:10-Exodus 18:27.

- Abraham and his family were chosen as the test for the promise that would bring blessing to all. The title of this dispensation comes from Hebrews 6:15; 11:9.

- The responsibility for the patriarchs were to believe God's promises, stay in the land given them, and serve him accordingly.

- Their failure came when they left the land and went into Egypt.

- Galatians 3:15-29 provides an explanation to the difference of separation between the dispensation of promise and the dispensation of the Law. Within the context of this passage, the Law does not nullify the covenant of promise but was added to help govern over transgressions or sins.

THE DISPENSATION OF THE MOSAIC LAW

- Scripture reference: Exodus 19:1-John 19:30

- The central figure of this dispensation was Moses, as he delivered the Law composed of the Ten Commandments and 613 other laws for Israel to abide by—known as the mosaic law.

- Romans 10:1-3 reflects on the failure of Israel, as well as the wording of the New Covenant found in Jeremiah 31:32-33.

  'Behold, days are coming,' declares the Lord, 'when I will make a new covenant with the house of Israel and with the house of Judah, not like the covenant which I made with their fathers in the day I took them by the hand to bring them out of the land of Egypt, My covenant which they broke, although I was a husband to them,' declares the Lord.

- Even with Israel breaking God's law, God dealt with them graciously. God's judgment came in the form of national disbursement into slavery. Ten tribes went into Assyrian captivity while the other two went into Babylonian captivity. Through the final rejection of Christ as the Messiah, Israel was ultimately scattered around the world until 1948, when the world gave legal recognition to the establishment of God's promised land to Israel, providing a mechanism for a future reunification of all the Jewish people once again. (Matthew 23:37-39)

- The Law was never a replacement for the promise God made to Abraham when he entered into a covenant agreement with him, but as Paul explains,

  What I am saying is this: the Law, which came four hundred and thirty years later, does not invalidate a covenant previously ratified by God, so as to nullify the promise. For if the inheritance is based on law, it is no longer based on a promise; but God has granted it to Abraham by means of a promise. Why the Law then? It was added because of transgressions, having been ordained through angels by the agency of a mediator, until the seed should come to whom the promise had been made.[353]

- The Law was never a means of justification by works, as expressed in Romans 2:19-21 and Galatians Chapter 3.

- Individuals were saved <u>under</u> the Law, but not <u>by</u> the Law. This is a key distinction that should be noted.

THE DISPENSATION OF GRACE

- Scripture reference: Jeremiah 31:31-34; Luke 22:20; Acts 2:1.

- The Dispensation of Grace is not a reflection of the first signs of God's

---

[353] Gal. 3:17-19.

grace in the world, but a period in which God demonstrates his grace through the fulfillment of the New Covenant, as expressed in Jeremiah 31:31-34.

'Behold, days are coming,' declares the Lord, 'when I will make a new covenant with the house of Israel and with the house of Judah, not like the covenant which I made with their fathers in the day I took them by the hand to bring them out of the land of Egypt, My covenant which they broke, although I was a husband to them,' declares the Lord. 'But this is the covenant which I will make with the house of Israel after those days,' declares the Lord, 'I will put My law within them, and on their heart I will write it; and I will be their God, and they shall be My people. 'And they shall not teach again, each man his neighbor and each man his brother, saying, 'Know the Lord,' for they shall all know Me, from the least of them to the greatest of them,' declares the Lord, 'for I will forgive their iniquity, and their sin I will remember no more.'

- The grace of God was demonstrated through Christ as we read,

For the grace of God has appeared, bringing salvation to all men, instructing us to deny ungodliness and worldly desires and to live sensibly, righteously and godly in the present age,

looking for the blessed hope and the appearing of the glory of our great God and Savior, Christ Jesus; who gave Himself for us, that He might redeem us from every lawless deed and purify for Himself a people for His own possession, zealous for good deeds.[354]

- The Apostle John tells us, "For the Law was given through Moses; grace and truth were realized through Jesus Christ."[355]

- The central figure of this dispensation is Jesus Christ.

- Humanity's responsibility during this dispensation is to repent and accept the gift of Christ's righteousness.

- The blessing of the Abrahamic covenant (Gen. 12:3) is entirely of grace. The offer of grace is to all, as we read in Romans 5:15-18:

But the free gift is not like the transgression. For if by the transgression of the one the many died, much more did the grace of God and the gift by the grace of the one Man, Jesus Christ, abound to the many. And the gift is not like that which came through the one who sinned; for on the one hand the judgment arose from one transgression resulting in condemnation, but on the other hand the free gift arose from many transgressions resulting in justification. For if

---

[354] Titus 2:11-14.

[355] John 1:17.

by the transgression of the one, death reigned through the one, much more those who receive the abundance of grace and of the gift of righteousness will reign in life through the One, Jesus Christ. So then as through one transgression there resulted condemnation to all men, even so through one act of righteousness there resulted justification of life to all men.

- The Judgment for rejection of the gospel message is the seven-year tribulation period as expressed in Revelation 19:11-19.

- This is a period where God is dealing with both Jews and Gentiles of the world.

THE DISPENSATION OF THE MILLENNIUM OR KINGDOM

- Scripture reference: Revelation 20:1-10.

- The nature of the Millennial Kingdom is to fulfill the Abrahamic and Davidic Covenants.

- The Central person of this dispensation is Jesus Christ as Lord and King, just as it was prophesied in Luke 1: 30-34:

    And the angel said to her, 'Do not be afraid, Mary; for you have found favor with God. And behold, you will conceive in your womb, and bear a son, and you shall name Him Jesus. He will be great, and will be called the Son of the Most High; and the Lord God will give Him the throne of His

father David; and He will reign over the house of Jacob forever; and His kingdom will have no end.'

- Humanity's responsibility will be to be obedient to the King and his laws for 1,000 years.

- Satan will be bound during this time until the ending of the period.

- This period will end with Satan being loosed and humanity's rebellion against God and Christ as King (Revelation 20:7-10).

- God's Judgement will manifest itself at the Great White Throne Judgment and the final cleansing of the world system by fire, ushering in a New Heaven and New Earth. (Revelation 20:11-15; 21:1)

CHAPTER REVIEW

All seven dispensations represent a stewardship in their own economies.

These periods of time have several characteristics in common, a test, a responsibility, a failure to live up to the responsibility, culminating in a judgment for failure.

Even though there are central characters in each of the dispensations, the responsibility seems to belong to all those who live under the various economies—read Second Corinthians Chapter 5.

Traditional Dispensational View

Dispensations	Scripture	Responsibility	Judgments
Innocence	Gen. 1:28-3:6	Keep Garden, No eating of the Fruit	Cast out of garden. Death-spiritual, physical
Conscience	Gen. 4:1-8:14	Stay obedient to God through conscience.	Flood destroys all living creatures.
Civil Government	Gen 8:15-11:9	Inhabit the Earth, use capital punishment	Scattered worldwide, language changed.
Patriarchal Rule	Gen. 11:10-Ex. 18:27	Stay in the land that was promised.	Bondage in Egypt, wander in wilderness.
Mosaic Law	Ex. 19:1-John 19:30	Stay obedient to the Law.	Captivity in slavery
Grace	Luke 22:20; Acts 2:1	Show Repentance and Faith in Christ.	Spiritual death as the second death.
Millennium	Revelation 20:1-10	Obedience to the King and his ruling authority	Final Judgment and death in the Lake of Fire.

Table 7.1

Progressive dispensationalism came on the scene in November 1986. The following is a breakdown of its theological position on dispensational economies.

Progressive Dispensational View [356]

Patriarchal	Mosaic	Ecclesiastical	Zionic
Adam to Mt. Sinai	Mt. Sinai to Christ's Ascension	Christ's Ascension to Second Coming	Part 1: Millennium Part 2: Eternal State

Table 7.2

[356] Ryrie, *Dispensationalism*, 196. (Reprint by permission.)

CHAPTER EIGHT

Biblical Evidence for Premillennialism

EVIDENCE FROM THE BIBLICAL COVENANTS

SCRIPTURAL USE OF THE WORD COVENANT

Covenants are spoken of throughout the Scriptures; from Genesis 6:18 to Revelation 11:19. The word is referenced 282 times in the Old Testament and 34 times in the New Testament.

Scripturally, covenants are made between two persons but can extend to outside entities. An example of this is found in Genesis 9: 8-12:

> Then God spoke to Noah and to his sons with him, saying, Now behold, I Myself do establish My covenant with you, and with your descendants after you; and with every living creature that is with you, the birds, the cattle, and every beast of the earth with you; of all that comes out of the ark, even every beast of the earth. And I establish My covenant with you; and all flesh shall never again be cut off by the water of the flood, neither shall there again be a flood to destroy the earth.

Covenants were made between God and his creation, and between one human and another. This can be seen in First Samuel 18:3 which states, "Then Jonathan made a covenant with David because he loved him as himself."

Within the discipline of Eschatology, covenants are made between God and individuals and affect those who follow, and are either conditional or unconditional.

THE TYPES OF DIVINE COVENANT

(1) Conditional Covenants—There is only one divine conditional covenant made in all of Scriptures—the Mosaic Covenant.

(2) Unconditional Covenants—There are four prophetic unconditional covenants made in Scripture. The Abrahamic, The Palestinian, The Davidic and The New Covenants.

The terms of these covenants are what makes them unique to themselves.

The covenant made with Moses was considered conditional because of God's wording and stipulations to Moses. Exodus 19:5-6 states: "Now then, if you will indeed obey My voice and keep My covenant, then you shall be My own possession among all the peoples, for all the earth is Mine; and you shall be to Me a kingdom of priests and a holy nation."

God goes on to stipulate a judgment if the terms are not kept. The keywords in this type covenant are *if* and *then*.

The other four covenants were unconditional and also based on the words stipulated. Genesis 12:1-3 is the first mention of the Abrahamic Covenant. This covenant was repeated in Genesis 17:1-8 as it reads,

> Now when Abram was ninety-nine years old, the Lord appeared to Abram and said to him,
> *I am God Almighty; Walk before Me, and be blameless. And I will establish My covenant between Me and you, And I will multiply you exceedingly.*
> And Abram fell on his face, and God talked with him, saying,
> *As for Me, behold, My covenant is with you, And you shall be the father of a multitude of nations. No longer shall your name be called Abram, But your name shall be Abraham; For I will make you the father of a multitude of nations.*
> And I will make you exceedingly fruitful, and I will make nations of you, and kings shall come forth from you. And I will establish My covenant between Me and you and your descendants after you throughout their generations for an everlasting covenant, to be God to you and to your descendants after you. And I will give to you and to your descendants after you, the land of your sojournings, all the land of Canaan, for an everlasting possession; and I will be their God.

The keywords here are *I will* and *everlasting*. Another important aspect to this covenant is there are no stipulations, conditions or demands made by God to Abraham. God simply states, *I will forever.*

The Davidic Covenant is found in Second Samuel 7:12-16 which reads,

> When your days are complete and you lie down with your fathers, I will raise up your descendant after you, who will come forth from you, and I will establish his kingdom. He shall build a house for My name, and I will establish the throne of his kingdom forever. I will be a father to him and he will be a son to Me; when he commits iniquity, I will correct him with the rod of men and the strokes of the sons of men, but My lovingkindness shall not depart from him, as I took it away from Saul, whom I removed from before you. And your house and your kingdom shall endure before Me forever; your throne shall be established forever.

Again, the keywords here are, *I will* and *forever*. There are no stipulations put upon King David toward this covenant. It is God simply saying, I will do this!

The New Covenant found in Jeremiah 31:31-34 reads as follows:

> Behold, days are coming, declares the Lord, when I will make a new covenant with the house of Israel and with the house of Judah, not like the covenant which I made with their fathers in the day I took them by the hand to bring them out of the land of Egypt, My covenant which they broke, although I was a husband to them, declares the Lord. But this is the covenant which I will make with the house of Israel after those days, declares the Lord, I will put My law within them, and on their heart I will write it; and I will be their God, and they shall be My people. And they shall not teach again, each man his neighbor and each man his brother, saying, Know the Lord, for they shall all know Me, from the least of them to the greatest of them, declares the Lord, for I will forgive their iniquity, and their sin I will remember no more.

Keywords spoken here are, *I will, I will, I will* and concludes with, *I will remember no more*—that is an everlasting, forever, phrase.

THE NATURE OF BIBLICAL COVENANTS

Biblical covenants were never spoken allegorically. They were spoken person to person and expected to be taken and understood literally.

This is evident through the response Jesus received, as recorded through the Gospels. The Jewish people of the day were expecting a literal Messiah to free them from the power of Rome and establish a literal kingdom, as promised to Abraham.

This reality is demonstrated through the prophecies about Jesus in Matthew chapter 2 that were all fulfilled literally at the time of Christ's birth and early childhood.

John the Baptist understood the prophecies of the Old Testament as he asks, "Are You the Expected One, or shall we look for someone else?" And Jesus answered and said to them, "Go and report to John what you hear and see: the blind receive sight and the lame walk, the lepers are cleansed and the deaf hear, and the dead are raised up, and the poor have the gospel preached to them. And blessed is he who keeps from stumbling over Me." (Matthew 11:3-6)

Biblical prophetic covenants are all eternal in nature. This is evident in Genesis 17, Second Samuel 23:5, Ezekiel 16:60, Jeremiah 32:40 and 50:5.

Biblical prophetic covenants are all unconditional, as recognized through their wording—*I will*, with no *if* stipulations.

COVENANTS THAT AFFECT END-TIME EVENTS

THE ABRAHAMIC COVENANT

The Abrahamic Covenant is the foundational covenant to God's eschatological and prophetic program. If the Abrahamic Covenant is seen as conditional or interpreted in Scripture as a covenant replaced by something else, then dispensational theology is null and void.

There are five principal areas about the Abrahamic Covenant needing to be discussed.

(1) Genesis Chapter 15 reveals two aspects to this covenant. One, the covenant was made to Abraham and his direct descendants. This covenant was not meant for those outside of Abraham's physical seed line. This is evident in verse 2 through 4 as Eliezer was not to be part of this covenant. Two, verse 18 reflects that the land promised to Abraham was much larger than they ever possessed, including the land currently being possessed today.

(2) The importance of the Abrahamic Covenant is demonstrated through its three-dimensional attributes. This is reflected in the three promises made to Abraham within this single covenant. These three promises are then amplified through their own individual covenants that came later in the historical timeline, as illustrated in the following table.

Promise	Covenant	Scripture
Land: Promised	Palestinian	Deut. 30
Seed: Great Nation	Davidic	II Sam. 7
Blessing: Universal	New Covenant	Jer. 31

Table 8.1

Note: The Abrahamic Covenant requires a distinct people, which translates to Abraham's seed line through Isaac inhabiting the promised land, to whom the promise was made.

(3) As shown from the previous table, the scope of the Abrahamic Covenant is three-fold. (i) A personal promise to Abraham of a physical seed line as expressed in Genesis 15. (ii) A national promise to the seed, in reference to the land as represented in Romans 9:6-8. (Seed defined—A spiritual seed by faith, as expressed in Galatians 3:8-9). It should be noted there is more than one meaning behind the term *seed* in scripture and each use of the word should be interpreted according to its context. (iii) A universal promise or blessing to all the nations of the world.

(4) The Abrahamic Covenant should always be understood as an unconditional covenant for the following reasons: (i) No conditions were ever stipulated. There are no conditional words like *if*, or *you shall*. (ii) This covenant is confirmed repeatedly, even through Israel's repeated disobedience (read Genesis 26:2-5; 1 Chronicles 16:16-18; Psalm 105:8-12; Jeremiah 31:35-37). (iii) Part of this covenant has already been fulfilled through Christ and the New Covenant,

despite Israel's temporary falling away. (iv) The covenant was visually established, based on faith with no human requirements. (v) The covenant was expressly stated to be eternal (Genesis 17:19, 1 Chronicles 16:16-17 and Psalm 105:8-10).

(5) The prophetic implications are six-fold. (i) The term Israel refers to the physical seed line of Abraham, representing the heirs to God's promise of the land. (ii) The nation of Israel must be preserved as an independent entity to receive its promised inheritance. (iii) Promises made to a physical seed line require a physical land to fulfill that promised inheritance. (iv) The covenant contained a universal blessing to the world, and not just to Israel. (v) The universal blessing provided a way for gentiles to be included in this covenant through Christ, the ultimate seed of Abraham. (vi) The physical seed line will inherit its covenant blessing when it receives its eternal King, spoken of in Matthew 23:39 and Romans 11:25-27.

THE PALESTINIAN COVENANT

What is referenced as the Palestinian Covenant is found in Deuteronomy 30:1-10. This covenant emphasizes God's promise to provide land to Israel through Abraham, and a permanent circumcised heart, representing the end result of the New Covenant to come.

There are three points of interest concerning this covenant. (i) This covenant reemphasizes the aspect of God's promise of LAND through the Abrahamic Covenant. (ii) Through the context of this passage, the emphasis of LAND and a circumcised heart speaks to events outside the true purpose of the Mosaic Covenant, as reflected in Galatians 3:17-20, which reads:

> What I am saying is this: the Law, which came four hundred and thirty years later, does not invalidate a covenant previously ratified by God, so as to nullify the promise. For if the inheritance is based on law, it is no longer based on a promise; but God has granted it to Abraham by means of a promise. Why the Law then? It was added because of transgressions, having been ordained through angels by the agency of a mediator, until the seed should come to whom the promise had been made. Now a mediator is not for one party only; whereas God is only one.

The conclusion to Paul's statement is, one covenant does not invalidate another unless it is conditional like the Mosaic Covenant, which the New Covenant replaced, read Jeremiah 31:31-33. (iii) There are six prophetic provisions provided within this covenant.

1) The nation would be driven out of the land due to unfaithfulness. (Duet. 28:63-68; 30:1-3)

2) There will be a future repentance of Israel. (Deuteronomy 28:28; 63-68; 30:1)

3) Israel will be converted as a nation. (Deuteronomy 30:6; Romans 11:26-27)

4) God will restore the nation to the land. (Deuteronomy 30:4-5)

5) Israel's enemies will be judged. (Deuteronomy 30:7)

6) Israel is to receive its full promised blessing. (Deuteronomy 30:9)

All these events have never been truly fulfilled up to the present time, making this covenant still future in nature.

THE DAVIDIC COVENANT

> When your days are complete and you lie down with your fathers, I will raise up your descendant after you, who will come forth from you, and I will establish his kingdom. He shall build a house for My name, and I will establish the throne of his kingdom forever. I will be a father to him and he will be a son to Me; when he commits iniquity, I will correct him with the rod of men and the strokes of the sons of men, but My lovingkindness shall not depart from him, as I took it away from Saul, whom I removed from before you. And your house and your kingdom shall endure before Me forever; your throne shall be established forever.[357]

This covenant made with David will be accomplished through the seed line of Abraham through the lineage of King David and ultimately fulfilled through Jesus Christ the King of Glory, just as the angel Gabriel proclaimed, approximately 900 years after the writing of Second Samuel, as we read,

> Now in the sixth month the angel Gabriel was sent from God to a city in Galilee, called Nazareth, to a virgin engaged to a man whose name

---

[357] 2 Sam. 7:12-16.

was Joseph, of the descendants of David; and the virgin's name was Mary. And coming in, he said to her, 'Hail, favored one! The Lord is with you.' But she was greatly troubled at this statement, and kept pondering what kind of salutation this might be. And the angel said to her, 'Do not be afraid, Mary; for you have found favor with God. And behold, you will conceive in your womb, and bear a son, and you shall name Him Jesus. He will be great, and will be called the Son of the Most High; and the Lord God will give Him the throne of His father David; and He will reign over the house of Jacob forever; and His kingdom will have no end.' [358]

Within the context of this covenant five provisions are established.

1) David's seed line will follow after him to establish his kingdom. (2 Sam. 7:12)

2) David's son would build the temple. (2 Sam. 7:13)

3) This son's kingdom will be established forever. (2 Sam. 7:13)

4) The throne will not be taken away despite the sins of the king. (2 Sam. 7:14)

5) David's house, throne and kingdom will be established forever. (2 Sam. 7:16)

There are four key prophetic features of the Davidic Covenant represented by four keywords.

1) David's House—David's lineage is established, never to be replaced by another family line.

2) David's Throne—The right to rule will always belong to the seed line of David.

3) David's Kingdom—Referring to David's political kingdom having authority over the nation of Israel.

4) Forever—Meaning the right to rule will never transfer to another family line. Its authority will exist for eternity. Despite the temporary gaps of time in God's plan, the covenant stands forever.

Unconditional aspects of the Davidic Covenant are as follows:

1) The reference made to be *eternal*, in Second Samuel 7:13-16, strongly suggests that the covenant is unconditional.

2) The reaffirmation of this covenant after repeated acts of disobedience points to an unconditional understanding (Amos 9:11-15; Luke 1:30-33).

3) The very words of the covenant suggest an unconditional understanding.

> I will be a father to him and he will be a son to Me; when he commits iniquity, I will correct him with the rod of men and the strokes of the sons of men, but My lovingkindness shall not depart from him, as I took it away from Saul, whom I removed from before you. And

---

[358] Luke 1:26-33.

your house and your kingdom shall endure before Me forever; your throne shall be established forever.[359]

4) The Davidic Covenant reemphasizes part of the Abrahamic Covenant, which is an unconditional covenant. By association, this would affirm the same to be true for the Davidic Covenant.

There is a conditional element to this covenant, which left open the question of whether David's offspring would continually occupy the throne until the messiah's appearance. It is only unconditional that David's seed line would always be the rightful offspring to the throne, not that the throne would be continuously occupied through a physical presence up to the coming of the messiah.

Christ as the final successor of the throne of David is not in dispute among Amillennialists and Premillennialists. The issue is how this will be accomplished.

The following are six arguments for a literal interpretation of the Davidic Covenant.

1) Parts of the Davidic Covenant were fulfilled literally.

2) King Solomon, the son of David, understood the covenant literally (2 Chronicles 6:14-16).

3) Old Testament prophets understood the covenant literally (Isaiah 9:6-7).

4) Those in Jesus' day interpreted the covenant literally (Luke 1:31-33; Matthew 20:21; Acts 1:6).

5) David's name and covenant promise is connected to Christ at his first advent, but Christ always inferred its fulfillment as being future to his current ministry. (Luke 1:31-34; Acts 1:6; Mark 15:43; Luke 19:11)

6) If one interprets the *Father's throne* and *David's throne* as synonyms, then the concept of the Davidic throne would be considered eternal with no beginning or ending. This does not fit the language of Second Samuel 7, which specifically states David's throne will have a beginning but will continue forever throughout eternity.

THE NEW COVENANT

Behold, days are coming, declares the Lord, when I will make a new covenant with the house of Israel and with the house of Judah, not like the covenant which I made with their fathers in the day I took them by the hand to bring them out of the land of Egypt, My covenant which they broke, although I was a husband to them, declares the Lord. But this is the covenant which I will make with the house of Israel after those days, declares the Lord, I will put My law within them, and on their heart I will write it; and I will be their God, and they shall be My people. And they shall not teach again, each man his neighbor and each man his brother, saying, 'Know the Lord,' for they shall all know Me, from the least of them to the greatest of them, declares the Lord, for I will forgive their iniquity, and their sin I will remember no more.[360]

---

[359] 2 Sam. 7:14-16.

[360] Jer. 31:31-34.

The New Covenant was made about 600 years before Christ and was the guarantor of a converted heart and the forgiveness of sins forever.

This covenant is the foundational covenant on which the New Testament is based and was reaffirmed by the prophet Ezekiel, most likely after the destruction of Jerusalem in 586 B.C. by King Nebuchadnezzar.[361] Ezekiel writes,

> And say to them, 'Thus says the Lord God, Behold, I will take the sons of Israel from among the nations where they have gone, and I will gather them from every side and bring them into their own land; and I will make them one nation in the land, on the mountains of Israel; and one king will be king for all of them; and they will no longer be two nations, and they will no longer be divided into two kingdoms. And they will no longer defile themselves with their idols, or with their detestable things, or with any of their transgressions; but I will deliver them from all their dwelling places in which they have sinned, and will cleanse them. And they will be My people, and I will be their God.
>
> And My servant David will be king over them, and they will all have one shepherd; and they will walk in My ordinances, and keep My statutes, and observe them. And they shall live on the land that I gave to Jacob My servant, in which your fathers lived; and they will live on it, they, and their sons, and their sons' sons, forever; and David My servant shall be their prince forever. And I will make a covenant of peace with them; it will be an everlasting covenant with them. And I will place them and multiply them, and will set My sanctuary in their midst forever. My dwelling place also will be with them; and I will be their God, and they will be My people. And the nations will know that I am the Lord who sanctifies Israel when My sanctuary is in their midst forever.[362]

It is evident that even in this prophecy of reaffirmation of the New Covenant, the Nation of Israel will physically be in a physical kingdom with a physical king ruling over them forever, as Christ will be the fulfiller of this promise, as their King in their promised LAND.

The New Covenant is seen as unconditional in four ways.

1) The covenant is based on the language of *I will.* There are no stipulations for anyone to do anything except for God himself.

2) The covenant is expressed in terms to be <u>unlike</u> the Mosaic Covenant—a conditional covenant.

3) Jeremiah reaffirms the covenant to be eternal in Chapter 32 verse 40.

4) The covenant amplifies the blessing aspect of the Abrahamic Covenant, tying itself to an everlasting covenant. Consequently, through this association, the New Covenant contains an everlasting attribute within itself.

---

[361] *New American Standard Bible,* The Open Bible Expanded Edition, "The Time of Ezekiel" (Nashville: Thomas Nelson Publishers, 1985), 783.

[362] Ezek. 37:21-28.

There are five provisions spoken of in the New Covenant.

1) Regeneration of the heart. (Jeremiah 31:33; 32:39)

2) The permanent forgiveness of sin. (Jeremiah 31:34)

3) Restoration to the land of Israel. (Jeremiah 32:37-42; Ezekiel 36:25-32.)

4) The result of this covenant will be the permanent indwelling of the Holy Spirit of God. (Jeremiah 31:33; Ezekiel 36:27; Hebrews 10:14-17)

5) A permanent teaching witness will occur inside every believer by faith. (Jeremiah 31:34; John 14:16-18, 26)

The New Covenant was made to Israel and Judah, the physical seed of Abraham (Jeremiah 31:31-ff). This is reaffirmed when it speaks to the issue of the Mosaic Covenant in verse 32. Both covenants were speaking to the same ancestry of people.

This covenant is an amplification of the blessing segment of the Abrahamic Covenant spoken in Genesis 12:3 and reaffirmed in Galatians 3:8.

There are eleven references to the New Covenant in the New Testament: Matthew 26:28, Mark 14:24; Luke 22:20, Romans 11:27; 1 Corinthians 11:25; 2 Corinthians 3:6 and Hebrews 8:8, 13; 9:15; 10:15-17; 12:24.

The fulfillment of this covenant for Israel begins at the start of the millennial kingdom. This is seen in the fact that the restoration of the land to Israel will be part of this covenant, as seen in Jeremiah Chapter 32. This is also reflected in the Apostle Paul's writings, found in Romans 11:25-27, which refers to the time of the Second Advent.

For I do not want you, brethren, to be uninformed of this mystery, lest you be wise in your own estimation, that a partial hardening has happened to Israel until the fulness of the Gentiles has come in; and thus all Israel will be saved; just as it is written,

"The Deliverer will come from Zion,
He will remove ungodliness from Jacob."

"And this is My covenant with them,
When I take away their sins."

This brings us to how the church Christ referenced in Matthew 16:18, fits into the New Covenant.

Romans 11:11-27 speaks to Israel's temporary rejection of Christ, and the allowing of the Gentiles to be part of the promise through a grafting in process.

This fulfills part of the Abrahamic Covenant's blessing aspect, as referenced in Genesis 12:3—that all nations will be blessed. Paul ties all these aspects together in Galatians 3:8-9 as he writes, "And the Scripture, foreseeing that God would justify the Gentiles by faith, preached the gospel beforehand to Abraham, saying, 'All the nations shall be blessed in you.' So then those who are of faith are blessed with Abraham, the believer."

It is evident that the Church is not fulfilling the first two aspects of the Abrahamic Covenant, nor any aspect of the Davidic Covenant. The church is not promised any inheritance of LAND, thereupon making the fulfillment of these covenants still future in nature.

There have been three Premillennial views expressed to explain the relationship of the church to the New Covenant.

1) The View of John Darby—The New Covenant was made to only Israel, and the church is only related to the blood of Christ who makes the covenant possible.

2) The View of Scofield—The New Covenant contains two parts. (i) The covenant is fulfilled in Israel in the future. (ii) The church, not seen in the Old Testament, will be part of the covenant now in this age.

3) The View of Charles Ryrie—There are two distinct covenants, one to the church and the other to Israel.

Within the evaluation of these views, the following seems to explain the church's role with the New Covenant without contradictions.

The Abrahamic Covenant consists of three covenant promises, with the third being a universal blessing which the Apostle Paul ties directly to the gospel of Christ.

The New Covenant speaks to and amplifies the three aspects of the Abrahamic Covenant to include the path forward in fulfilling all three promises within a single covenant. Hence, the New Covenant is partially fulfilled by the universal blessing providing the New Testament Church a place in God's fold as a branch grafted into the true vine, and the remaining promises of the Abrahamic Covenant will be fulfilled in the future with Israel through the New Covenant at the start of the millennial kingdom.

This explanation fits more with Scofield's perspective and within the context of the Scripture as a whole, while making the most sense with relationship to the grafting in processes expressed in Romans 11:17-21.

In the end, it is most evident that the Church or body of Christ is a separate entity from the Nation of Israel and this can be demonstrated through the proper understanding of the four prophetic covenants made between God and Abraham and his seed line.

f

Evidence for Premillennialism in the New Testament Gospels

SOME BACKGROUND

The gospel of Matthew was written by Jesus' chosen disciple Matthew—a tax collector. It is believed the final version of Matthew was completed between 58 and 68 A.D. and was widely accepted as authentic by those living at the time of its writing.[363]

The target audience were Matthew's Jewish countrymen, in hopes of convincing them that Jesus was the Christ, the long sought-after Messiah, as he presents Jesus as Israel's promised messiah King throughout his writings.

Matthew uses the phrase, *the kingdom of heaven* twenty-eight times in his book. This phrase appears nowhere else in the New Testament. Matthew demonstrates Jesus' qualifications to be the fulfilling Messiah by using almost 130 inferences through Old Testament quotes and allusions to the fact. Matthew demonstrates that Jesus was the climax to the prophets and ties Christ to the Davidic Covenant nine times.[364]

It should be noted that the Jewish people of the day believed in a literal view of Old Testament prophecies concerning the coming Messiah and the promised Kingdom to come.

The following outline is a synopsis of an eschatological viewpoint of premillennialism as demonstrated through the Gospel of Matthew.

I. Chapter 1—Christ's Legal Right to the Throne.

   Key Verse: 1:1

   Note: Jesus was born the <u>legal</u> heir to the Throne of David, through the kingly seed line from Abraham to David to Solomon to his earthly father Joseph.

II. Chapter 2—Christ's Royal Right to the Throne.

   Key Verses: 2 and 5

---

[363] *New American Standard Bible*, The Open Bible Expanded Edition, "The Author and Time of Matthew" (Nashville: Thomas Nelson Publishers, 1985), 959.

[364] *New American Standard Bible*, The Open Bible Expanded Edition, "The Christ of Matthew," 959.

Note: Jesus was born in the City of Bethlehem as prophesied in Micah 5:2.

III. Chapter 3—Christ's Divine Right to the Throne

    Key Verses: 1-2, 17

- Vs. 1 — From the beginning Jesus' ministry is directly associated with John the Baptist.

- Vs. 2 — John announces the nearness of the Kingdom.

- Vs. 16-17 — The doctrine of the trinity is seen for the first time as Jesus is given the Father's approval as his divine Son—the Messiah that came.

IV. Chapter 4—Christ's Moral Right to the Throne.

    Key Verses: 1 and 17

- Vs. 1-11 — The purpose of the temptation of Christ was to prove he was sinless. Secondly, to provide an example to others in the arena of temptation.

- Vs. 17 — The message of Christ and John the Baptist was the same, repent and make moral preparation for the kingdom of heaven.

V. Chapter 5-7—Christ's Judicial Right to the Throne.

    Key Verses: 7:28-29

Note: Within these chapters, Jesus is demonstrating his ability to interpret the Scripture correctly, as he speaks as one with authority in his interpretations.

A. Chapter 5—Christ Rejects the Pharisees' Interpretation of the Law, not the law itself. This is evident in 5:17 where he states, "Do not think that I came to abolish the Law or the Prophets; I did not come to abolish, but to fulfill."

B. Chapter 6:1-18—Christ Rejects the Pharisees' Practice.

- Ver. 1-4—Their alms.
- Ver. 5-15—Their prayers.
- Ver. 16-18—Their fasting.

C. Chapter 6:19 - Ch. 7—Christ Instructs those Who would be his Disciples.

Note: Verses 28-29 — Jesus spoke with authority as he taught and interpreted the Scriptures, interacting with the Scriptures through His divine authority as the living Word as he makes the statement, *but I say.*

VI. Chapter 8-10—Christ's Prophetic Right to the Throne.

Note: From this point on, Jesus proves his divine authority within his interpretations of the Scriptures by performing miracles that fulfill Old Testament prophecies.

A.   Chapter 8:1-22—The Miracles of Healing

- Leper—Jewish person—Illustrates sin. Ver. 1-4
- Palsy—Centurion's servant—Illustrates helplessness. Vs. 5-13
- Fever—Peter's mother-in-law—Illustrates restlessness. Vs. 14-18 (Testing of Discipleship in Vs. 19-22)

B.   Chapter 8:23-Ch. 9:8—The Miracles of Power

- The storm on the Sea calmed—Power over nature.
- The demon-possessed man delivered—Power over Satan's kingdom.
- The palsied man healed and forgiven—Power over sickness and sin.

Note: (Matthew called, disciples eat with sinners—9:9-17)

C.   Chapter 9:18-38—The Miracles of Compassion

- The woman with issues of blood—Health (9:18-26).
- The Raising of Jairus' daughter—Life (9:18-26; Luke 5:22-43).
- The blind man healed—Sight (9:27-38).

D. Chapter 10—The Miracles of the Disciples

- This demonstrates that not only did Jesus have power, He also had the authority to give that power to others.

- This chapter is not the commissioning of the Church, but the commissioning of Christ's disciples to perform a specific ministry toward the Jews at the time of their discipleship (See Luke 2:35-39).

- Verses 17-42—Jesus as a prophet speaks to a future time beyond the church age, to the time of the tribulation period before the second advent.

VII. Chapter 11—Christ Anticipates His Rejection as King

Key Verse: 2

- As John the Baptist was rejected, so Jesus would be as well—just as he anticipated.

- Verse 5—Jesus fulfills what was prophesied in Isaiah 29:17-19; 35:5-6; and 61:1-3.

- Verse 10—John is declared to be the forerunner of the messiah. (Malachi 3:1; Isaiah 40:3)

- Verse 14—John the Baptist is seen as the person fulfilling this prophecy through the words of Christ himself.

- Verse 20— "Then began" is a time indicator that Christ began to change his approach to the Nation of Israel because they refused to repent.

VIII. Chapter 12—Christ Pronounces the Unpardonable Sin

Key Verses: 23-24

Note: Jesus' response to the sin of the Pharisees was a climatic event, building up to this point throughout his ministry. It was an attitude of total rebellion against God and his program. The accusation that the Holy Spirit's powers were the result of Satan's controlling influence was the final act of arrogance toward God and Jesus. This act cut them off from the true vine, as spoken of in John 15. This was the turning point. Jesus now began moving toward offering the kingdom to outsiders, as reflected in His pronouncement of the coming Church to Peter in Chapter 16. Jesus then tells two parables in chapter 21 about the Landowners, and in chapter 22 about the Marriage Feast, providing an understanding that the Kingdom of God was now being offered to others, just as Paul spoke of in Romans Chapter 11.

- Vs. 22—Jesus performs a triple miracle.

- Vs. 23—The question expected a negative answer. Possibly because of their own unbelief or because of the hostility of the Pharisees.

- Vs. 31—Jesus pronounces the unpardonable sin.

- Vs. 38—After all the miracles, Jewish leadership still required a sign to prove his authority.

- Vs. 39—Jesus states there will be no more signs but that of Jonah.

IX. Chapter 13—Christ Depicts the Postponement of the Kingdom in Seven Parables.

Key Verse: 1

Note 1: With the Kingdom now rejected by Israel, Jesus reveals an intercalation of time between his rejection as the messiah—the son of David—and the establishment of his Kingdom. Through study of the Scriptures, this time gap is represented by more than just the *Church Age*.

Question: Now that the Kingdom has been rejected, the question arises, was the offer of the Kingdom legitimate, was it real?

Answer: The fact that God has foreknowledge of future events and acts upon that knowledge in advance does not negate the sincerity of the offer. An example of this can be seen in God dealing with the Pharaoh of Egypt as God offered ten chances for him to comply with Moses' demands. In the end, the Scriptures tell us that God only hardened Pharaoh's heart five times out of the ten. Meaning there were opportunities for Pharaoh to comply on his own, but he refused (Exodus 9:12; 10:20, 27; 11:10; 14:8). This is a true representation of the sovereignty of God and the responsibility of man. This question ultimately falls to the debate between the Calvinist and Armenian perspectives.

Note 2: The meaning of "Mystery" found in verse 11 should be compared to Colossians 1:26 and Ephesians 3:3-7 to help understand this concept. A revealed mystery in the New Testament is a hidden truth existing in the Old Testament that is now being revealed in the present.

Note 3: Matthew 13:34-35 speaks to the question of why Jesus spoke in parables after Israel's rejection of Christ.

Question: Why did Jesus speak in parables?

Answer: There are three reasons that can be found in verses 10-13 and verse 35. (i) To reveal the mystery of the kingdom to his disciples. (ii) To hide the mystery of the kingdom from non-disciples. (iii) To fulfill the Old Testament prophecy found in Psalm 78:2.

The Emphasis in the Parables

- Verses 1-23—The Sower—The spread of the gospel and opposition to the Word.

- Verses 24-30—The Wheat and the Tares—There are false professors among the elect of God (See verses 36-43).

  Note: Vs. 24—The phrase "is likened unto" (KJV), when speaking of the Kingdom, reflects a change in Jesus' past presentation of the Kingdom when he used to say the Kingdom "is at hand" (Matthew 3:2; 4:17 and 10:7).

- Verses 31-32—The Grain of Mustard Seed—Showing that the coming Kingdom is progressive in nature. The Kingdom starts with Christ in the hearts of believers that grow into his universal church as the body or bride of Christ, then in time the Kingdom will finally appear.

- Verses 33-35—The Leaven—False doctrine influences the whole.

  Note: Leaven usually represents evil. Examples: Matthew 16:6, 12—evil doctrine; First Corinthians 5:6-8—evil actions; Luke 12:1—evil attitude.

- Verse 43—The first word, "Then," reflects a time element in reference to the subject of the "mystery" spoken of in verse 11. The mystery timeframe runs from the time of the rejection of the messiah to the time of the Second Advent.

- Verse 44—The Hidden Treasure—The remnant represents Christ's purchase and preservation of Israel (See Exodus 19:5). The fact that Israel failed to keep the Mosaic Covenant does not negate the concept that God will preserve himself a remnant, just as he has always done with Israel throughout history. (Read Romans 11:1-5)

- Verse 45-46—The Pearl of Great Price—This pearl represents the church, the body of Christ.

- Verse 47-52—The Dragnet—The good will be separated from the bad. Warren W. Wiersbe makes the following observations:

  The preaching of the Gospel in the world does not convert the world. It is like a huge dragnet that gathers all kinds of fish, some good and some bad. The professing church today has in it both true and false believers (the Parable of the Tares) and good and bad. At the end of the age, God will separate the true believers from the false and the good from the bad. When Jesus Christ returns to earth, to fight the battle of Armageddon (Rev 19:11-ff), He will separate believers and unbelievers already on the earth.[365]

X. Chapter 14-15—Christ provides more miracles to the common people.

- Verses 14:15-21—The five thousand fed.
- Verses 14:22-23—Jesus walks on the water.

    Note: Vs. 15:21—What Israel would not have or recognize the Canaanite or Syrophoenician woman wanted, as she recognizes Jesus as "the son of David."

- Verses 15:32-39—The four thousand fed.

XI. Chapter 16—Christ predicts his church and his death on the Cross.

Key Verses: 18 and 21

- Verse 13—This takes place in Caesarea Philippi, a Gentile area.

- Verse 18—Jesus pronounces a New Testament concept for the first time, called the church, just six months before his crucifixion. We learn later that this church is synonymous with the term the "body of Christ." Colossians 1:24 reads, "Now I rejoice in my sufferings for your sake, and in my flesh I do my share on behalf of His body (which is the church) in filling up that which is lacking in Christ's afflictions."

- Verse 21—This is the first time Christ made mention of his coming death in the book of Matthew.

- Verse 22—Peter is thinking about the Kingdom, not the need for the cross.

- Verse 24—The ground rules for true discipleship are explained.

- Verse 27—Jesus announces his return as something new. Then in verse 28 He prophesied an event in the future that was fulfilled in Chapter 17.

---

[365] Warren W. Wiersbe, "Matthew 13:47-50," in *The Bible Exposition Commentary* (Colorado Springs, Colorado: Chariot Victor Publishing, an imprint of Cook Communication Ministries, 1989); available from PC Study Bible V5.0E for Windows; Biblesoft Inc.; 1988-2007. (www.biblesoft.com)

XII. Chapter 17—Christ gives a miniature picture of the Kingdom through his transfiguration.

> **Note:** "Matthew and Mark state that the Transfiguration took place "six days later," while Luke says, "some eight days after" (Luke 9:28). There is no contradiction; Luke's statement is the Jewish equivalent of "about a week later." During that week, the disciples must have pondered and discussed what Jesus meant by His death and resurrection. No doubt they were also wondering what would happen to the Old Testament promises about the kingdom. If Jesus were going to build a church, what would happen to the promised kingdom?" [366]

- Verse 9—Christ mentions his death for the second time.

XIII. Chapter 18-20—Christ provides the disciples additional teaching.

XIV. Chapter 21—Christ's official and formal presentation of himself as King to the Nation of Israel.

> **Note:** Zechariah 9:9

> "Rejoice greatly, O daughter of Zion!
> Shout in triumph, O daughter of Jerusalem!
> Behold, your king is coming to you;
> He is just and endowed with salvation,
> Humble, and mounted on a donkey,
> Even on a colt, the foal of a donkey."

> Key Verses: 5 and 23

- Verse 13— "My house" The Temple is to be the headquarters of the Kingdom. (Read Ezekiel Ch. 40-48)

- Verse 23—This question provides the background for all that follows through Chapter 23.

- Verse 25—Jesus once again associates himself with John the Baptist. They know John's testimony about who Jesus was. If they had answered Jesus' question truthfully, they would have answered their own question about Jesus' authority.

---

[366] Warren W. Wiersbe, "Matthew 17:1-13," in *The Bible Exposition Commentary*.

- Verse 28-32—These verses indirectly answer the Pharisee's question to the origin of Jesus authority. The Pharisee's issue was not Jesus' authority, but their own lack of repentance.

- Verse 37-44—The point is that the Pharisees have rejected God's Son; they will kill him and thus experience God's judgment.

- Verse 45—In verse 31 and 41 the Pharisees admitted their guilt without realizing what they have done. Now they realize what they have done.

XV. Chapter 22—Christ is officially and formally rejected as King by the Nation.

Key Verse: 15

Note: Jesus' accusers cannot find anything in his descent or his character that can be used to deny his messiahship. They must resort to trying to find some fault in his speech.

- Verses 16-22—The Herodians with a political question.
- Verses 23-33—The Sadducees with a rationalistic question.
- Verses 34-40—The Pharisees with a religious question.
- Verses 45-46—Jesus now asks them a question. If the Messiah is only David's son, then why did the Spirit move David to worship him, calling him Lord. The Messiah must be a deity. Thus, Jesus answers the question of his authority.

XVI. Chapter 23—Christ's official and formal rejection from the Nation for his Kingdom.

Key Verses: 37-39

- Verse 1— "Then" is a word used in reference to after their refusal to repent.

- Verse 37—The issue was not with Jesus' offer, but that they "would not."

- Verse 38— "House" = reference to the Nation of Israel.
        "Desolate" = meaning forsaken, barren (Read Isaiah 62:4).

- Verse 39— "not see me until or henceforth"—This is a phrase representing Christ's temporary stay or pause on the coming promised kingdom.

"Till"—There will come a time when being bypassed will end (Read Romans 11:25-27).

"Blessed is he that comes in the name of the Lord."—This is in reference to the Nation of Israel's repentance, not the church.

XVII. Chapter 24—Christ gives signs of the end of the Age of postponement.

Key Verse: 3

- Verse 1—The Temple was to be the center of the future kingdom. (Read Ezekiel Ch. 38-40)

- Verse 2— "see ye not" in the KJV means, don't you understand.

    "These things"—The Greek word is ταῦτα, a gender neutral term, accordingly the antecedent cannot be the building because the Greek word for building is feminine.

    Christ's reference to "these things" seem to go back to his statements in Chapter 23:37-39 where Jesus is pronouncing a stay on the coming kingdom and his presence before Israel as King until they repent with an attitude which says, "Blessed is He who comes in the name of the Lord!" (Matthew 23:39b)

- Verse 3—The answers to the following questions are the subject of this discourse. When shall these things be? What shall be the sign of thy coming and of the end of the Age?

    Keywords in verse 3 are:

    "These things"—Same explanation as for verse 2. Referencing an event tied to Israel's repentance.

    "world"—This word has the meaning of Age.

    "end of the age" (συντέλεια τοῦ αι.τοὐτ.)—Within this phrase, the Age is referring to "the end, or rather consummation of the age preceding Christ's return, which connects the resurrection of the dead, the last judgment, the demolition of this world and its restoration to a more excellent condition (cf. 4 Esd 7:43), Mt. 13:39,49; 24:3; 28:20."[367]

---

[367] Grimm S. and Wilke S., "συντέλεια τοῦ αι.τοὐτ," in *Clovis Novi Testamenti, A New Testament Lexicon*, revised and enlarged, trans. by Joseph Henry Thayer, D.D. (New York: Harper & Brothers, 1889), 19.

"sign"—Something that would let them know his coming was near.

"coming"—They are not asking about the rapture. They are asking about the coming which is connected with Israel's change of heart by saying, "blessed is He that cometh in the name of the Lord."

Note: Within this prophecy Christ does not mention anything that does not take place in the 70th week of Daniel.

- Verses 4-8—These verses picture conditions in the first half of Daniel's 70th week.

- Verses 9-14—The last half of Daniel's 70th week is described.

  Verse 9— "Then"—representing a sequence of time.

  Verse 14— "this gospel of the Kingdom…" is not representing the identical gospel message of today but is proclaiming the nearness of the kingdom.

  Verse 14— "Then shall the end come," referencing the end of the age postponed that they asked about in verse 3, which is connected with Christ's Second Advent.

- Verses 15-31—The last half of Daniel's 70th week is retraced in greater detail.

  Verse 15—See Daniel 9:27.

  Verse 21—The last half of Daniel's 70th week is known as the "Great Tribulation."

- Verses 32-25:30—This section is parenthetical. That is, it does not advance the narrative. It characterizes people and attitudes as the time of the second coming.

  Verse 32—"fig tree"—Compare this term with Luke 21:29, showing that this fig tree has no significant symbolism to Israel.

  Verse 33— "all these things." This refers to the events spoken of in the first 31 verses of the chapter. "These things" refers to the sign of the second coming given by Jesus, not the founding of Israel as a nation in 1948.

Verses 37-41—This passage is often misunderstood as a reference to the rapture. This passage is not making reference to the rapture.

*Three reasons why this is not referencing the rapture.

(i) The context.

(ii) The comparison with people in Noah's day. The ones taken in Noah's day were the last taken in judgment, the saved were left. By comparison, it is the saved who are left to enter the Kingdom.

(iii) There is no specific mention of the rapture. It does not say they will be caught up with Christ. There is no reference of any one going to heaven nor is there any reference to a resurrection or glorification.

Note: The point of the passage is that life will be going on with no real thought of judgment by God until it is too late.

XVIII. Chapter 25—The time of the realization of the Kingdom.

Key Verse: 34

- Verse 1— "then." Compare with verses 24:37 and 40. The time period is the same, taking place after the tribulation period.

- Verses 1-13—The lost in Israel will be excluded from the Kingdom. Only those who are ready at Christ's coming will enter with Christ and His bride.

- Verse 31—Notice the time indicator.

- Verses 31-46—The judgment of the Nations (Gentiles) = éthnee or ethnos, this word "nation (NT: 1484)" is found about 28 times in the New Testament.

"This section explains to us how Jesus Christ will judge the Gentile nation.... This means that the nations will be gathered before Jesus Christ, but He will judge them as individuals. This will not be a judgment of groups (Germany, Italy, Japan, etc.), but of individuals within these nations.... The judgment here in Matthew 25 takes place before the kingdom is established on earth, for the saved are told to 'inherit the kingdom' (Matthew 25:34). The White Throne Judgment will take place after the 1,000 - year reign of Christ (Rev. 20:7 ff)."[368]

---

[368] Warren W. Wiersbe, "Matthew 25:31-46," in *The Bible Exposition Commentary*.

There are three groups of people seen in this judgment.

"Sheep" Representing saved gentiles.
"Goat" Representing the lost.
"My brethren" Represents Jewish brethren or Israel.

The following commentary provides some context as to who the brethren are that Jesus is speaking about.

"And the King shall answer and say unto them, Verily I say unto you, Inasmuch as ye have done it unto one of the least of these my brethren, ye have done it unto me. Astonishing dialogue this between the King, from the Throne of His glory, and His wondering people! 'I was an hungered, and ye gave Me meat,' etc.—'Not we,' they reply, 'We never did that, Lord: We were born out of due time, and enjoyed not the privilege of ministering unto Thee.'"[369]

XIX. Chapter 26—The King betrayed and arrested.

XX. Chapter 27—The King tried and crucified.

XXI. Chapter 28—The King resurrected and ascended.

---

[369] *Jamieson, Fausset and Brown Commentary*, vol. 2 "Matthew 25:40," 60.

SECTION II

CHAPTER TEN

The Distinction Between Israel and the Church

THE IMPORTANCE OF A DISTINCTION BETWEEN ISRAEL AND THE CHURCH

THE IMPORTANCE OF THIS DISTINCTION TO THE PREMILLENNIAL SYSTEM OF INTERPRETATION

The premillennial system of interpretation relies heavily on the understanding that the nation or people identified with Israel of the Old Testament are a separate entity or group from the New Testament Church established by Christ.

This is a critical point within dispensational theology for two reasons. First, it is the only conclusion one can come to when interpreting the Scriptures from a literal Grammatico-historical method. Paul Lee Tan (Th.D.) expresses it this way,

> The Scriptures, when normally read, describe Israel and the church as two distinct entities. This is so apparent that even covenant theologians admit that only by spiritualizing may the fusion between Israel and the church be upheld.
>
> When the apostle Paul introduces the church in the New

Testament as a mystery "kept secret since the world began" (Rom. 16:25), "hidden from ages and from generations" (Col. 1:26), and revealed only in New Testament times, he is distinguishing it as an entity apart from the nation Israel.[370]

The second reason for the importance of this position is the foundation it lays for the doctrine of a pre-tribulation rapture. Tan writes,

> Dispensational theologians are pretribulational on the distinction between Israel and the church. Covenant premillennialists must necessarily be posttribulational because they see the New Testament church as part of the one-people of God and yet somewhat distinct. Covenant amillennialists are always posttribulational.[371]

THE IMPORTANCE OF THE TERM "CHURCH" TO THIS DISTINCTION

The question of a pre-tribulation versus post-tribulation rapture is more a matter of ecclesiology than eschatology.

Milton S. Terry (S.T.D.) provides this explanation based on the primary meaning of words within the Greek text.

---

[370] Tan, *The Interpretation of Prophecy*, 251-252.

[371] Ibid., 246-247.

Take, for example, that commonly occurring New Testament word ἐκκλησία, commonly rendered church. Compounded of ἐκ, *out of,* and καλεῖν, to *call,* or summon, it was first used of an assembly of the citizens of a Greek community, summoned together by a crier, for the transaction of business pertaining to the public welfare. ...The verb καλεῖν denotes that the assembly was legally called..., summoned for the purpose of deliberating in lawful conclave. ...the Septuagint translators generally render קָהָל by ἐκκλησία, and thus by an obvious process, ἐκκλησία came to represent among the Hellenists the Old Testament concept of "the congregation of the people of Israel," as usually denoted by the Hebrew word קָהָל. Hence it was natural for Steven to speak of the congregation of Israel, which Moses led out of Egypt, as "the ἐκκλησία in the wilderness" (Acts vii, 38), and equally natural for the word to become the common designation of the Christian community of converts from Judaism and the world. Into this New Testament sense of the world, it was also important that the full force of ἐκ and καλεῖν (κλῆσις, κλητός) should continue. As the old Greek assembly was called by a public herald (κῆρυξ), so "the Church of God (or of the Lord), which he purchased with his own blood" (Acts xx, 28), is the congregation of those who are "called to be saints" (κλητοὶ αγίοι,

Rom. i, 7), "called out of darkness into the marvelous light" (1 Pet. ii, 9), called "unto his kingdom and glory" (1 Thess. ii, 12), and called by the voice of an authorized herald or preacher (Rom. x, 14, 15: 1 Tim. ii, 7).[372]

It is evident that the history of the original language behind the word used for *church* has transitioned to represent the body of Christ of the New Testament. A group hidden in God and revealed by Christ in Matthew 16:18.

This church is identified by the Apostle Paul as he writes,

> Now I rejoice in my sufferings for your sake, and in my flesh I do my share on behalf of His body (which is the church) in filling up that which is lacking in Christ's afflictions. Of this church I was made a minister according to the stewardship from God bestowed on me for your benefit, that I might fully carry out the preaching of the word of God, that is, the mystery which has been hidden from the past ages and generations; but has now been manifested to His saints, to whom God willed to make known what is the riches of the glory of this mystery among the Gentiles, which is Christ in you, the hope of glory.[373]

As the Apostle Paul proclaims that the church (the body of Christ) is represented by the mystery of "Christ in you, the hope of glory," it should be understood that this statement is not associated with the Jewish population but with the Gentiles the Apostle is ministering to.

The only way to conclude anything different is to allegorize this concept,

[372] Terry, *Biblical Hermeneutics*, 74-75.

[373] Col. 1:24-27.

thereupon moving into a world of speculation regarding the true meaning of this body, as intended by Christ himself.

If this term represented all saints of all ages, allegorizing would be necessary to obtain this interpretation and the rapture would be a moot doctrine. At the same time, if this term represents, as the Apostle suggests, there are two separate groups, whom Christ identified this way: "And I have other sheep, which are not of this fold; I must bring them also, and they shall hear My voice; and they shall become one flock with one shepherd." (John 10:16)

The end result of this teaching is reflected in a pre-tribulational position.

THE USAGE OF THE WORD FOR "CHURCH," EKKLEESÍA SUPPORTS THIS DISTINCTION

The term ἐκκλησία (ekkleesía) as found in Acts 19:39 references an assembly of people with no spiritual connotation. In Acts 7:38 we find the same word used in connection to an Old Testament Jewish assembly out in the wilderness, also with no spiritual connotation.

This word is also used in Acts 11:26 and Galatians 1:2, translated as *church*, referring to a location Christians were meeting at, and in Ephesians 1:22, reflecting a concept of interest.

This form of the word carries the *dative case*, telling us that it is speaking more to time, location or making reference to some interest.

Jesus pronounces, for the first time, the concept of a church that will be directly associated with himself, as found in Matthew 16:18. The word he used was ἐκκλησίαν (ekkleesían). This term seems to be used in reference to physical churches made up of a local assembly of <u>believers</u> as found in Acts 8:1, 11:22, 1 Corinthians 15:9 and Galatians 1:13.

This form of the word carries the *accusative case*, telling us that it is directed toward someone(s), and adds or limits some form of direction with respect to time, place, things, and manner of behavior.

This brings us to a third term ἐκκλησίας (ekkleesías), which specifically makes reference to the body of Christ (universal) or a spiritual unified connection with God. We see this in Acts 12:1 and Hebrews 2:12, which is found in an Old Testament quote from Psalm 22:22; "I will tell of Thy name to my brethren; In the midst of the assembly I will praise Thee." This verse represents a worship time within a spiritual body, and carries with it a prophetic connotation referring to the body of Christ, as a result of Christ's suffering that purchased the body, as referenced in Psalm 22. Jamieson, Fausset, and Brown Commentary expresses it this way:

> The language of complaint is turned to that of rejoicing in the assured prospect from relief of suffering and triumph over his enemies. The use of the words in the first clause of v. 1 by our saviour on the cross, and the quotation of v. 18 by John (19:24), and of v. 22 by Paul (Hebrews 2:12), as fulfilled in His history, clearly intimate the prophetical and Messianic purport of the Psalm.[374]

---

[374] *A commentary, critical and explanatory, on the Old and New Testaments*, vol. 1, "Psalm 22:22," by Rev. Robert Jamieson, Rev. A. R. Fausset, and Rev. David Brown (New York: S.S. Scranton and company, 1873), 353; available from http://hdl.handle.net/2027/miun.ajg3934.0002.001; Internet; accessed 29 January 2019.

This form of the word carries the *genitive case*, which describes relationships between substantives.

The fourth term used within its own context is similar to the first, ἐκκλησία (ekkleesía), as found in Colossians 1:24. This makes sense since it is referencing Christ as the Head of this group he started.

This form of the word carries a *nominative case*, reflecting the relationship between subjects.

In summary, the term for the church must be taken in the context of its usage, and when read in an English translation, requires the review of the Greek text to see the parsing attributes (Genitive, Accusative, Nominative, Dative), which helps us understand better how the word relates in context to the overall discussion. When understood in this light, the understanding that there is no connection between Israel and the New Testament church that Christ established becomes much clearer.

There does seem to be a spiritual connection between the Old and New Testament in reference to these two groups, but there is no literal historic connection to reflect that the Nation of Israel and the current New Testament church are the same continuous group in history, or that one has replaced the other. Paul refutes that concept in Romans Chapter 11, along with Jesus' comment that he has two separate folds of sheep that will be united one future day through himself (John 10:16).

ARGUMENTS IN SUPPORT OF THE DISTINCTION BETWEEN ISRAEL AND THE CHURCH

THE FUTURE REFERENCE OF THE CHURCH

Matthew 16:18 speaks about the church as future, meaning not yet established. "I also say to you that you are Peter, and upon this rock I will build My church; and the gates of Hades will not overpower it."

As Jesus states here, he will begin to build his church, starting with his disciples. This statement supports the concept that the church is a New Testament entity not associated with Old Testament saints or Israel as a Nation.

THE CHURCH IS DISTINGUISHED FROM OTHER ENTITIES

First Corinthians 10:32-33 states: "Give no offense either to Jews or to Greeks or to the church of God; just as I also please all men in all things, not seeking my own profit but the profit of the many, so that they may be saved." Through this passage the Apostle Paul infers there is a difference between Jews, Greeks (Gentiles) and the Church.

Hebrews 12:18-24 contrasts the Mosaic temple system with the concept of the Church and the New Covenant. This contrast reflects a distinction between Israel and the church of God of the New Testament.

Ephesians 2:11-22 reflects that the covenant of promise belongs to the Jews (Israel), and that the Gentiles will be grafted in and offered a place in God's Kingdom. This concept supports the teaching that Israel was not replaced by the church in terms of salvation or the beneficiaries of that promise or the New Covenant. Both entities will become one, as the beneficiaries in the Kingdom of God.

EVIDENCE OF A PARENTHESIS OF TIME BETWEEN THE FIRST AND SECOND ADVENT

Psalm 61:1-11 speaks about the Advents of Christ, with Christ proclaiming the partial fulfillment of Psalm 61:1-2 in Luke 4:18-21, leaving a gap in the remaining portion of the prophecy. This is also reflected in Malachi 3:1-2.

The evidence for this gap or parenthesis of time is reflected in:

a.) Daniel's seventy-week prophecy—Daniel 9:24-27.

   1) This prophecy speaks to the destiny of the Nation of Israel.

   2) The Messiah is cut off after the 69th week, and the prince of the world (Satan) has free rule during the 70th week.

   3) The 69 weeks were fulfilled literally, with an expectation that the 70th week would be as well. To hold any other view would be inconsistent with scriptural interpretation.

b.) The fact that the prophets were aware of their lack of understanding of this gap—First Peter 1:10-12 shows that they understood that the messiah would suffer before the Kingdom would come.

c.) Additional illustrations of this parenthesis.

   1) Compare Hosea 3:4-5 with Malachi 3:1-2.

   2) Compare Hosea 5:15 with 6:1.

   3) Psalm 22:1-21—The suffering of Christ at the First Advent.

   4) Psalm 22:22 is fulfilled in Matthew 4:23.

   5) Psalm 22:23-ff reflects millennial conditions.

With the lack of mention or understanding of a church age in the Old Testament prophecies, it would be reasonable to conclude that the Church and Israel are two separate entities, and that the prophecies of old were speaking to Israel and not the New Testament church.

THE MYSTERY OF THE NEW TESTAMENT CHURCH SUPPORTS ITS DISTINCTION

Jesus first mention these mysteries in Matthew 13:11. "Jesus answered them, 'To you it has been granted to know the mysteries of the kingdom of heaven, but to them it has not been granted.'" The Apostle Paul picks up on this theme by saying, "This mystery is great; but I am speaking with reference to Christ and the church" (Ephesians 5:32). Paul writes,

> By referring to this, when you read you can understand my insight into the mystery of Christ, which in other generations was not made known to the sons of men, as it has now been revealed to His holy apostles and prophets in the Spirit; to be specific, that the Gentiles are fellow heirs and fellow members of the body, and fellow partakers of the promise in Christ Jesus through the gospel, of which I was made a minister, according to the gift of

God's grace which was given to me according to the working of His power. To me, the very least of all saints, this grace was given, to preach to the Gentiles the unfathomable riches of Christ, and to bring to light what is the administration of the mystery which for ages has been hidden in God who created all things; so that the manifold wisdom of God might now be made known through the church to the rulers and the authorities in the heavenly places.[375]

The Apostle Paul reflects here that the mystery of Christ and the Church have been hidden from those living in past ages, but a new administration or dispensation is being revealed.

The concept of New Testament mysteries is best explained by Paul in his letter to the church at Colossae when he wrote,

Now I rejoice in my sufferings for your sake, and in my flesh I do my share on behalf of His body, which is the church, in filling up what is lacking in Christ's afflictions. Of this church I was made a minister according to the stewardship from God bestowed on me for your benefit, so that I might fully carry out the preaching of the word of God, that is, the mystery which has been hidden from the past ages and generations, but has now been manifested to His saints, to whom God willed to make known what is the riches of the glory of this mystery among the Gentiles, which is Christ in you, the hope of glory.[376]

A short synopsis of this concept are the mysteries revealed in the New Testament, where truths hidden from times past are now revealed in the New Testament. The subject matter of these mysteries were Christ, the Church and the Holy Spirit, who was introduced to the world by Christ in John 14:16-17, where Jesus states:

I will ask the Father, and He will give you another Helper, that He may be with you forever; that is the Spirit of truth, whom the world cannot receive, because it does not see Him or know Him, but you know Him because He abides with you and will be in you.

Jesus goes on to explain that this Helper is the Holy Spirit in John 14:25-26.

The concept of revealed mysteries carries with it two elements of theological fact. The first is the fact that both Jew and Gentile will be one in Christ as a single body. As Christ put it, he must combine his two folds of sheep into one group. The second fact is, this body will be united through *Christ in you, the hope of glory.*

To conclude this section, it should be noted that Israel and its destiny is clearly outlined in the Old Testament prophecies. While the destiny of the Church, as revealed through the New Testament, has emerged on a separate track, both to be united in the millennial Kingdom.

THE TRANSLATION OR RAPTURE OF THE SAINTS IS NOT CONNECTED TO ISRAEL

The content of the mystery of the *translation* can be found in First Corinthians 15:51-53 which reads,

Behold, I tell you a mystery; we will not all sleep, but we will all be

---

[375] Eph. 3: 4-10.

[376] Col. 1: 24-27.

changed, in a moment, in the twinkling of an eye, at the last trumpet; for the trumpet will sound, and the dead will be raised imperishable, and we will be changed. For this perishable must put on the imperishable, and this mortal must put on immortality.

The context of this *translation* (verses 50-58) is speaking of entering a spiritual or heavenly kingdom, a place where Christ currently resides, one that cannot be accessed without this bodily transformation. Jesus' resurrected body was different from his earthly body, just as our bodies will be changed to enter the same domain where Jesus currently sits at the right hand of the Father.

This mystery or understanding the difference of an earthly body versus a heavenly body is explained in verses 35 through 49.

The significance of the mystery of this translation is as follows.

(a) The nature of the *translation* event is spiritual, transforming the human body from a natural body to a spiritual or glorified body.

(b) The nature of the Millennial Kingdom is earthly, allowing for a natural body inhabitance of those who were not part of the *translation* event, as expressed in Isaiah 65:20-25.

The mystery *translation* is spoken of as a hope, as found in Titus 2:13 and First Thessalonians 4:13-18, which reads:

But we do not want you to be uninformed, brethren, about those who are asleep, that you may not grieve, as do the rest who have no hope. For if we believe that Jesus died and rose again, even so God will bring with Him those who have fallen asleep in Jesus. For this we say to you by the word of the Lord, that we who are alive, and remain until the coming of the Lord, shall not precede those who have fallen asleep. For the Lord Himself will descend from heaven with a shout, with the voice of the archangel, and with the trumpet of God; and the dead in Christ shall rise first. Then we who are alive and remain shall be caught up together with them in the clouds to meet the Lord in the air, and thus we shall always be with the Lord. Therefore comfort one another with these words.

The nature of the *translation,* or rapture is a spiritual transformation of the body to co-exist with the Lord Jesus Christ in his current state. Therefore, Paul speaks of a hope that would come in the midst of difficult times.

This hope lends itself to a pre-tribulational perspective, as the saints at the time of Paul's writing were already going through great persecution, even unto death. Therefore, Paul was providing hope that they would one day be with Christ. Paul writes,

For God has not destined us for wrath, but for obtaining salvation through our Lord Jesus Christ, who died for us, that whether we are awake or asleep, we may live together with Him. Therefore encourage one another, and build up one another, just as you also are doing.[377]

This stands in contrast to Old Testament prophecies that spoke in terms of a coming Millennial Kingdom that was earthly in nature, not as a future hope, but as a promise of inheritance and physical possession. This was the understanding of the Old Testament saints of Israel, as covenanted with Abraham and King David. (Genesis 12:1-3, 17:1-8; 2 Samuel 7:7-17)

The contrasts between what was promised, the church in the hope to be with Christ, and the Old Testament Covenants made with Israel, demonstrate two separate economies taking place. One economy representing the *Church Age* and the other representing the *Millennial Kingdom*.

In the end, the support for Israel and the Church as being two separate entities through these concepts is evidentiary clear.

THE CHURCH AS THE "BRIDE OF CHRIST"—A MYSTERY— SUPPORTS THIS DISTINCTION

Ephesians 5:22-33 provides the analogy of the relationship between Christ and the Church, with a marriage between a man and woman—a mystery as verse 32 states: "This mystery is great; but I am speaking with reference to Christ and the church."

This relationship was never spoken of in past prophecies or tied to any covenant. This relationship came about as the result of the New Covenant, which represents the permanent forgiveness of sins and the personal indwelling of the Holy Spirit.

It is clear this relationship has nothing to do with the Davidic Covenant—the inheritance of land forever. Yes, the church will ultimately be part of the Kingdom, but under a difference set of circumstances.

Israel has often been seen as the wife of Jehovah within the Old Testament—an adulteress and unfaithful. While the church of the New Testament is seen as a pure virgin, espoused to Christ as his bride to be as expressed in Second Corinthians 11:2, "For I am jealous for you with a godly jealousy; for I betrothed you to one husband that to Christ I might present you as a pure virgin."

These contrasting concepts support the view that Israel and the church are functioning on two separate tracks, heading toward unification, as one body, at the end of the age.

CONCLUSION ON THE DISTINCTION BETWEEN ISRAEL AND THE CHURCH

The Scriptures maintain a clear distinction between Israel and the Church. The biblical evidence as a whole, demonstrate this distinction through the use of the term *church*, to the plain statement of Jesus in Matthew 16:18, to the existence of *un-translated* saints at the Second Advent.

All these distinctions provided within this discussion point to the fact of two distinct bodies, running side by side to the end. Their promises and futures cannot be interchanged. This is basic to the question, does the Church go through the tribulation or does the rapture come first?

---

[377] 1 Thess. 5:9-11.

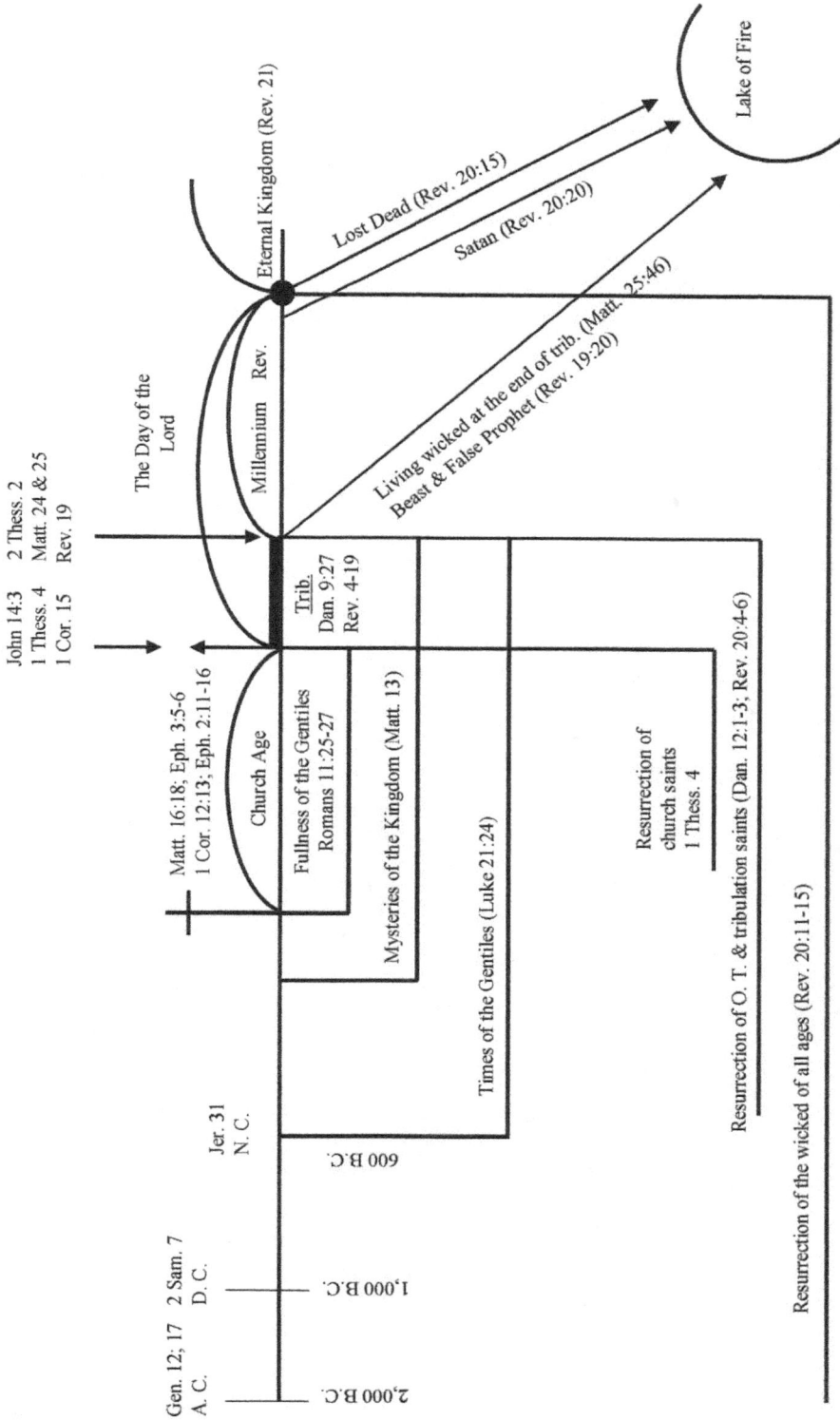

Fig. 10.1

CHAPTER ELEVEN

The Day of the Lord and the Day of Christ

THE DAY OF THE LORD

THE SCOPE OF THE TERM

The Day of the Lord as it relates to end-time events is that extended period beginning with God's dealing with Israel and the Gentile world after the rapture, starting from the beginning of the tribulation period, then extending through the Tribulation, Second Advent, and Millennium age.

The prophet Zephaniah states:

Near is the great day of the Lord, Near and coming very quickly; Listen, the day of the Lord! In it the warrior cries out bitterly. A day of wrath is that day, A day of trouble and distress, A day of destruction and desolation, A day of darkness and gloom, A day of clouds and thick darkness, A day of trumpet and battle cry, Against the fortified cities And the high corner towers. And I will bring distress on men, So that they will walk like the blind, Because they have sinned against the Lord; And their blood will be poured out like dust, And their flesh like dung. Neither their silver nor their gold Will be able to deliver them On the day of the Lord's wrath; And all the earth will be devoured In the fire of His jealousy, For He will make a complete end, Indeed a terrifying one, Of all the inhabitants of the earth.[378]

The prophet Zechariah expresses it this way,

Behold, a day is coming for the Lord when the spoil taken from you will be divided among you. For I will gather all the nations against Jerusalem to battle, and the city will be captured, the houses plundered, the women ravished, and half of the city exiled, but the rest of the people will not be cut off from the city. Then the Lord will go forth and fight against those nations, as when He fights on a day of battle. And in that day His feet will stand on the Mount of Olives, which is in front of Jerusalem on the east; and the Mount of Olives will be split in its middle from east to west by a very large valley, so that half of the mountain will move toward the

---

[378] Zeph. 1:14-18.

north and the other half toward the south. [379]

The Apostle Peter writes,

But the day of the Lord will come like a thief, in which the heavens will pass away with a roar and the elements will be destroyed with intense heat, and the earth and its works will be burned up. Since all these things are to be destroyed in this way, what sort of people ought you to be in holy conduct and godliness, looking for and hastening the coming of the day of God, on account of which the heavens will be destroyed by burning, and the elements will melt with intense heat! But according to His promise we are looking for new heavens and a new earth, in which righteousness dwells.[380]

DIFFERING TIME PERIODS REPRESENTED WITHIN THE DAY OF THE LORD

The *Day of the Lord* is spoken of throughout the Scriptures. We find this term used over 100 times, either directly or in a descriptive format.

For the benefit of further independent study on this topic, the following list of Scripture passages is provided in alphanumeric order:

1 Corinthians 1:8; 1 Thessalonians 5:1-8; 2 Peter 2:9; 2 Peter 3:10-12; 2 Thessalonians 2:3; 2 Timothy 1:12; Acts 2:17-21; Amos 5:18-20; Amos 9:11; Daniel 12:1-2; Ezekiel 13:5; Ezekiel 30:3-4; Ezekiel 30:9-10; Ezekiel 38:14-16; Haggai 2:23; Hosea 3:5; Isaiah 11:10-14; Isaiah 13:4-9; Isaiah 19:16-17; Isaiah 2:12-17; Isaiah 24:21-22; Isaiah 26:1-6; Isaiah 27:1; Isaiah 27:12-13; Isaiah 4:2-6; Isaiah 5:26-30; Jeremiah 30:4-8; Jeremiah 30:9-11; Jeremiah 46:10; Job 20:28-29; Joel 1:15; Joel 2:10-11; Joel 2:1-2; Joel 2:23-27; Joel 3:9-14; John 11:24; John 12:48; John 6:40; Luke 12:39-40; Luke 21:11-12; Luke 21:20-22; Luke 21:31; Malachi 4:1-3; Malachi 4:4-5; Mark 13:19-20; Mark 13:24-27; Mark 13:29; Mark 13:32; Matthew 24:20-21; Matthew 24:30-31; Matthew 24:33; Matthew 24:43-44; Matthew 7:22-23; Micah 4:6-8; Micah 5:8-9; Obadiah 1:15-16; Proverbs 11:4; Revelation 20:7-9; Revelation 22:5; Revelation 6:15-17; Romans 2:16; Romans 2:5; Zechariah 12:10-11; Zechariah 14:1-2; Zechariah 14:20-21; Zechariah 9:16-17; Zephaniah 1:14-18; Zephaniah 2:1-3; Zephaniah 3:11-13; Zephaniah 3:14-20; Zephaniah 3:8.[381]

The key passages on this subject are: Isaiah 2:12, 13:6-9; Joel 1:15, 2:1-11, 31, 3:14; Amos 5:18-20; Obadiah vs. 15; Zephaniah 1:7, 14-16; Zechariah 14:1-2; Malachi 4:5; Acts 2:20; 1 Thessalonians 5:2; 2 Thessalonians 2:2 and 2 Peter 3:10.

Through these verses collectively, we find that the concept of judgment is the theme. The tribulation judgment is seen in Zephaniah 1:14-18. The Second Advent judgment is described in Zechariah 14:1-4 and the Millennial judgment is expressed in Second Peter 3:10-13, which ties the millennium to the *Day of the Lord*—a judgment which takes place just before the creation of the New Heaven and New Earth that ushers in the Eternal State.

---

[379] Zech. 14:1-4.

[380] 2 Peter 3:10-13.

[381] Scripture references compiled by https://bible.knowing-jesus.com/topics/Day-Of-The-Lord; and was edited for accuracy for this work; Internet; accessed 9 March 2019. Note: This list of passages was not incorporated in the Scripture Index.

EVENTS THAT TAKE PLACE WITHIN THE PERIOD CALLED THE "DAY OF THE LORD"

J. Dwight Pentecost provides us a list of events that takes place within the period called the *Day of the Lord*, as summarized here:

[The federation of states of the Roman Empire (Daniel Chapters 2 and 7); the rise of political power of this Roman rule that forges a covenant with Israel (Daniel 9:27; Revelation 13:1-10); the rise of a false religion and its prophets (Revelation 13:11-18); God's seal judgements unleashed on the world (Revelation Chapter 6); God's choosing of 144,000 witnesses (Revelation 7); God's trumpet judgments (Revelation Chapters 8-11); the rise of God's witnesses (Revelation Chapter 11); the persecution of Israel (Revelation Chapter 12); God's bowl judgments poured out on the earth (Revelation Chapter 16); the overthrow of the false church (Revelation Chapters 17 & 18); the war of Armageddon (Ezekiel Chapters 38 & 39; Revelation 16:16, 19:17-21); the gospel of the kingdom preached (Matthew Chapters 24 & 25).

There are also events tied to the Second Advent which are the return of the Lord (Matthew 24:29-30); the resurrection of Old Testament and tribulation saints (John 6:39-40; Revelation 20:4); the destruction of the Beast, False Prophets and their armies (Revelation 19:11-21); the judgment of the nations (Matthew 25:31-46); the regathering of Israel (Ezekiel 37:1-14); the judgment of living Israel (Ezekiel 20:33-38); the restoration of Israel to their land (Amos 9:15); the binding of Satan (Revelation 20:2-3).

And finally there are events tied to the millennial Kingdom such as, the final revolt of Satan (Revelation 20:11-15) and the purging of the earth (2 Peter 3:10-13).] [382]

THE DAY OF CHRIST

SCOPE OF THE TERM

The term *Day of Christ* is not tied to any event but refers to a period of time coinciding with the rapture of the church and continuing into the Eternal State.

THE IDEA OF REWARD

This term seems to convey reward and blessing as it relates to the New Testament saints—the church.

C. I. Scofield makes this comment,

The expression "day of Christ," occurs in the following passages: 1 Cor. 1:8; 5:5; 2 Cor. 1:14; Phil. 1:6, 10; 2:16. A.V. has "day of Christ," 2 Thess. 2:2, incorrectly, for "day of the Lord" (Isa. 2:12; Rev. 19:11-21). The "day of Christ" related wholly to the reward and blessing of saints at His coming, as "day of the Lord" is connected with judgment. [383]

With regard to Scofield's remarks concerning Second Thessalonians 2:2, it should be noted that it can be difficult to determine the proper translation of the word for *Christ* or *Lord* in this passage.

Joseph H. Thayer (D.D.) was a Professor of New Testament Criticism and Interpretation at Harvard University at the time of the publication of his Lexicon in 1889. Dr. Thayer makes this observation concerning the word κύριος (κυρίου, ὁ).

---

[382] Pentecost, *Things to Come*, 231.

[383] C. I. Scofield, "Note 2," *The Scofield Reference Bible* (New York: Oxford University Press, 1909), 1212.

There is nothing strange in the appearance of the term in the narrative of occurrences after his resurrection: Luke 24:34; John 20:2,18,20,25; 21:7,12. d. There are some who hold that Paul (except in his quotations from the O. T. viz. Rom. 4:8; 9:28; 11:34; 1 Cor 1:31; 2:16; 3:20; 10:26; 2 Cor 6:17; 10:17; 2 Tim. 2:19) uses the title κύριος everywhere not of God, but of Christ.[384]

It would appear that the term κύριος carries two connotations. First, the idea of having power or authority over others. Second, a title of honor, respect and reverence.[385] Therefore, how one translates this term is a matter of researching the background and context in which it is used. It is most likely that the 47 translators of the King James Bible, published in A.D. 1611 got it right when they translated this word in Second Thessalonians 2:2 as *Christ*.

CONCLUSION CONCERNING THE TWO TERMS

When conducting word studies within the Scriptures, one soon discovers that words mean things. This is evident in God's designed choice of the original languages of the Scriptures—purpose does exist.

Hebrew and Greek are very precise languages. For example, in Greek there are four primary words that represent the concept of *love*. There also seems to be a distinction between the *day of the Lord* and *the day of Christ* that some do not see or recognize.

The difference in terms seem to reflect the difference between the concept of judgment as represented in the *day of the*

Lord, and the concept of *translation, glorification* and an *examination time* with Christ, as connected to the term *day of Christ*.

Within these concepts it is reasonable to conclude there are individual purposes for both terms to exist and be translated as two separate terms.

It is evident through a closer study that each of these eschatological terms represent two concepts that are unrelated to the content of the timeframe they represent. This can be seen in the place, people and subject matter emphasized within these terms. The following table will reflect such differences and conclude this segment of our discussion.

Day of the Lord	Day of Christ
Place: Earth	Place: Heaven
People: Israel/Gentiles	People: The Church
Emphasis: Judgment	Emphasis: Rewards

Table 11.1

[384] Grimm's Wilke's *Clovis Novi Testamenti, A Greek-English Lexicon of the New Testament*, trans. Joseph Henry Thayer, D.D. (New York: American Book Company, 1889), 366.
[385] Ibid., 365.

Chapter Twelve

The Tribulation Period

THE TRIBULATION AS REVEALED IN THE OLD TESTAMENT

THE FIRST REFERENCE TO THE TRIBULATION

But from there you will seek the Lord your God, and you will find Him if you search for Him with all your heart and all your soul. When you are in distress and all these things have come upon you, in the latter days, you will return to the Lord your God and listen to His voice. For the Lord your God is a compassionate God; He will not fail you nor destroy you nor forget the covenant with your fathers which He swore to them. (Deuteronomy 4:29-31)

There are two takeaways from this text. One purpose of the tribulation is to turn Israel back to God, while a second purpose is to prepare for God's fulfillment of the Abrahamic covenant.

THE PROPHECY OF JEREMIAH— JEREMIAH 30:4-11

Now these are the words which the Lord spoke concerning Israel and concerning Judah, "For thus says the Lord, 'I have heard a sound of terror, Of dread, and there is no peace. 'Ask now, and see, If a male can give birth. Why do I see every man With his hands on his loins, as a woman in childbirth? And why have all faces turned pale? 'Alas! for that day is great, There is none like it; And it is the time of Jacob's distress, But he will be saved from it. 'And it shall come about on that day,' declares the Lord of hosts, 'that I will break his yoke from off their neck, and will tear off their bonds; and strangers shall no longer make them their slaves. But they shall serve the Lord their God, and David their king, whom I will raise up for them.' 'And fear not, O Jacob My servant,' declares the Lord, 'And do not be dismayed, O Israel; For behold, I will save you from afar, And your offspring from the land of their captivity. And Jacob shall return, and shall be quiet and at ease, And no one shall make him afraid. 'For I am with you,' declares the Lord, 'to save you; For I will destroy completely all the nations where I have scattered you, Only I will not destroy you completely. But I will chasten you justly, And will by no means leave you unpunished.'"[386]

---

[386] Jer. 30:4-11.

Four key concepts preside within the context of this passage.

(1) The tribulation induces terror and anguish on the part of those living.

(2) The tribulation is distinct from any other time in Israel's history.

(3) The tribulation destroys gentile dominion over Israel.

(4) The tribulation is followed by the millennium, as seen with Israel restored to their land.

It should be noted that the *Eternal State* does not follow the *Time of Trouble*. Instead, Israel is restored to the land. This shows the necessity of a period such as the millennium to accomplish this, and is an argument that would oppose an Amillennialism perspective.

THE PROPHECY OF DANIEL— DANIEL 9:24-27

Seventy weeks have been decreed for your people and your holy city, to finish the transgression, to make an end of sin, to make atonement for iniquity, to bring in everlasting righteousness, to seal up vision and prophecy, and to anoint the most holy place. So you are to know and discern that from the issuing of a decree to restore and rebuild Jerusalem until Messiah the Prince there will be seven weeks and sixty-two weeks; it will be built again, with plaza and moat, even in times of distress. Then after the sixty-two weeks the Messiah will be cut off and have nothing, and the people of the

prince who is to come will destroy the city and the sanctuary. And its end will come with a flood; even to the end there will be war; desolations are determined. And he will make a firm covenant with the many for one week, but in the middle of the week he will put a stop to sacrifice and grain offering; and on the wing of abominations will come one who makes desolate, even until a complete destruction, one that is decreed, is poured out on the one who makes desolate.[387]

There are four key points to consider within this text.

1) The sixty-nine *weeks* of Daniel 9:24-26 demonstrated through its fulfillment that the unit of time reflects a single day as equivalent to one year.

2) The 70th week is a seven-year period, if understood in the same way as the first 69 weeks. This interpretation is also supported by Daniel 12:11.

3) After the first 69 weeks, the Messiah is cut off and the city and temple are destroyed, but this occurs before the 70th week begins. Thus, there must be a time gap between the 69th and 70th week.

4) The 70th week begins with a covenant between the prince and Israel at the start of the tribulation period.

The covenant made in this text consists of three elements.

1) It is a covenant of protection and religious liberty.

---

[387] Dan. 9:24-27.

2) It allows for temple sacrifices in the temple.

3) The covenant will be broken in the middle of the seven years. This event is tied to two concepts:

(a) The possible connection with the defiling of the temple by the antichrist in Second Thessalonians Chapter 2.

(b) The breaking of the covenant marks the beginning of the Great Tribulation, spoken of in Matthew 24:15-21 and Revelation 7:14.

DETAILS OF THE TRIBULATION PERIOD FROM DANIEL

Daniel 7:7-8 reads:

After this I kept looking in the night visions, and behold, a fourth beast, dreadful and terrifying and extremely strong; and it had large iron teeth. It devoured and crushed, and trampled down the remainder with its feet; and it was different from all the beasts that were before it, and it had ten horns. While I was contemplating the horns, behold, another horn, a little one, came up among them, and three of the first horns were pulled out by the roots before it; and behold, this horn possessed eyes like the eyes of a man, and a mouth uttering great boasts.

As express in chapter six, Scripture interprets Scripture, as Daniel explains the meaning behind this passage in verses 19 through 28:

Then I desired to know the exact meaning of the fourth beast, which was different from all the others,

exceedingly dreadful, with its teeth of iron and its claws of bronze, and which devoured, crushed, and trampled down the remainder with its feet, and the meaning of the ten horns that were on its head, and the other horn which came up, and before which three of them fell, namely, that horn which had eyes and a mouth uttering great boasts, and which was larger in appearance than its associates. I kept looking, and that horn was waging war with the saints and overpowering them until the Ancient of Days came, and judgment was passed in favor of the saints of the Highest One, and the time arrived when the saints took possession of the kingdom. As for the ten horns, out of this kingdom ten kings will arise; and another will arise after them, and he will be different from the previous ones and will subdue three kings. And he will speak out against the Most High and wear down the saints of the Highest One, and he will intend to make alterations in times and in law; and they will be given into his hand for a time, times, and half a time. But the court will sit for judgment, and his dominion will be taken away, annihilated and destroyed forever. Then the sovereignty, the dominion, and the greatness of all the kingdoms under the whole heaven will be given to the people of the saints of the Highest One; His kingdom will be an everlasting kingdom, and all the dominions will serve and obey Him. At this point the revelation ended.

The apostle John also expands on this prophecy in Revelation 17:12-13 as he writes, "And the ten horns which you saw are ten kings, who have not yet received a kingdom, but they receive authority as kings with the beast for one hour. These have one purpose and they give their power and authority to the beast."

From Daniel's prophecy, it would appear there will be a time of a great struggle and war, resulting in possessing a physical kingdom, not a spiritual one, with all nations under the control of a final King—which is Jesus Christ. It should also be noted that Satan will be bound for all the millennial kingdom years (Revelation 20:2), and the talk about war during that timeframe does not exist until the very end. The result of that struggle is not the possession of the kingdom, but the ushering in of the *Eternal State*. Therefore, talk of a tribulation period outside the millennium must exist in a literal sense.

Daniel goes on to provide additional information about the Great Tribulation timeframe in Daniel 11:36-45 and 12:11-13. Daniel's prophecy is then affirmed by the apostle John in Revelation 11:2 and 12:6.

DETAILS OF THE TRIBULATION PERIOD FROM THE MINOR PROPHETS

Zephaniah 1:14-18 reads,

> Near is the great day of the Lord, Near and coming very quickly; Listen, the day of the Lord! In it the warrior cries out bitterly. A day of wrath is that day, A day of trouble and distress, A day of destruction and desolation, A day of darkness and gloom, A day of clouds and thick darkness, A day of trumpet and battle cry, Against the fortified cities And the high corner towers. And I will bring distress on men, So that they will walk like the blind, Because they have sinned against the Lord;

And their blood will be poured out like dust, And their flesh like dung. Neither their silver nor their gold Will be able to deliver them On the day of the Lord's wrath; And all the earth will be devoured In the fire of His jealousy, For He will make a complete end, Indeed a terrifying one, Of all the inhabitants of the earth.

This is not a description of the millennial period but of something else that can only fit into the time of tribulation.

The prophet Zechariah writes,

> "And it will come about in all the land," Declares the Lord, "That two parts in it will be cut off and perish; But the third will be left in it. And I will bring the third part through the fire, Refine them as silver is refined, And test them as gold is tested. They will call on My name, And I will answer them; I will say, 'They are My people,' And they will say, 'The Lord is my God.'"

> Behold, a day is coming for the Lord when the spoil taken from you will be divided among you. For I will gather all the nations against Jerusalem to battle, and the city will be captured, the houses plundered, the women ravished, and half of the city exiled, but the rest of the people will not be cut off from the city. Then the Lord will go forth and fight against those nations, as when He fights on a day of battle. And in that day His feet will stand on the Mount of Olives, which is in front of Jerusalem on the east; and the Mount of Olives will be split in its middle from east to west by a very large valley, so that half of the

mountain will move toward the north and the other half toward the south. And you will flee by the valley of My mountains, for the valley of the mountains will reach to Azel; yes, you will flee just as you fled before the earthquake in the days of Uzziah king of Judah. Then the Lord, my God, will come, and all the holy ones with Him![388]

This appears to be a description of the last days of the tribulation, with Christ returning to establish his millennial Kingdom. The question is, who are the holy ones coming back with him?

The Hebrew word קרשים can mean sacred—Leviticus 11:44-45, 19:2; 20:7, 26; 21:6 and Numbers 15:40; sacred ones, saints—Deuteronomy 33:3, Psalm 16:3, 34:10 and Daniel 8:24; angels—Psalm 89:6, 8; Job 5:1; 15:15; Zechariah 14:5 and Daniel 8:13.[389]

The word in Zechariah is translated *holy ones*, with the assumption that it must be speaking of angels, even though the same word is also translated in Deuteronomy 33:3 as *holy ones*, but this context is self-defined as being God's people or saints.

This leaves the question of how should Zechariah 14:5 be understood? The answer that seems most logical is by comparing the context of the passage in relation to the whole of Scripture.

Within the context of this study, it would not be unreasonable to interpret this term as representing both angels and saints, as suggested by other Scriptures that speak to this event within other prophecies, such as Revelation 19:11-16 where it speaks of

the armies of God returning with Christ just before the millennium begins; while in Second Thessalonians 2:1-12 the context is the Christians of Paul's day did not expect to enter the *day of the Lord*, a time of judgment, a time when God will send a *deluding influence* so those within this period will believe a lie.

With Paul calming down those who believed the *day of the Lord* had already arrived, this seems to indicate that Paul was assuring them they will not be part of those days of judgment. Therefore, if the rapture occurs before the tribulation, then at some point those who were raptured must also return with Christ at the second advent, leaving open the possibility that Zechariah's prophecy of the *holy ones* coming would include saints.

The prophet Amos speaks to this period as he writes,

> Alas, you who are longing for the day of the Lord, For what purpose will the day of the Lord be to you? It will be darkness and not light;
>
> As when a man flees from a lion, And a bear meets him, Or goes home, leans his hand against the wall, And a snake bites him.
>
> Will not the day of the Lord be darkness instead of light, Even gloom with no brightness in it? [390]

---

388 Zech. 13:8-14:5.
389 William Gesenius, "קרשים," *A Hebrew and English Lexicon of the Old Testament*, ed. Francis Brown, D.D., S. R. Driver D.D. and Charles A. Briggs, D.D., trans. Edward Robinson (New York:

Boston and New York Houghton Mifflin Company, 1907), 892.
390 Amos 5:18-20.

THE TRIBULATION AS REVEALED IN THE NEW TESTAMENT

CHRIST'S OLIVET DISCOURSE

Within the context of Matthew 24:14-30 we learn six key elements concerning the tribulation period.

1) The Olivet Discourse provides specific details presented as signs of the Lord's coming at his Second Advent.

2) Matthew 24:15 reads, "Therefore when you see the abomination of desolation which was spoken of through Daniel the prophet, standing in the holy place (let the reader understand)." This reflects back to Daniel 9:27, providing support for the concept that Jesus' comments in Matthew 24 are referencing Daniel's prophecy of the seventieth week.

3) Matthew 24:21 reflects on the fact that this period will be a time of unprecedented trouble.

4) Matthew 24:14, 20 indicates that the events of this period are influenced by divine control.

5) Luke 21:24 speaks to this same timeframe, which supports the concept that this period will be a time of final Gentile domination over the world, and ultimately over Israel.

6) Matthew 24:29-30 reads,

But immediately after the tribulation of those days the sun will be darkened, and the moon will not give its light, and the stars will fall from the sky, and the powers of the heavens will be shaken, and then the sign of the Son of Man will appear in the sky, and then all the tribes of the earth will mourn, and they will see the Son of Man coming on the clouds of the sky with power and great glory.

This passage reflects on the fact that the tribulation period will usher in the coming of the Lord at his Second Advent.

PAUL'S FIRST EPISTLE TO THE THESSALONIANS

Paul's writings in First Thessalonians 5:1-11 present five concepts associated with the tribulation period.

1) Paul reminds the Christians at Thessalonica what they already knew, which most likely came through Jesus' teachings stated in Matthew 24:36, "But of that day and hour no one knows, not even the angels of heaven, nor the Son, but the Father alone." This He stated in reference to his return and the establishment of the Kingdom. The opening statement in Matthew 24:36 is also similar to the statement made in Acts 1:7, which reads, "He said to them, 'It is not for you to know times or epochs which the Father has fixed by His own authority;'" which he said as he ascended into heaven.

2) Paul is now using the term, *the day of the Lord*; indicating that the *end-times* are now in view, with an emphasis shifting to judgment on the world.

3) Verse 3 indicates a sudden and unexpected destruction during a time of supposed peace and safety. Paul uses

the term *they*, in sharp contrast to *we*, as Paul separates himself and his readers with this pronoun choice of words.

4) Paul separates the believer from the unbeliever in verse 5, pointing out that the believers are not appointed to face the wrath of God.

5) Paul presents a syllogism in verses 1 through 11, where he describes this period of *the day of the Lord* as a time of destruction because of God's wrath. And this period is not for those who are of the light or day, but for those in darkness. Therefore, those of the light are not appointed for God's wrath and judgement but will instead be with Christ for eternity.

To summarize these points, believers will not be on earth at the time of God pouring out his wrath on the earth. For this to take place there must be a rapture before this period and the next, which is the Millennial Kingdom.

THE NATURE OF THE TRIBULATION

The following list represent attributes associated with the tribulation period.

1. Wrath—Zephaniah 1:15-18; 1 Thessalonians 1:10; 5:9; Revelation 6:16-17; 14:10; 15:1, 7; 16:1, 19.

    "… and to wait for His Son from heaven, whom He raised from the dead, that is Jesus, who delivers us from the wrath to come." (1 Thess. 1:10)

2. Judgment—Revelation 14:7; 15:4; 16:5, 7; 19:2.

    "And he said with a loud voice, 'Fear God, and give Him glory, because the hour of His judgment has come; and worship Him who made the heaven and the earth and sea and springs of waters'" (Rev. 14:7)

3. Indignation—Isaiah 26:20-21; 34:1-3.

    "Come, my people, enter into your rooms, And close your doors behind you; Hide for a little while, Until indignation runs its course. For behold, the Lord is about to come out from His place To punish the inhabitants of the earth for their iniquity; And the earth will reveal her bloodshed, And will no longer cover her slain." (Isa. 26:20-21)

4. Trial—Revelation 3:10.

    "Because you have kept the word of My perseverance, I also will keep you from the hour of testing, that hour which is about to come upon the whole world, to test those who dwell upon the earth." (Rev. 3:10)

5. Trouble—Jeremiah 30:7; Zephaniah 1:14-15; Daniel 12:1.

    "Alas! for that day is great, so that none is like it: it is even the time of Jacob's trouble; but he shall be saved out of it." (Jer. 30:7; KJV)

6. Destruction—Joel 1:15; 1 Thessalonians 5:3.

    "Alas for the day! For the day of the Lord is near, And it will come as destruction from the Almighty." (Joel 1:15)

7. Darkness—Joel 2:2; Amos 5:18.

    "A day of darkness and gloom, A day of clouds and thick darkness. As the dawn is spread over the mountains, So there is a great and mighty people; There has never been anything like it, Nor will there be again after it To the years of many generations." (Joel 2:2)

8. Desolation—Daniel 9:27; Zephaniah 1:14-15.

"And he will make a firm covenant with the many for one week, but in the middle of the week he will put a stop to sacrifice and grain offering; and on the wing of abominations will come one who makes desolate, even until a complete destruction, one that is decreed, is poured out on the one who makes desolate." (Dan. 9:27)

9. Overturning—Isaiah 24:1-4, 19-21.

"Behold, the Lord maketh the earth empty, and maketh it waste, and turneth it upside down, and scattereth abroad the inhabitants thereof." (Isa. 24:1; KJV)

10. Punishment—Isaiah 24:20-21.

"So it will happen in that day, That the Lord will punish the host of heaven, on high, And the kings of the earth, on earth." (Isa. 24:21)

THE PURPOSE OF THE TRIBULATION

TO PROVIDE THE FINAL OPPORTUNITY FOR SALVATION TO BOTH JEWS AND GENTILES WHO WILL POPULATE THE KINGDOM

The tribulation will drive Israel to a place where they will call him blessed and bless the Lord in fulfillment of Matthew 23:39.

It will be a time where 144,000 Jewish witnesses will be sealed to go forth in

testimony of the Lamb of God, as described in Revelation 7:1-8.

The tribulation will prepare the nation of Israel for its messiah and the promised Kingdom to come. (Matthew 25:1-13)

The tribulation will also be a time for those Gentiles who have not yet heard the Gospel to be saved under the witness of the 144,000 Jewish witnesses.

And one of the elders answered, saying to me, 'These who are clothed in the white robes, who are they, and from where have they come?' And I said to him, 'My lord, you know.' And he said to me, 'These are the ones who come out of the great tribulation, and they have washed their robes and made them white in the blood of the Lamb.' (Rev. 7:9-14)

The final judgment of the gentiles will come at the end of this period, as expressed in Matthew 25:31-46.

TO POUR OUT JUDGMENT UPON THE UNBELIEVING INDIVIDUALS AND NATIONS.

Revelation 3:10 states: "Because you have kept the word of My perseverance, I also will keep you from the hour of testing, that hour which is about to come upon the whole world, to test those who dwell upon the earth."

John goes on to tell us why this period will come to pass, as he writes,

And the kings of the earth and the great men and the commanders and the rich and the strong and every slave and free man, hid themselves in the caves and among the rocks of the mountains; and they said to the mountains and to the rocks, 'Fall on us and hide us from the presence of

Him who sits on the throne, and from the wrath of the Lamb; for the great day of their wrath has come; and who is able to stand'? [391]

Then finally we read in Second Thessalonians 2:8-12,

> And then that lawless one will be revealed whom the Lord will slay with the breath of His mouth and bring to an end by the appearance of His coming; that is, the one whose coming is in accord with the activity of Satan, with all power and signs and false wonders, and with all the deception of wickedness for those who perish, because they did not receive the love of the truth so as to be saved. And for this reason God will send upon them a deluding influence so that they might believe what is false, in order that they all may be judged who did not believe the truth, but took pleasure in wickedness.

We are told that God will save some out of the tribulation period, while at the same time God will send a lie or dilution upon others, that they may ultimately be judged. It would stand to reason if this lie fell to everyone, no one would be saved and Revelation 7 would then be a false statement. Therefore, the question remains, who are the ones that believe this lie?

If one evaluates these concepts in the context of Second Thessalonians 2:10—"and with all the deception of wickedness for those who perish, because they did not receive the love of the truth so as to be saved;" with the theological teachings from a human perspective in areas such as, *Sovereignty*, *justness*, *mercy* and *love*, it would stand to reason that the lie falls upon those

gentiles who have heard the gospel and about the love of God in the past but rejected it up to this time.

This fits the same scenario that occurred with the religious rulers of Jesus' day, where they made a final decision to reject Christ, resulting in Christ moving his focus away from them and directing it toward others. (See Chapter 9; VIII)

The tribulation then becomes a time for those who have never heard the gospel message, providing them an opportunity to be saved by the Lamb of God through the 144,000 Jewish witnesses.

THE SOURCE OF THE TRIBULATION

Who are the major players in the tribulation? Is this event just happening in the natural course of historical events, or is there more to it than that?

The following are three driving forces behind these events, and as you will see, men are powerless to prevent it.

1) God is the primary source in bringing about this period, as he uses his power and authority to pour out his wrath in judgment on the world. Isaiah 24:1 states, "Behold, the Lord lays the earth waste, devastates it, distorts its surface, and scatters its inhabitants." The prophet Joel declares, "Alas for the day! For the day of the Lord is near, And it will come as destruction from the Almighty (Joel 1:15)." The words of the prophet Zephaniah proclaim,

> Neither their silver nor their gold Will be able to deliver them On the day of the Lord's wrath; And all the earth will be devoured In the fire of His jealousy, For He

---

[391] Rev. 6:15-17.

will make a complete end, Indeed a terrifying one, Of all the inhabitants of the earth.[392]

Other Scripture that reference God's involvement are listed here: Revelation 6:16-17; 11:18; 14:7, 19; 15:4, 7; 16:1, 7, 19; 19:1-2.

2) Satan is also involved, as he provides the beast power and authority to make war against the saints and control the world. Revelation Chapter 13:3, 4, and 7 reads,

> And I saw one of his heads as if it had been slain, and his fatal wound was healed. And the whole earth was amazed and followed after the beast; and they worshiped the dragon, because he gave his authority to the beast; and they worshiped the beast, saying, 'Who is like the beast, and who is able to wage war with him?'... And it was given to him to make war with the saints and to overcome them; and authority over every tribe and people and tongue and nation was given to him.

3) And finally, Satan, as the prince of this world makes war against Israel, because his time is short, knowing God will soon bring final judgment upon himself.

> For this reason, rejoice, O heavens and you who dwell in them. Woe to the earth and the sea, because the devil has come down to you, having great wrath, knowing that he has only a short time. And when the dragon saw that he was thrown down to the earth, he persecuted the woman who gave birth to the male child. And the two wings of the great eagle were given to the woman, in order that she might fly into the wilderness to her place, where she was nourished for a time and times and half a time, from the presence of the serpent. And the serpent poured water like a river out of his mouth after the woman, so that he might cause her to be swept away with the flood. And the earth helped the woman, and the earth opened its mouth and drank up the river which the dragon poured out of his mouth. And the dragon was enraged with the woman, and went off to make war with the rest of her offspring, who keep the commandments of God and hold to the testimony of Jesus.[393]

---

[392] Zeph. 1:18.

[393] Rev. 12:12-17.

CHAPTER THIRTEEN

The Rapture and Related Events

VIEWS CONCERNING THE RAPTURE IN RELATION TO THE TRIBULATION

THE PARTIAL RAPTURE VIEW

This view holds that only those with faith associated with the church will be raptured before the tribulation. The rest will be raptured during or at the end of the tribulation. This view holds that the tribulation is a reward for service and not part of salvation. Hebrews 9:28 is the Scripture used to support this perspective.

The refutation of this view comes through the interpretation of First Thessalonians 4:13-18 and 5:9-10 which reads, "For God has not destined us for wrath, but for obtaining salvation through our Lord Jesus Christ, who died for us, that whether we are awake or asleep, we may live together with Him." The refutation that can be used is threefold, based on verse 10.

1) Verse 10 starts with the phrase *Who died for us*. The omission of these words would not change the general sense of the passage. The words *who*, and *us*, are given to clarify the truth that salvation is its own consummation; salvation is by grace alone.

The sacrificial death of Christ is the only ground upon which any believer will be caught away at the rapture. The Rapture is a part of our salvation, not a reward for spiritual living.

2) The word *that* (ἵνα), creates a purpose clause meaning, *in order that* we may live with Christ. This ties Christ's action directly to our future existence with him; therefore, it is not based on our actions.

3) The terms *wake* and *sleep*, used in this context, makes reference to Paul's discussion back in First Thessalonians 4:13-18 which reads,

But we do not want you to be uninformed, brethren, about those who are asleep, that you may not grieve, as do the rest who have no hope. For if we believe that Jesus died and rose again, even so God will bring with Him those who have fallen asleep in Jesus. For this we say to you by the word of the Lord, that we who are alive, and remain until the coming of the Lord, shall not precede those who have fallen asleep. For the Lord Himself will descend from heaven with a shout, with the voice of the archangel, and with the trumpet of God; and the dead in Christ shall rise first. Then we who are alive and remain shall be caught up together with them in the clouds to meet the Lord in the air, and thus we shall always be with the

Lord. Therefore comfort one another with these words.

The terms *wake* and *sleep* in verse 10 are not referring to the concept of watching as found in verse 6 (KJV). This is because the terms *sleep* and *watch* in verse 6 (KJV) are associated with those who are lost and saved. Verse 7 associates *sleep* with darkness and *darkness* is associated with those who are lost. The terms used in verse 10 suggests that no matter what state one is in (alive or dead in Christ), they will be with Christ for eternity.

The deliverance from God's wrath is solely based on Christ's work on the cross and man's response in faith toward that work. The apostle Paul's point is simply this, we are secure in Christ, not in ourselves. This is the reason it is a true hope of comfort. If the terms of our rapture were based on our efforts then our hope would not be hope but distress; accordingly, one purpose for Paul's letter was to reinforce this point.

MID-TRIBULATION RAPTURE VIEW

The mid-tribulation rapture view is defined as the rapture taking place at the midpoint of the seven-year tribulation period.

There are five characteristics associated with this perspective and listed as follows:

1) The seventh trumpet judgment in Revelation Chapter 11 is regarded as the beginning of the Great Tribulation—the last 3 ½ years of the period.

2) This view holds that the seventh trumpet of Revelation 11 is the same trumpet spoken of in First Corinthians Chapter 15.

3) This view holds the position that the rapture of the church takes place within the timeframe of Revelation Chapter 11.

4) This view believes that God's program for Israel and the Church overlap in time.

5) This view rejects the doctrine of the imminent return of Christ and holds it to be an unscriptural teaching.

POST-TRIBULATION RAPTURE VIEW

The post-tribulational perspective is defined through its view that the church continues on earth until the Second Advent of Christ, then the church will be caught up in the clouds, at which time they will return with Christ to the earth.

There are seven characteristics associated with this view as follows:

1) This view denies the distinctives of dispensationalism.

2) This view denies the distinction between Israel and the Church.

3) This view denies the scriptural narrative of the nature and purpose of the tribulation period.

4) This view rejects the scriptural interpretation describing the rapture and Second Advent as two distinct events. Those holding this view see both as the same event.

5) Those who hold this view make one of two choices in their interpretation. (i) They must either deny the doctrine of the imminent return of Christ and believe in signs yet to be fulfilled, or (ii)

They must spiritualize the tribulation and make it part of the church age.

6) There are some holding this view who deny any future fulfillment of Daniel's prophecy concerning the 70th week.

7) This view must apply passages that outline God's program for Israel to the Church. Example: Matthew Chapters 24 and 25 with Revelation Chapters 4 through 19.

There are three major points of argument used in support of the post-tribulation rapture perspective.

1) The argument for historical support. This view is held by the majority of the current church, which includes both Catholic and Protestants, and uses the argument that the pre-tribulational view was not studied until the 1900s. This then becomes an argument against the progressive revelation interpretation. An example of this is the mysteries revealed by Christ and the Apostle Paul, as recorded in the New Testament books of John, Colossians and Ephesians. Those who reject those revealed mysteries also reject progressive revelation interpretations. It should also be noted that the pre-tribulational perspective is simply a small adjustment to the historical premillennialist position and has a majority acceptance among this group.

2) It is argued that the church was born in persecution and tribulation, therefore this period would be no different for the church—historically. They view pre-tribulationalists as simply wanting to escape this period of suffering, making the pre-tribulation rapture view more emotional than scriptural.

With reference to this argument, it should be noted that the difference between these two perspectives are that the suffering of the church throughout history was based on Satan's attacks, all in the context of Jesus' words in John 15:20 which reads, "Remember the word that I said to you, 'A slave is not greater than his master.' If they persecuted Me, they will also persecute you; if they kept My word, they will keep yours also." The context of the Tribulation period is the tribulation is not directly tied to Satan but to God, in the context of these words: "He who believes in the Son has eternal life; but he who does not obey the Son shall not see life, but the wrath of God abides on him" (John 3:36). The tribulation period will be a result of the wrath of God pouring out his judgment, which the church is not under. The ultimate position of a pre-tribulation rapture is not based on emotion but on the understanding of the whole counsel of God.

3) Some Scriptures used in support of a post-tribulation rapture are: Matthew 13:24-30, 36-43. It should be noted that these passages, in relationship to Revelation Chapter 14 would be a closer support for a mid-tribulation rapture. Daniel 12:1-3 speaks to the resurrection of the dead which takes place after the tribulation period, called the end of the age. This does not speak to any living saints and their plight. John Walvoord makes the observation that resurrections associated with the second coming of Christ never refer to the saints of the New Testament

church.[394] Revelation 20:4-6 speaks to a resurrection that occurs after the tribulation but before the millennium. Scripture states this is called the first resurrection, and most likely from the context of this passage, that this is making reference to the first of its kind since the start of the tribulation period. Make note of who is being raised and the type of deaths and events that took place during the tribulation. This is not the first resurrection from an historical time perspective, for clearly another resurrection took place at the time Christ was raised from the dead, as the Scriptures state, "And behold, the veil of the temple was torn in two from top to bottom, and the earth shook; and the rocks were split, and the tombs were opened; and many bodies of the saints who had fallen asleep were raised; and coming out of the tombs after His resurrection they entered the holy city and appeared to many." (Matthew 27:51-53)

PRE-TRIBULATION RAPTURE VIEW

The pre-tribulation rapture view holds the position that all the church, also defined as the *body of Christ*, will be raptured before the beginning of the tribulation period.

The remaining portion of this chapter will supply the arguments in support of this view.

REASONS WHY THE CHURCH DOES NOT GO THROUGH THE TRIBULATION PERIOD ON EARTH

THE DOCTRINE OF IMMINENCE

The doctrine of Imminence is partly based on Christ's words recorded in John 14:3 which reads, "And if I go and prepare a place for you, I will come again, and receive you to Myself; that where I am, there you may be also." Within this context there are no stipulations or signs required for Christ to return. The same is true in Acts 1:6-11 when the disciples were told that Jesus would return the same way he left; in this context Christ left in peace as he ascended into heaven. The same will be true when he returns for his church, Christ will come in peace and take his body or bride home, just as he promised in John Chapter 14. Within both Scripture passages, the talk of the Kingdom was put on hold, or ignored altogether. The Apostle Paul expresses it this way,

> For they themselves report about us what kind of a reception we had with you, and how you turned to God from idols to serve a living and true God, and to wait for His Son from heaven, whom He raised from the dead, that is Jesus, who delivers us from the wrath to come.[395]

This is in sharp contrast to Christ's Second Advent return as spoken of in Revelation 19:11-18 and Isaiah 63:1-4. The Revelation passage proclaims the purpose of Christ's return will be to wage war and

---

[394] John F. Walvoord, *The Rapture Question*, rev ed. (Grand Rapids: Zondervan Publishing House, 1979), 206.

[395] 1 Thess. 1:9-10.

describes his return as riding a white horse and "clothed with a robe dipped in blood." This is not how Christ left. According to the writer of Acts Chapter 1, Christ did not leave to wage war but to prepare a place for his saints. Therefore, by comparison, these events cannot be the same according to the Scriptures.

It should also be noted that the description of these events are all spoken of as literally taking place; the words of Jesus and later the two witnesses who told the disciples what to expect at his return spoke in literal terms—not dreams or visions—so as to be understood in a literal vernacular.

The imminent return of Jesus Christ means there are no signs or events that need to take place for Christ's peaceful return to receive his church to himself. This is in stark contrast to the Second Advent return where Christ lists signs to look for as described in Matthew 24:3-29.

Another aspect to the doctrine of Imminence is it is always presented as a hope. This is seen in First Corinthians 1:7; First Thessalonians 1:9-10; 4:13-18 and Titus 2:12-13.

THE WORK OF THE HOLY SPIRIT DURING THE CHURCH AGE

Jesus Christ introduces the Holy Spirit to the world in John 14:16-18, 25-26 as he says,

> And I will ask the Father, and He will give you another Helper, that He may be with you forever; that is the Spirit of truth, whom the world cannot receive, because it does not behold Him or know Him, but you know Him because He abides with you, and will be in you. I will not leave you as orphans; I will come to you.... These things I have spoken to you, while abiding with you. But

the Helper, the Holy Spirit, whom the Father will send in My name, He will teach you all things, and bring to your remembrance all that I said to you.

Jesus further explains this introduction in John 16:7-15 when he says,

> But I tell you the truth, it is to your advantage that I go away; for if I do not go away, the Helper shall not come to you; but if I go, I will send Him to you. And He, when He comes, will convict the world concerning sin, and righteousness, and judgment; concerning sin, because they do not believe in Me; and concerning righteousness, because I go to the Father, and you no longer behold Me; and concerning judgment, because the ruler of this world has been judged. I have many more things to say to you, but you cannot bear them now. But when He, the Spirit of truth, comes, He will guide you into all the truth; for He will not speak on His own initiative, but whatever He hears, He will speak; and He will disclose to you what is to come. He shall glorify Me; for He shall take of Mine, and shall disclose it to you. All things that the Father has are Mine; therefore I said, that He takes of Mine, and will disclose it to you.

Two concepts to remember within Christ's introduction. (i) The Holy Spirit will be a key player in the fulfillment of the New Covenant, with Christ as the foundation and fulfiller of the Covenant, and the Holy Spirit as the enforcer and guarantor of that same covenant (2 Corinthians 1:22; Ephesians 1:13-14; 4:30). The individual believer will know Christ because of the work of the Holy Spirit, just as the New Covenant proclaims in Jeremiah 31:33-34 as it reads,

> But this is the covenant which I will make with the house of Israel after those days, declares the Lord, I will put My law within them, and on their heart I will write it; and I will be their God, and they shall be My people. And they shall not teach again, each man his neighbor and each man his brother, saying, 'Know the Lord,' for they shall all know Me, from the least of them to the greatest of them, declares the Lord, for I will forgive their iniquity, and their sin I will remember no more.

It is the Holy Spirit who will allow us to know God from the heart and be the teacher of all believers in Christ, as Christ provides the means to permanent forgiveness. This unique ministry of the Holy Spirit could only take place after Christ's work was completed on earth, when the New Covenant was established by Christ and the sealing event through the Holy Spirit on the day of Pentecost, 50 days later. This sealing ministry of the Holy Spirit is unique only to the Church prior to the return of Christ.

(ii) The other aspect of the Holy Spirit's ministry will be to reprove and convict the world of sin.

> And He, when He comes, will convict the world concerning sin, and righteousness, and judgment; concerning sin, because they do not believe in Me; and concerning righteousness, because I go to the Father, and you no longer behold Me; and concerning judgment,

because the ruler of this world has been judged.[396]

Because of this unique relationship to the Church, when the Church is raptured the present ministry of the Holy Spirit associated with the Church will end. This is most likely the cause behind the statement made in Second Thessalonians 2:3-7 which reads,

> Let no one in any way deceive you, for it will not come unless the apostasy comes first, and the man of lawlessness is revealed, the son of destruction, who opposes and exalts himself above every so-called god or object of worship, so that he takes his seat in the temple of God, displaying himself as being God. Do you not remember that while I was still with you, I was telling you these things? And you know what restrains him now, so that in his time he may be revealed. For the mystery of lawlessness is already at work; only he who now restrains will do so until he is taken out of the way.

The question within this discussion is, who is the one that restrains? There are two indicators within this text that may provide us some answers. First, this restrainer is referenced as *He*, which is similar to Christ's introduction to the Holy Spirit. Remember Christ words?

> And I will ask the Father, and He will give you another Helper, that He may be with you forever; that is the Spirit of truth, whom the world cannot receive, because it does not behold Him or know Him, but you know Him because He abides with

---

[396] John 16:8-11.

you, and will be in you. (John 14:16-17)

Second, the restrainer is said to have the power to suppress iniquity to the point that the *man of sin* could not be revealed so long as He is around.

To provide this much restraint against sin in the world would require a worldwide reach or presence. This could only come from an attribute or power not associated with any other being known to us in Scripture other than God. Certainly, a single angel would not have such presence or power capable of providing such restraint. Angels are not omnipresent or omniscient beings, qualities that most certainly would be required to carry out such a task.

With these facts in mind, to conclude that the restrainer Paul is referencing is the Holy Spirit of God would be a reasonable conclusion. Although there have been some other suggestions such as the restrainer representing the Roman Empire or some other form of human government, this could only be concluded if one spiritualizes the text by equating the term *He*, to represent an entity and not a living being. Another suggestion is that the term *He* represents Satan, even though this would go against Christ's analogy in Matthew 12:26 which says, "And if Satan casts out Satan, he is divided against himself; how then shall his kingdom stand?"

If one allows good hermeneutical principles to stand, the only conclusion to be made concerning this text is the restrainer of Second Thessalonians Chapter 2 is the Holy Spirit of God.

The next question that comes to mind is, to what extent is the restrainer or Holy Spirit to be withdrawn?

The answer lies with understanding the ministry of the Holy Spirit with the Church. The Holy Spirit will stop his practice of indwelling and baptizing new believers in Christ during this period, and the church's witness will be replaced by 144,000 Jews chosen from all twelve tribes of Israel, along with the two prophets who appear sometime in the beginning of the tribulation.

Other evidence of the Holy Spirit's removal can be seen through the lack of humanity's repentance recorded for us in Revelation Chapters 9 and 14. This, along with the fact that those who repented came out of the Great Tribulation—the last 3 ½ years (Revelation 7:9-13). This is about the same time God's hand-picked witnesses (144,000), whom God sealed, come on the scene.

Another question that needs to be asked is, if the church is still on the earth during the tribulation period, why does God need to appoint 144,000 witnesses or even need the two prophets to appear? If the answer is that these 144,000 represent the church, the question would then be, are there only 144,000 individuals to represent the whole church that exists today? And how does the church fit into the concept of the twelve tribes of Israel? I realize there are those who have thought up answers to some of these questions, but not through a literal hermeneutic. If the 144,000 does not represent the church but the church is present, this leads to the question of, Why are the Jewish witnesses sealed from the harm of God's wrath (Ezek. 9:4-5) while the Christian church is left to suffer under God's judgment on the world? Another question that should be asked is, if the Holy Spirit is still working the same way he did during the church age, then why has no one repented before the mid-point? The obvious answer would be, because the Holy

Spirit is no longer working in the same way he had before. For the Apostle John states,

> And the rest of mankind, who were not killed by these plagues, did not repent of the works of their hands, so as not to worship demons, and the idols of gold and of silver and of brass and of stone and of wood, which can neither see nor hear nor walk; and they did not repent of their murders nor of their sorceries nor of their immorality nor of their thefts.[397]

It should be remembered that one of the purposes of the tribulation period is to bring judgment to the world, not repentance. John says no one who is alive repented. If the church is present, would they not have repented? The much broader question would be, why would the church need to repent? Have they not already been saved?

The most obvious question that comes to mind for those who do not hold to this position is, how do those who do repent get saved if the Holy Spirit is not indwelling them? The following answer may surprise some, but is true all the same, according to the Scriptures.

The indwelling of the Holy Spirit is not an action required for salvation. The Scriptures state that we are saved through faith in the work of Jesus Christ on the cross at Calvary, plus nothing and minus nothing. The conditions of salvation are repentance and faith. This is supported by the whole of Scripture. We are then told in the New Testament that we are sealed until the day of redemption by the Holy Spirit with promise. For the Scriptures state,

> In Him, you also, after listening to the message of truth, the gospel of your salvation—having also believed, you were sealed in Him with the Holy Spirit of promise, who is given as a pledge of our inheritance, with a view to the redemption of God's own possession, to the praise of His glory.[398]

During the tribulation period those who repent will be saved through faith in Christ. The only difference is, they will not be sealed by the Holy Spirit of promise, just as the Old Testament saints were not sealed. Those during the tribulation period will need to prove their faith through their actions of not recanting their faith, or become apostates throughout the rest of this period of testing. This is what is meant in Matthew 24:13, "But the one who endures to the end, he shall be saved." This is not speaking to a works salvation, but as James expresses it,

> But someone may well say, 'You have faith, and I have works; show me your faith without the works, and I will show you my faith by my works.' You believe that God is one. You do well; the demons also believe, and shudder. But are you willing to recognize, you foolish fellow, that faith without works is useless? Was not Abraham our father justified by works, when he offered up Isaac his son on the altar? You see that faith was working with his works, and as a result of the works, faith was perfected; and the Scripture was fulfilled which says, 'And Abraham believed God, and it was reckoned to him as righteousness, and he was called the friend of God.' You see that a man

---

[397] Rev. 9:20-21.

[398] Eph. 1:13-14.

is justified by works, and not by faith alone. And in the same way was not Rahab the harlot also justified by works, when she received the messengers and sent them out by another way? For just as the body without the spirit is dead, so also faith without works is dead.[399]

By the time of the millennial kingdom, all those who enter in, either with natural or spiritual bodies, will be indwelt by the Holy Spirit, as the New Covenant promises for both the church and the remaining remnant of Israel.

Why would this be true? Jesus stated that once the Holy Spirit enters a person, He will remain there forever (John 14:16). Therefore, those who are part of God's flock known as the church are already indwelt. Then, through the first resurrection and those still alive following the tribulation period will be deemed ransomed through Christ by faith and will also be indwelt by the Holy Spirit, for the millennial kingdom is described as governed by Christ as the Holy Spirit rests on him. (Isa. 11:1-2)

At this point, the New Covenant will be fully fulfilled as both flocks of Christ will be united under Christ as they enter into the millennial kingdom.

These questions and type of details have always been the sticking point for those who do not hold to a dispensational theology. The key to understanding these questions is to come to the Scriptures as a whole, through a literal hermeneutical approach and not to forget the *whys* in theology, which could be better understood by following Timothy's instructions. "Study to show thyself approved unto God, a workman that needeth not to be ashamed,

rightly dividing the word of truth" (2 Timothy 2:15; KJV). And remember, there are no contradictions in Scripture. For biblical truth to be true, it must agree with all other biblical truth.

THE ARGUMENTS FROM INTERMEDIATE EVENTS ON EARTH

Based on Matthew 25:31-46, there are some events taking place that require understanding from a time element perspective.

For those holding the view that the rapture will take place just before the Second Advent, two things should be considered. The nature of the rapture is that all who are saved at that time will be caught up with Christ and then return with him to establish Christ's Kingdom.

The first issue is, when Christ comes at the Second Advent, there are already saved individuals on the earth, as represented by the difference between the sheep and the goats. The question becomes, where did the sheep come from if the rapture just happened? The second issue is, the sheep and the goats are being separated based on actions they both have taken in their everyday lives. The question here would be, if the rapture just happened, when did these sheep that are already present have time to perform the acts they are being rewarded for?

The scriptural answer can be found in a syllogism based on an argument from the intermediate events.

First Corinthians 15:51 speaks to an event that translates all believers on earth to a new body that will be taken up to be with Christ.

Matthew 25:31-32 states that when Christ comes back to the earth, there will

---

[399] James 2:18-26.

already be individuals on the earth referenced as sheep and goats, which represent the saved and the lost, as they are presented in their natural earthly bodily state.

Therefore, within these two passages there are two sets of believers coming from two separate sets of circumstances. The rapture, which changed the saints into a glorified bodily state, and those found on the earth still in their natural bodily state.

The only conclusion one could infer is, there must be a time gap between these two events and these two events represent two separate groups of people.

THE RAPTURE IN SECOND THESSALONIANS 2

Second Thessalonians Chapter 2 presents a problem for post-tribulationalists. The argument is presented this way.

If Paul taught a post-tribulation rapture view to the current church, the idea of the day of the Lord having begun should have shown them that the rapture was near. Instead, it created a panic. The implication is that before the false teachers came, members of the church at Thessalonica did not expect to enter the day of the Lord.

Paul goes on to explain that before the day of the Lord comes, two things need to take place. First, as expressed in verse 3, "Let no one in any way deceive you, for it will not come unless the apostasy comes first, and the man of lawlessness is revealed, the son of destruction…." Second, Paul then explains in verse 7 and 8 that the man of sin or lawlessness cannot be revealed until the restrainer is removed.

> For the mystery of lawlessness is already at work; only he who now restrains will do so until he is taken out of the way. And then that lawless one will be revealed whom the Lord

will slay with the breath of His mouth and bring to an end by the appearance of His coming….

It should still be evident to the church today that these two events have not yet taken place, and the blessed hope proclaimed by the Apostle Paul still remains, awaiting fulfillment.

THE ARGUMENT FROM THE 24 ELDERS—REVELATION CHAPTER 4

John opens the Revelation of Jesus Christ with instructions found in Revelation 1:19 which states, "Write therefore the things which you have seen, and the things which are, and the things which shall take place after these things."

John writes about his vision in Chapter 1, the current state of the church in Chapter 2 and 3, then goes on to write Christ's Revelation, prophesying about things to come in the future in Chapters 4 through 22.

As John is invited into heaven in a vision, he sees 24 thrones with 24 Elders sitting on those thrones robed in white, wearing golden crowns, all which represents rewards (Rev. 4:4). The question is, who are these 24 Elders and where did they come from?

The answer lies within the Scriptures themselves, as we see future events starting with Chapter 4, leaving the current period in the past.

It is evident that the 24 Elders exist with Christ before the tribulation period begins, which from a pre-tribulation perspective means they represent the presence of the church in heaven with Christ. This interpretation is supported through four factual points.

1) The song of the redeemed expressed in Revelation 5:8-10 indicate the 24 Elders are redeemed individuals.

2) The Crowns are seen as rewards for service and are tied to the redeemed.

3) The white raiment or garments represents righteous acts of living, tied to the redeemed as expressed in Revelation 19:8.

4) The Elders are also defined in three distinct ways: (i) The Elders are contrasted with angels in Revelation 5:11. (ii) The Elders are seated on thrones (Rev. 4:4), where angels are always standing or moving about. (iii) The Elders are said to be redeemed. (Rev. 5:8-9)

Therefore, the Elders are not angels, nor do they represent anyone from the first resurrection since that takes place at the time of Christ's second coming, which has not occurred yet. This only leaves New Testament saints alive or resurrected at the time of the rapture. It should also be noted that the Elders will be returning with Christ at his Second Advent and are said to be present during the millennium. (Rev. 19:14; Isa. 24:23)

EVENTS IN HEAVEN THAT ARE BETWEEN THE RAPTURE AND THE SECOND ADVENT

Revelation 19:7-11 reveals that the marriage of the Lamb takes place before the Second Advent. John then tells us in verse 14, "And the armies which are in heaven, clothed in fine linen, white and clean, were following Him on white horses." It has already been established that those clothed in white are the redeemed, and in this verse the redeemed are part of God's army ascending on the earth with Christ at his Second Advent.

The point to be noted here is that the marriage of the Lamb takes place before the Second Advent, not during or after, which is an argument opposing a post-tribulation position.

THE ABSENCE OF LANGUAGE

It should be noted there is no explicit mention of the church on earth during the tribulation period, as expressed in Revelation Chapters 4 through 19.

THE DIRECT PROMISE TO THE CHURCH OF DELIVERANCE FROM THE WRATH OF GOD

The wrath of God is a term reserved for the wicked or lost, as described in the Scriptures. The Apostle Paul expresses it this way,

> But because of your stubbornness and unrepentant heart you are storing up wrath for yourself in the day of wrath and revelation of the righteous judgment of God, who will render to every man according to his deeds: to those who by perseverance in doing good seek for glory and honor and immortality, eternal life; but to those who are selfishly ambitious and do not obey the truth, but obey unrighteousness, wrath and indignation.[400]

John the Baptist provides this statement about the religious rulers of his day as they tried to discredit him from the very beginning of his ministry. "But when he saw many of the Pharisees and Sadducees coming for baptism, he said to them, 'You

---

[400] Rom. 2:5-8.

brood of vipers, who warned you to flee from the wrath to come?'" [401]

Some suggest that the wrath of God is subdued through one's salvation, making no provision for any future event involving God's wrath. The context of these Scriptures reflect that God's wrath will be on full display at some future event. Accordingly, the believer or the church is provided the following hope.

"For God has not destined us for wrath, but for obtaining salvation through our Lord Jesus Christ, who died for us, that whether we are awake or asleep, we may live together with Him." (1 Thess. 5:9-10)

"Much more then, having now been justified by His blood, we shall be saved from the wrath of God through Him." (Rom. 5:9)

"Because you have kept the word of My perseverance, I also will keep you from the hour of testing, that hour which is about to come upon the whole world, to test those who dwell upon the earth." (Rev. 3:10)

Revelation 3:10 reflects on the fact that the church will not be part of God's wrath or time of testing that will be poured out on the earth during the tribulation period.

THE NATURE OF THE TRIBULATION PERIOD

The nature of the tribulation period is expressed as the outpouring of God's wrath. Revelation 6:15-17 states:

> And the kings of the earth and the great men and the commanders and the rich and the strong and every slave and free man, hid themselves in the caves and among the rocks of the mountains; and they said to the mountains and to the rocks, 'Fall on us and hide us from the presence of Him who sits on the throne, and

from the wrath of the Lamb; for the great day of their wrath has come; and who is able to stand?'

We read in Revelation 16:19, "And the great city was split into three parts, and the cities of the nations fell. And Babylon the great was remembered before God, to give her the cup of the wine of His fierce wrath." It is evident that God's wrath or anger against sin will come in a physical, not just a spiritual manner. The question in this study is, will the church be part of this period? According to the Scriptures, as interpreted from a dispensational theological perspective, the answer is no!

THE FAILURE OF THE BOOK OF REVELATION TO CONNECT THE RAPTURE WITH THE SECOND ADVENT

The major theme of the book of Revelation is the tribulation period and God's program for carrying out his wrath and judgment on the world. The Second Advent precedes these actions, bringing an end to God's wrath and ushering in the millennial kingdom. Within all these activities the Rapture is never mentioned, and the church is alluded to as already being with Christ, from the beginning of this period as part of God's army. (Rev. 4:4; 19:14)

WHAT HAPPENS AT THE RAPTURE?

Jesus tells his disciples in John 14:2-3 that he is leaving to prepare a place for them in heaven and promises to return. The Apostle Paul informs us in First Corinthians 15:51-57 of a mystery, that we will not all die but will be changed along with the dead in Christ. This is known to the dispensationalist as the rapture, the

[401] Matt. 3:7.

return for the church that he promised in John Chapter 14.

During this event, the living saints will be taken from the earth to heaven in bodily form. The dead in Christ (church saints) will be raised from the dead in bodily form to be with the Lord. This is evident in First Corinthians 15:42-49; 15:53-54, and First John 3:2.

This bodily change for the living and the resurrection of the dead in Christ is not speaking about the Old Testament saints of Daniel Chapter 12, or the tribulation saints spoken of in Revelation Chapter 20. Those resurrections take place at the end of the age, which is at the end of the tribulation period. (Matthew 13:39-40, 49; 24:3)

EVENTS IN HEAVEN FOLLOWING THE RAPTURE OF THE CHURCH

THE JUDGMENT SEAT OF CHRIST

The term "judgment seat" comes from the Greek word bema, which was the platform in Greek towns where orations were made or decisions handed down by rulers (see Matt 27:19; Acts 12:21; 18:12). It was also the place where the awards were given out to the winners in the annual Olympic Games. This "judgment seat" must not be confused with the Great White Throne from which Christ will judge the wicked (Rev 20:11-15). Because of the gracious work of Christ on the cross, believers will not face their sins (John 5:24; Rom. 8:1); but we will have to give an account

of our works and service to the Lord.[402]

The Apostle Paul writes, "For we must all appear before the judgment seat of Christ, that each one may be recompensed for his deeds in the body, according to what he has done, whether good or bad" (2 Cor. 5:10). This concept of judgment for the believer is clarified by Paul in his first letter to the Corinthian church , as he writes,

For we are God's fellow workers; you are God's field, God's building.

According to the grace of God which was given to me, as a wise master builder I laid a foundation, and another is building upon it. But let each man be careful how he builds upon it. For no man can lay a foundation other than the one which is laid, which is Jesus Christ. Now if any man builds upon the foundation with gold, silver, precious stones, wood, hay, straw, each man's work will become evident; for the day will show it, because it is to be revealed with fire; and the fire itself will test the quality of each man's work. If any man's work which he has built upon it remains, he shall receive a reward. If any man's work is burned up, he shall suffer loss; but he himself shall be saved, yet so as through fire.[403]

The time at which the judgment seat of Christ takes place is immediately following the *translation* of the church through the rapture event.

This assessment is based on the following arguments. (i) Luke 14:14 states:

---

[402] Warren W. Wiersbe, "2 Corinthians 5:9-13," in *The Bible Exposition Commentary*.

[403] 1 Cor. 3:9-15.

And He also went on to say to the one who had invited Him, 'When you give a luncheon or a dinner, do not invite your friends or your brothers or your relatives or rich neighbors, lest they also invite you in return, and repayment come to you. But when you give a reception, invite the poor, the crippled, the lame, the blind, and you will be blessed, since they do not have the means to repay you; for you will be repaid at the resurrection of the righteous.'

Jesus tells us that at the *resurrection of the righteous* there will be a time of reward. The principle here is that rewards for the Christian are directly associated with their resurrection. First Thessalonians 4:13-17 ties the Christian's resurrection to the rapture. This then provides a connection between the bema seat and the rapture. (ii) Revelation 19:8-9 states,

And it was given to her to clothe herself in fine linen, bright and clean; for the linen is the righteous acts of the saints. And he said to me, "Write, 'Blessed are those who are invited to the marriage supper of the Lamb.'" And he said to me, 'These are true words of God.'

This passage reflects that the saint's righteous acts have already been recognized and rewarded at the marriage supper of the Lamb. This event takes place before the Second Advent. (iii) First Corinthians 4:5, Revelation 22:12 and Second Timothy 4:8 which reads, "in the future there is laid up for me the crown of righteousness, which the Lord, the righteous Judge, will award to me on that day; and not only to me, but also to all who have loved His appearing." These passages are all associated with the concept that there will be a day of reward and evaluation at the coming of Christ.

When all three arguments are evaluated together, the timeframe of the bema seat judgment fits the context of occurring after the rapture and before the Second Advent.

The place the bema takes place is in the heavenlies. This assessment comes from understanding the relationship of First Thessalonians 4:17 with Revelation 4:4.

The judge presiding over the bema seat is Jesus Christ. (2 Corinthians 5:10-11; John 5:22)

The subjects at the bema seat of Christ will be the *body of Christ* or the *Church*. (2 Corinthians 5:10)

The reasons for the judgment seat of Christ can be seen in four concepts.

1) This event is not to determine whether someone is saved or lost (Revelation 8:1; John 5:24).

2) This event is not to make Christians accountable for their sins (John 5:24; 2 Corinthians 5:10; Romans 8:1; Hebrews 10:1-19).

3) This event is to individually and publicly manifest one's life of service as a believer.

4) This event is to judge the works of the believers to determine whether they are worthy of reward.

The result of this examination at the bema seat is two-fold.

1) The believer's works of service will be judged based on one's motives (1 Corinthians 4:5; James 4:3).

2) The second result is rewards lost (1 Corinthians 3:15).

There are four specific areas mentioned in life that bring about a reward in the New Testament.

1) A reward for practiced self-control over one's life (1 Corinthians 9:24-27).

2) A crown of life for those who persevere under trials (James 1:12).

3) A crown of righteousness for those that love Christ's appearing (2 Timothy 4:8).

4) A crown of glory for those who shepherd the flock of Christ out of correct motives as expressed in First Peter 5:1-5.

THE NATURE AND PURPOSE OF THE REWARDS AT THE JUDGMENT SEAT OF CHRIST.

The purpose for rewards can be seen in Revelation 4:10-11, as the 24 Elders cast their crowns before the throne of the Lord in praise and worship to his glory.

The nature of the rewards is based on Second Peter 1:1-11, where verses 2 through 4 provide the key context to this reality.

> Grace and peace be multiplied to you in the knowledge of God and of Jesus our Lord; seeing that His divine power has granted to us everything pertaining to life and godliness, through the true knowledge of Him who called us by His own glory and excellence. For by these He has granted to us His precious and magnificent promises, in order that by them you might become partakers of the divine nature, having escaped the corruption that is in the world by lust.

The end result of any reward granted is based on God's enabling of the believer through his nature in us.

THE MARRIAGE OF THE LAMB

The marriage of the Lamb is based on the following Scriptures: John 6:39; 2 Corinthians 11:2; Ephesians 5:25-33; Revelation 19:7-9, and Revelation 21:1-22:7.

The time period of the *marriage of the Lamb* is between the rapture and the Second Advent of Christ. This can be seen through the Church's anticipation for this union in Second Corinthians 11:2, and the reunion taking place before the Second Advent spoken of in Revelation 19:7, and after the bema seat spoken of in Revelation Chapter 19.

The place of the *marriage of the Lamb* is in heaven. The church is seen returning to earth with Christ at the Second Advent in Revelation 19:7-14. This fits the concept presented by the Apostle Paul as he writes,

> For our citizenship is in heaven, from which also we eagerly wait for a Savior, the Lord Jesus Christ; who will transform the body of our humble state into conformity with the body of His glory, by the exertion of the power that He has even to subject all things to Himself.[404]

The participants in the marriage are Christ and the Church. This is evident in Second Corinthians 11:2.

It should be noted that Israel (O. T. Saints) are not part of this event nor are those who come out of the tribulation period. This is because neither will be

---

[404] Phil. 3:20-21.

resurrected until the Second Advent. This can be seen in Daniel 12:1-3, 11-13; Isaiah 26:19-21, and Revelation 20:4-6.

The distinction between the marriage and the marriage supper can be seen in the context in which they are presented. As stated before, the marriage of the Lamb takes place in heaven, consummating the relationship between Christ and his body—the Church. The marriage supper is an event on earth involving Israel and the saints who come out of the tribulation period as participants, and takes place after the Second Advent, symbolizing the Kingdom itself. This can be seen in Matthew 22:1-14; Luke 14:16-24, and Matthew 25:1-13.

It should be noted that there are some who hold that the marriage supper takes place before the Second Advent.

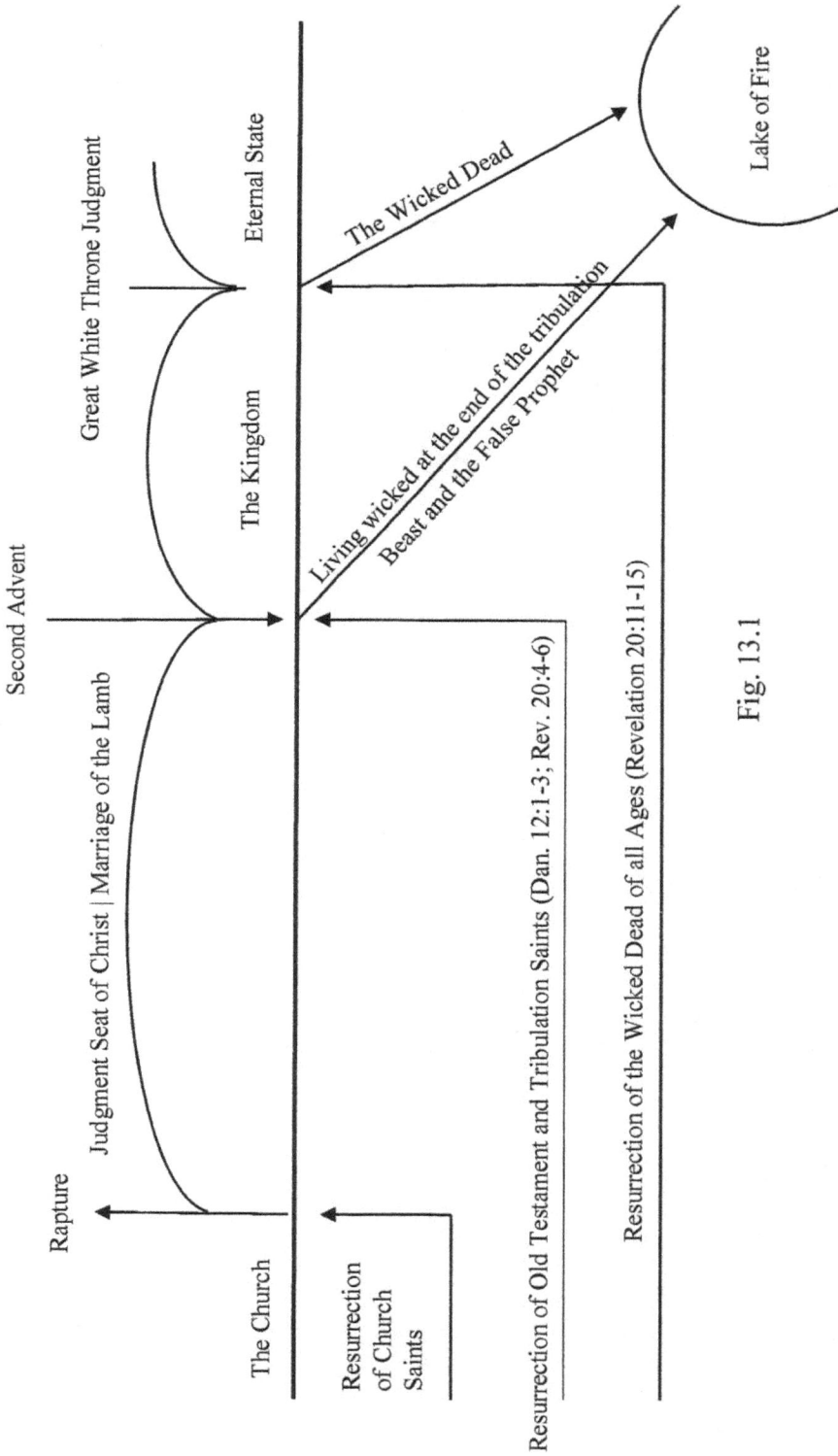

Fig. 13.1

CHAPTER FOURTEEN

The Second Advent and Related Events

JUDGMENTS ASSOCIATED WITH THE SECOND ADVENT

BACKGROUND ON BIBLICAL JUDGMENTS

The Apostle Paul spoke to the people of Athens about their culture and how they recognized an unknown God, who he introduced to them as the creator of all things, and is now making himself known to clear up their ignorance. Paul then makes this declaration to them,

> Therefore having overlooked the times of ignorance, God is now declaring to men that all everywhere should repent, because He has fixed a day in which He will judge the world in righteousness through a Man whom He has appointed, having furnished proof to all men by raising Him from the dead.[405]

This declaration of Pauls' is supported by the Psalmist who wrote,

> Say among the nations, 'The Lord reigns; Indeed, the world is firmly established, it will not be moved; He will judge the peoples with equity.'

Let the heavens be glad, and let the earth rejoice; Let the sea roar, and all it contains; Let the field exult, and all that is in it. Then all the trees of the forest will sing for joy Before the Lord, for He is coming; For He is coming to judge the earth. He will judge the world in righteousness, And the peoples in His faithfulness.[406]

The message of Paul and the Psalmist is simply this, God is righteous and just, and has sole authority over his creation, and has appointed Jesus Christ, his only Son to have the final say regarding the final judgment on the world.

The Scriptures speak about many types of judgments within its own writings. Therefore, a survey may be the best approach to bring a better understanding to this subject matter.

Some judgments are brought by a judge while others are self-imposed. But in the end, judgments all serve the same purpose, to correct wrong action based on God's standards or to punish the guilty and provide justice to the wronged.

Within the context of the Scriptures regarding eschatology, the guilty are all of humanity along with Satan and his angels, and the wronged is God himself.

---

[405] Acts 17:30-31.

[406] Ps. 96:10-13.

The past and current judgments within Scripture are explained in the following manner.

Within the context of the study of eschatology, the New Testament provides a record of the foundational judgment that provides the standard to understanding all other judgments to follow. This judgment took place on a cross at Calvary over 2,000 years ago, when Christ was crucified unto death, then three days later arose again through his resurrection. The purpose of this judgment unto death was to pay the penalty for all of humanity's sins, thus satisfying God's righteousness and reconciling a Holy God to his creation. The reason for this judgment on Christ is expressed as follows:

> Therefore, just as through one man sin entered into the world, and death through sin, and so death spread to all men, because all sinned — for until the Law sin was in the world; but sin is not imputed when there is no law. Nevertheless death reigned from Adam until Moses, even over those who had not sinned in the likeness of the offense of Adam, who is a type of Him who was to come. But the free gift is not like the transgression. For if by the transgression of the one the many died, much more did the grace of God and the gift by the grace of the one Man, Jesus Christ, abound to the many. And the gift is not like that which came through the one who sinned; for on the one hand the judgment arose from one transgression resulting in condemnation, but on the other hand the free gift arose from many transgressions resulting in justification.[407]

By Christ taking humanity's punishment for sin, God's judgment resulted in humanity having the opportunity to be justified before God, resulting in reconciliation between God and his creation (2 Corinthians 5:18-19).

It is through Christ's actions on behalf of his creation that all other judgments are justified and right. This past judgment provides the context to all other future judgment activity.

As Christians, we are told to judge ourselves so God will have no need to judge us later. These type of judgments have nothing to do with condemnation of the soul (Romans 8:1), but are to bring the Christian's life in line with God's Holiness in reconciliation for fellowship. This can be seen in First Corinthians 11:28-31.

> But let a man examine himself, and so let him eat of the bread and drink of the cup. For he who eats and drinks, eats and drinks judgment to himself, if he does not judge the body rightly. For this reason many among you are weak and sick, and a number sleep. But if we judged ourselves rightly, we should not be judged.

This concept is better understood through the writer of Hebrews 12:1-8 as he writes,

> Therefore, since we have so great a cloud of witnesses surrounding us, let us also lay aside every encumbrance, and the sin which so easily entangles us, and let us run with endurance the race that is set before us, fixing our eyes on Jesus,

---

[407] Rom. 5:12-16.

the author and perfecter of faith, who for the joy set before Him endured the cross, despising the shame, and has sat down at the right hand of the throne of God. For consider Him who has endured such hostility by sinners against Himself, so that you may not grow weary and lose heart. You have not yet resisted to the point of shedding blood in your striving against sin; and you have forgotten the exhortation which is addressed to you as sons,

'My son, do not regard lightly the discipline of the Lord, Nor faint when you are reproved by Him; For those whom the Lord loves He disciplines, And He scourges every son whom He receives.'

It is for discipline that you endure; God deals with you as with sons; for what son is there whom his father does not discipline? But if you are without discipline, of which all have become partakers, then you are illegitimate children and not sons.

The Scriptures go on to speak about future judgments for both the believer and unbeliever. Seven judgments are spoken of in the Scriptures and they are listed as follows:

1) The judgment on the believer's works at the judgment seat of Christ (1 Corinthians 3:11-15).

2) The judgment of the anti-Christ and his forces at the Second Advent (2 Thessalonians 2:3-11; Revelation 19:19-20).

3) The judgment of the living nation of Israel (Ezekiel 20:37-38; Zechariah 13:8-9).

4) The judgment of the living gentile nations (Matthew 25:37-38; Isaiah 34:1-2; Joel 3:1-2).

5) The judgment on the fallen angels (Jude 6; 1 Corinthians 6:3). This judgment will take place on that *great day*, which is the same as *the day of the Lord*. The place is unknown, and the details are unclear, but the Scriptures tell us that in some way the saints will have a part in pronouncing these judgments.

6) The judgment of Satan through his being bound for 1,000 years, then at the end his final sentence will be pronounced and he will be thrown into the Lake of Fire (Revelation 20:1-3, 10).

7) The judgment of the Great White Throne (Revelation 20:11-15).

SPECIFIC JUDGMENTS AT THE SECOND ADVENT

THE JUDGMENT ON THE ANTI-CHRIST AND HIS FORCES

God's judgment on the anti-Christ and his forces are seen through God's wrath, as demonstrated in Revelation 6:15-17; 1 Thessalonians 5:1-3; 2 Thessalonians 2:8-10, and then by fire for all of eternity, as spoken of in Revelation 19:20-21; 20:10.

THE JUDGMENT ON THE LIVING NATION OF ISRAEL

There are many who can claim Abraham as their father, but the people referenced here are the descendants of Isaac, the only son of Abraham through Sarah. And from this group there will be a small remnant judged worthy to enter into the promised Kingdom. This is partially evident through the choosing of the 144,000 Jewish witnesses at the mid-point of the tribulation period. Paul's explanation of who the remnant are is expressed this way:

> But it is not as though the word of God has failed. For they are not all Israel who are descended from Israel; neither are they all children because they are Abraham's descendants, but: 'through Isaac your descendants will be named.' That is, it is not the children of the flesh who are children of God, but the children of the promise are regarded as descendants.[408]

Paul goes on to quote the prophet Isaiah as he writes,

> And Isaiah cries out concerning Israel, 'Though the number of the sons of Israel be as the sand of the sea, it is the remnant that will be saved; for the Lord will execute His word upon the earth, thoroughly and quickly.'[409]

J. Dwight Pentecost (Th.D.) provides some insight as to the timeframe of this judgment, gleaned from Matthew Chapters 24 and 25. Matthew 24:4-26 speaks to the tribulation period. Matthew 24:27-30 speaks to Christ's Second Advent. Matthew 24:31 speaks to the regathering of Israel. Matthew 25:1-30 speaks to the judgment of Israel. Matthew 25:31-46 speaks to the judgment on the Gentiles. Then finally the millennial kingdom is established.[410]

This judgment takes place in the wilderness of the people, which is symbolic of where God's judgment on Israel had taken place in the past. This is expressed through Israel's prophets as they have written in Zechariah 14:4-5 and Ezekiel 20:34-38.

The prophet Ezekiel tells us who will enter the kingdom as he writes,

> And I shall make you pass under the rod, and I shall bring you into the bond of the covenant; and I shall purge from you the rebels and those who transgress against Me; I shall bring them out of the land where they sojourn, but they will not enter the land of Israel. Thus you will know that I am the Lord.[411]

Jesus provides an analogy through parables, indicating which Israelites will not be entering the millennial kingdom in Matthew 25:1-30.

The reason for this judgment is to separate the true sons of Abraham from the false ones. This concept is expressed in Malachi 3:2-5 which reads,

> But who can endure the day of His coming? And who can stand when He appears? For He is like a refiner's fire and like fullers' soap. And He will sit as a smelter and purifier of silver, and He will purify the sons of Levi and refine them like gold and silver, so that they may present to the Lord offerings in righteousness. Then the offering of Judah and Jerusalem will be pleasing to the Lord, as in the days of old and as in former years. Then I will draw near to you for judgment; and I will be a swift witness against the

---

[408] Rom. 9:6-8.
[409] Rom. 9:27-29.

[410] Pentecost, *Things to Come*, 413.
[411] Ezek. 20:37-38.

sorcerers and against the adulterers and against those who swear falsely, and against those who oppress the wage earner in his wages, the widow and the orphan, and those who turn aside the alien, and do not fear Me, says the Lord of hosts.

The tribulation period will not only be used to drive Israel to their God but to test Israel to see who is, and who is not a true son of Abraham at the judgment before the King.

THE JUDGMENT ON THE LIVING GENTILES

This Judgment occurs for those gentiles who survived the tribulation period. The time of this judgment comes after the judging of the Jews who also survived the tribulation, but before the millennial kingdom. This is tied to the concept of the *brethren* mentioned in Matthew Chapter 25, within the context of Matthew 25:31-46 (key verse 40) and Joel 3:1-2.

Warren W. Wiersbe helps clarify this by commenting,

> If we keep in mind the three groups in the account, it will help to solve this problem: There were sheep, goats, and brethren. Who are these people that the King dares to call "My brethren"? It seems likely that they are the believing Jews from the Tribulation period. These are people who will hear the message of the 144,000 and trust Jesus Christ. Since these believing Jews will not receive the "mark of the beast" (Rev 13:16-17), they will be unable to buy

or sell. How, then, can they survive? Through the loving care of the Gentiles who have trusted Christ and who care for His brethren.[412]

This judgment takes place on the earth as Matthew 25:31-32 suggests: "But when the Son of Man comes in His glory, and all the angels with Him, then He will sit on His glorious throne. And all the nations will be gathered before Him...." The prophet Joel states in Joel 3:2, 12 that this event will take place in the valley of Jehoshaphat. Zechariah 14:4 speaks of a very large valley that Christ will stand near as he comes and stands on the Mount of Olives.

Jamieson, Fausset and Brown make the observation that the valley of Jehoshaphat is also known as the valley of blessing (2 Chronicles 20:26), an expanse between the Mount of Olives and Jerusalem, and it carries a history of victory (2 Chronicles 20:21-22, 26), foreshadowing Jerusalem's final victory over all her enemies. They also point out that *Jehoshaphat* means *the judgment of Yahweh*, which may be used in general terms to express that this place will be the final judgment of Israel's foes.[413]

The subjects of this judgment are the living gentiles. The term used is *nations* ἔθνη (éthnee) and is translated thirty-seven times in the KJV New Testament. This term is not referring to governments, but rather groups of individuals representing ethnicities worldwide who are foreign to the Jewish people.

The basis of this judgment seems to be one's faith through action, as the Lord explains his decision will be based on how individuals treated his brethren in life, that

[412] Warren W. Wiersbe, "Matthew 24:45-25:30," in *The Bible Exposition Commentary*.

[413] *A Commentary Critical, Experimental, and Practical On The Old and New Testaments*, s.v. "Joel 3:2," by Jamieson, Fausset, and Brown (S.S.

Scranton, Hartford, 1877); reprint, *Jamieson, Fausset, and Brown Commentary* (Grand Rapids: William B. Eerdmans Publishing Company, 1993) [Electronic Database]; available from Biblesoft, Inc.

is, how the gentiles as individuals treated the Jews during the tribulation period (Matthew 25:40,45). This should not be seen as a salvation by works, but faith demonstrated by one's works. Jesus expressed the concept this way:

> You will know them by their fruits. Grapes are not gathered from thorn bushes, nor figs from thistles, are they? Even so, every good tree bears good fruit; but the bad tree bears bad fruit. A good tree cannot produce bad fruit, nor can a bad tree produce good fruit. Every tree that does not bear good fruit is cut down and thrown into the fire. So then, you will know them by their fruits. Not everyone who says to Me, 'Lord, Lord,' will enter the kingdom of heaven; but he who does the will of My Father who is in heaven. Many will say to Me on that day, 'Lord, Lord, did we not prophesy in Your name, and in Your name cast out demons, and in Your name perform many miracles?' And then I will declare to them, 'I never knew you; depart from Me, you who practice lawlessness.' [414]

The result of this judgment can be seen through the separation of the sheep and the goats. The sheep are granted eternal life with Christ and the goats are cast into the lake of fire, which is the same place the beast and false prophet reside at this point and where the devil and his angels will end up (Matthew 25:41; Revelation 19:20; 20:10). At this point in time, all those deemed as sheep and brethren will move into the millennial kingdom, while all those who remain alive and deemed to be goats will receive their final punishment, which is the Lake of Fire. For the living wicked this is their final judgment, bypassing the great white throne judgment.

RESURRECTIONS ASSOCIATED WITH THE SECOND ADVENT

THE RESURRECTION PROGRAM

God's program for how and when he will resurrect the dead is explained in First Corinthians 15:20-24.

> But now Christ has been raised from the dead, the first fruits of those who are asleep. For since by a man came death, by a man also came the resurrection of the dead. For as in Adam all die, so also in Christ all shall be made alive. But each in his own order: Christ the first fruits, after that those who are Christ's at His coming, then comes the end, when He delivers up the kingdom to the God and Father, when He has abolished all rule and all authority and power.

We see here that the resurrections come in an orderly fashion in their own timeframe. Starting with the reason for all resurrections, Christ himself being the first fruits, followed by the resurrection of the dead in Christ at his coming (rapture), then comes the resurrection of Old Testament Saints at the Second Advent. Finally, we see all the remaining souls of the living and the dead standing before Christ at the end of the millennium at the Great White Throne Judgment (Revelation 20:11-15).

The Apostle Paul goes on to explain some concepts behind the resurrections in First Corinthians 15:35-49.

---

[414] Matt. 7:16-23.

The sequence of resurrection events are as follows.

THE FIRST RESURRECTION— THREE ASPECTS

The first resurrection should not be confused with the resurrection *unto life,* as referenced in John 5:29. Within the context of John Chapter 5, Jesus is making the point that he has the authority and power to *resurrect to life* all souls, either to eternal life or to eternal damnation. For Christ to make this point makes perfect sense since the Sadducees of Christ's day did not believe in the resurrection of the dead, and the Jews were challenging his authority as the Son of God.

As to the initial aspect of the *first resurrection*, its purpose is partly based on Hebrews Chapter 11, which is a testimony to the faith of Old Testament saints, who in the end, never received what was promised. "And all these, having gained approval through their faith, did not receive what was promised, because God had provided something better for us, so that apart from us they should not be made perfect" (Hebrews 11:39).

Now, because of Christ's resurrection and Second Advent, these Old Testament saints can finally obtain what was promised them through the Abrahamic and Davidic Covenants, on top of eternal life through the New Covenant, which is what Paul was referencing when he said, "because God had provided something better." All this starts for them through the first resurrection of the dead, just before they enter into the millennial kingdom (Revelation 20:6).

The second aspect to the *first resurrection* is found in Daniel 12:1-2 and Isaiah 26:19-21, which speaks to the resurrection and judgment of the rest of Israel, which will be based on God's written records from their historical beginning that started with Abraham and his wife Sarah. This can be seen through a reading of Daniel 12:1-2.

> Now at that time Michael, the great prince who stands guard over the sons of your people, will arise. And there will be a time of distress such as never occurred since there was a nation until that time; and at that time your people, everyone who is found written in the book, will be rescued. And many of those who sleep in the dust of the ground will awake, these to everlasting life, but the others to disgrace and everlasting contempt.

The context of this passage suggests that Daniel's prophecy is directed to the nation of Israel. The time of distress is the tribulation period, and this resurrection and judgment refers to the Nation of Israel and not to any other gentile entity.

The third aspect is found in Revelation 20:4-5, which speaks to the resurrection of all the saints, both Jew and gentile, who died during the tribulation period.

These three aspects make up the first resurrection, and most likely occurs in some sequential order after the tribulation and Second Advent, just before the beginning of the millennial kingdom.

THE RE-ESTABLISHMENT OF THE DAVIDIC KINGDOM

The Davidic Kingdom was promised by an eternal covenant in Second Samuel Chapter 7, which reinforced the Abrahamic Covenant that promised the deed to the land it would reside on.

The book of Amos was written around (760-753 B.C.), when the prophet writes,

> 'In that day I will raise up the fallen booth of David, And wall up

its breaches; I will also raise up its ruins, And rebuild it as in the days of old; That they may possess the remnant of Edom And all the nations who are called by My name,' Declares the Lord who does this.

Behold, 'days are coming,' declares the Lord, 'When the plowman will overtake the reaper And the treader of grapes him who sows seed; When the mountains will drip sweet wine, And all the hills will be dissolved. Also I will restore the captivity of My people Israel, And they will rebuild the ruined cities and live in them, They will also plant vineyards and drink their wine, And make gardens and eat their fruit. I will also plant them on their land, And they will not again be rooted out from their land Which I have given them,' Says the Lord your God.[415]

Since this prophecy occurred before the nation's captivity or the destruction of its cities, how do we know what period fits this prophecy? Was not Israel reestablished as a nation in 1948? The answer lies with the reestablishment of the Davidic kingdom or the rule by a king. Luke 1:31-33 states,

And behold, you will conceive in your womb, and bear a son, and you shall name Him Jesus. He will be great, and will be called the Son of the Most High; and the Lord God will give Him the throne of His father David; and He will reign over the house of Jacob forever; and His kingdom will have no end.

It is evident from this passage that the reestablishment of the Davidic kingdom will all be under Christ as its final King.

Another point that should be noted is, Israel today does not possess anywhere near all the land Abraham was promised in Genesis 15:18-21. This leaves Amos' prophecy still future.

THE SPIRITUAL REVIVAL OF ISRAEL

The spiritual revival of the Nation comes through the New Covenant found in Jeremiah 31:31-34. The Apostle Paul explains it this way:

For I do not want you, brethren, to be uninformed of this mystery, lest you be wise in your own estimation, that a partial hardening has happened to Israel until the fulness of the Gentiles has come in; and thus all Israel will be saved; just as it is written,

The Deliverer will come from Zion,
He will remove ungodliness from Jacob.
And this is My covenant with them,
When I take away their sins.

From the standpoint of the gospel they are enemies for your sake, but from the standpoint of God's choice they are beloved for the sake of the fathers; for the gifts and the calling of God are irrevocable.

The prophet Ezekiel clarifies this mystery by his pronouncement found in Ezekiel 39:25-29 which reads,

Therefore thus says the Lord God, Now I shall restore the fortunes of Jacob, and have mercy on the whole house of Israel; and I shall be jealous for My holy name.

---

[415] Amos 9:11-15.

And they shall forget their disgrace and all their treachery which they perpetrated against Me, when they live securely on their own land with no one to make them afraid. When I bring them back from the peoples and gather them from the lands of their enemies, then I shall be sanctified through them in the sight of the many nations. Then they will know that I am the Lord their God because I made them go into exile among the nations, and then gathered them again to their own land; and I will leave none of them there any longer. And I will not hide My face from them any longer, for I shall have poured out My Spirit on the house of Israel," declares the Lord God.

The fulfillment of this prophecy will take place during the millennium, since this will be the only time they will not be afraid of other nations, and they as a nation will collectively recognize their God and King.

A JUDGMENT ON SATAN

Revelation 20:1-3 describes Satan's temporary imprisonment for a 1,000 year period, then will be released for a short time to wage the final war on God.

CHAPTER FIFTEEN

The Millennium and Beyond

THE PURPOSE OF THE MILLENNIUM

The millennium period serves three purposes. One, to fulfill God's promises he established in the Abrahamic, Davidic and New Covenants (Genesis Chapters 12, 15, 17; 2 Samuel Chapter 7; Jeremiah Chapter 31). Second, to uphold God's truthfulness of his words as pronounced in all his ordained prophecies concerning Israel, the church, and all that pertains to God's plan for his creation to the end of the age. Moses records it this way, "God is not a man, that He should lie, Nor a son of man, that He should repent; Has He said, and will He not do it? Or has He spoken, and will He not make it good?" [416] The Apostle Paul testifies to God's character in a greeting to Titus as he writes, "In hope of eternal life, which God, that cannot lie, promised before the world began…." (Titus 1:2; KJV).

The concept that God cannot lie is critical to an understanding of God and his purposes. If there is no millennium in the form of a literal 1,000 years and God does not honor his covenants made to Israel, then God would be a liar and the trustworthiness of the Scripture would be in serious question.

If the millennial age is not meant to come to pass in a literal format, then why did God send the angel Gabriel to Mary with the following proclamation?

And the angel said to her, "Do not be afraid, Mary; for you have found favor with God. And behold, you will conceive in your womb, and bear a son, and you shall name Him Jesus. He will be great, and will be called the Son of the Most High; and the Lord God will give Him the throne of His father David; and He will reign over the house of Jacob forever; and His kingdom will have no end. [417]

The millennial kingdom represents the throne of David and the house of Jacob, to which Christ will be its final King. The purpose? To fulfill the covenant promise to his servant and friend, King David (2 Sam. 7:13; 1 Chron. 28:7; Ps. 89:35-37; Isa. 9:7). It should also be noted that David, as one of the resurrected Old Testament saints, will be part of this kingdom. And according to Revelation 20:6, he will be a priest and reign with Christ, among others. Ezekiel 37:25 states, "and David My servant shall be their prince forever." This supports Isaiah as he writes, "Behold, a king will reign righteously, And princes will rule justly. And each will be like a refuge from the wind, And a shelter of water in a dry

---

[416] Num. 23:19.

[417] Luke 1:30-33.

country, Like the shade of a huge rock in a parched land." [418]

The third purpose of the millennium is to demonstrate that man in his natural state is indeed totally depraved. This is reflected at the end of the millennial period, as the nations led by Satan will commence war on the current saints on the earth, just as Revelation 20:7-9 expresses it.

This rebellion takes place after God establishes a perfect government and a perfect environment for 1,000 years.

Who are the saints Satan will wage war on? First, the saints expressed in Revelation 20:6, as it states, "Blessed and holy is the one who has a part in the first resurrection; over these the second death has no power, but they will be priests of God and of Christ and will reign with Him for a thousand years." And second, those who survived the tribulation period and entered into the millennial kingdom alive.

The church saints will be present, not in mortal bodies but in glorified bodies, as they have been raptured and came back with Christ at his Second Advent.

Another question that should be asked is, who will be the ones Satan is leading to war, if all who entered the millennial kingdom are God's saints? The only possible answer could be, the unrepentant children and subsequent descendants of the original saints (Isa. 11:8) who entered the kingdom still in their mortal bodies.

THE RELATIONSHIP OF CHRIST TO THE MILLENNIUM

CHRIST AS KING

The Apostle Paul tells us the following concerning Christ and his kingdom.

For as in Adam all die, so also in Christ all shall be made alive. But each in his own order: Christ the first fruits, after that those who are Christ's at His coming, then comes the end, when He delivers up the kingdom to the God and Father, when He has abolished all rule and all authority and power. For He must reign until He has put all His enemies under His feet. The last enemy that will be abolished is death.[419]

The Apostle John writes, "And the seventh angel sounded; and there arose loud voices in heaven, saying, 'The kingdom of the world has become the kingdom of our Lord, and of His Christ; and He will reign forever and ever.'"[420]

These statements of the Apostles are supported by the Old Testament prophet Daniel who wrote,

I kept looking in the night visions, And behold, with the clouds of heaven One like a Son of Man was coming, And He came up to the Ancient of Days And was presented before Him. And to Him was given dominion, Glory and a kingdom, That all the peoples, nations, and men of every language Might serve Him. His dominion is an everlasting dominion Which will not pass away; And His kingdom is one Which will not be destroyed.[421]

CHRIST WILL BE MANIFESTED

The Old Testament prophets showed through their writings who would be magnified over the kingdom. Isaiah writes, "Then the moon will be abashed and the

---

[418] Isa. 32:1-2.
[419] 1 Cor. 15:22-26.

[420] Rev. 11:15.
[421] Dan. 7:13-14.

sun ashamed, For the Lord of hosts will reign on Mount Zion and in Jerusalem, And His glory will be before His elders." [422] Jeremiah continues this theme as he writes, "In His days Judah will be saved, And Israel will dwell securely; And this is His name by which He will be called, The Lord our righteousness." [423]

CHARACTERISTICS OF THE MILLENNIUM

THE PHYSICAL CHARACTERISTICS OF THE KINGDOM

And the wolf will dwell with the lamb, And the leopard will lie down with the kid, And the calf and the young lion and the fatling together; And a little boy will lead them. Also the cow and the bear will graze; Their young will lie down together; And the lion will eat straw like the ox. And the nursing child will play by the hole of the cobra, And the weaned child will put his hand on the viper's den. They will not hurt or destroy in all My holy mountain, For the earth will be full of the knowledge of the Lord As the waters cover the sea.[424]

There are several characteristics listed that we need to expand on. First, the world will be at peace, as demonstrated through the relationship of all the animals. There are no longer adversarial roles among the animals. They are all peaceful, even toward human life (Hosea 2:18; Ezekiel 34:25; Romans 14:17). Second, there will be human birth and children in this kingdom. This is significant because Jesus tells us, "For in the resurrection they neither marry, nor are given in marriage, but are like angels in heaven." [425] This tells us that those who died and have been resurrected or changed through the rapture will never have children again. Therefore, only those who lived through the tribulation period and remain in their mortal bodies as they enter the millennial kingdom will be able to procreate. Third, there is water covering the sea. This is significant because by the time the New Heaven and New Earth come on the scene, the Apostle John tells us there will be no more sea, as he writes, "And I saw a new heaven and a new earth; for the first heaven and the first earth passed away, and there is no longer any sea." (Revelation 21:1).

All these characteristics describe the millennial period and tells us that it must be of a different time and place from the eternal state; unless of course, one chooses to interpret these verses through spiritualization or allegorizing these passages to come to a different conclusion. Otherwise, from a common-sense literal perspective, this interpretation is the most consistent with Scripture as a whole.

Another item of conjecture is, will the mortal and the spiritual intermingle and live among one another? This is hard to say, one thing we do know is the roles the spiritual beings will play, and that is as judges and priests. Therefore, it is most likely those in spiritual bodies will serve God at the tabernacle or as part of the governing body under the King.

One last item to be talked about are the physical cities, and yes the temple with all it brings to the discussion, such as the sacrifices that will take place there. This is, and will be, the most controversial element to a dispensational theology. The question is, how should it be approached? The

---

[422] Isa. 24:23.
[423] Jer. 23:6.

[424] Isa. 11:6-9.
[425] Matt. 22:30.

answer is, in the same manner as the rest of its theology, from a Historical-grammatical perspective.

The simplest place to begin is with the prophet Jeremiah as he writes,

> In those days Judah shall be saved, and Jerusalem shall dwell in safety; and this is the name by which she shall be called: the Lord is our righteousness. For thus says the Lord, 'David shall never lack a man to sit on the throne of the house of Israel; and the Levitical priests shall never lack a man before Me to offer burnt offerings, to burn grain offerings, and to prepare sacrifices continually.' [426]

It is obvious from this passage and others that a temple that includes sacrifices are on God's agenda (Ezek. 43:18-46:24; Isa. 56:7; 66:20-23; Zech. 14:16-21). Therefore, in our understanding of current theological perspectives, how should this be viewed in light of Christ and his sacrifice, which is stated to be once and for all (Heb. 7:27; 9:12).

John Walvoord offers this observation:

> Those that consider the millennial sacrifices as a ritual which will be literally observed in the millennium invest the sacrifices with the central meaning of a memorial looking back to the one offering of Christ. The millennial sacrifices are no more expiatory than were the Mosaic sacrifices which preceded the Cross. If it has been fitting for the church on the present age to have a memorial of the death of Christ in the Lord's Supper, it is suggested that it would be suitable also to have a memorial of possibly

a different character in the millennium in keeping with the Jewish characteristics of the period. [427]

It needs to be remembered that the kingdom is set up for the Jewish people as part of their promised inheritance. The temple is God's, and he has prepared it beforehand to be a place on earth for them (Ezek. 40:1-46:24). The scripture states that all those in the first resurrection will be God's representatives in the kingdom as priests. Throughout history God's temple always included priests, and there is no such thing as a temple without priests and sacrifices offered up to God. Within God's kingdom these sacrifices are not offered to cover sin, but to honor and please God as he himself instructs and requires as part of the worship experience. Who is mankind to say this cannot be so? When clearly God expected other types of offerings in honor of himself.

Another term for *offerings* is *sacrifices*. When we hear this term we immediately think in terms of atonement for sin, but with further research we learn the following:

> SACRIFICE—Sacrifice is thus a complex and comprehensive term. In its simplest form it may be defined as "a gift to God." It is a presentation to Deity of some material object, the possession of the offerer, as an act of worship.... it may be... a prayer, an expression of dependence, obligation and thanksgiving. It may express repentance, faith, adoration, or all of these combined. It was the one and only way of approach to God. Theophrastus defines it as

---

[426] Jer. 33:16-18.

[427] Walvoord, *The Millennial Kingdom*, 311-312.

expressing homage, gratitude and need.[428]

It is clear from this view that the temple sacrifices during the tribulation and millennial periods do not necessarily represent blood attornment offerings for sin.

From within the Scriptures, they could offer another view concerning the temple during the tribulation. Based on past Jewish heritage, the Jews set up temple sacrifices continuing with Mosaic Law practices, but for the first three and a half years the Scriptures state no one repents (Rev. 9:20-21), then at the midpoint, the prince in Daniel 9 desecrates the temple and God moves away from the temple scene to 144,000 Jewish witnesses sealed from harm as they proclaim the gospel of the Kingdom with Jesus as the Messiah. From this point forward, the temple sacrifices become a moot point for the remaining three and a half years during this time of testing. The discussion concerning a temple presence will continue later in this chapter.

THE SPIRITUAL CHARACTERISTICS OF THE MILLENNIUM

> Then a shoot will spring from the stem of Jesse, And a branch from his roots will bear fruit. And the Spirit of the Lord will rest on Him, The spirit of wisdom and understanding, The spirit of counsel and strength, The spirit of knowledge and the fear of the Lord. And He will delight in the fear of the Lord, And He will not judge by what His eyes see, Nor make a decision by what His ears hear; But with righteousness He will judge the poor, And decide with fairness for the afflicted of the earth; And He will strike the earth with the rod of His mouth, And with the breath of His lips He will slay the wicked. Also righteousness will be the belt about His loins, And faithfulness the belt about His waist.[429]

This is the spirit by which Christ will rule the kingdom, steeped in righteousness, wisdom, knowledge, strength and faithfulness to his own holy nature. The spiritual atmosphere will be one of righteousness (Matthew 25:37; Isaiah 60:21 and Psalm 72:7); of obedience (Jeremiah 31:33-34; Psalm 110:1-3); of holiness (Zechariah 14:20; Joel 3:17); of truth (John 14:6; Psalm 85:10; Zechariah 8:3), and full of the Holy Spirit (Ezekiel 36:27; 37:14; Jeremiah 31:33).

THE GOVERNMENT OF THE MILLENNIUM

THE FORM OF GOVERNMENT

A theocratic monarchy would be the best way to describe the kingdom's governance model. God, through Christ will be the ruling king and final authority on all matters. Revelation 11:15 states: "And the seventh angel sounded; and there arose loud voices in heaven, saying, 'The kingdom of the world has become the kingdom of our Lord, and of His Christ; and He will reign forever and ever.'" Isaiah proclaims,

> For a child will be born to us, a son will be given to us; And the government will rest on His

---

[428] *International Standard Bible Encyclopaedia*, s.v. "Sacrifice," In the Old Testament, I. Terms and Definitions [Electronic Database]; available from Biblesoft, Inc.

[429] Isa. 11:1-5.

shoulders; And His name will be called Wonderful Counselor, Mighty God, Eternal Father, Prince of Peace. There will be no end to the increase of His government or of peace, On the throne of David and over his kingdom, To establish it and to uphold it with justice and righteousness From then on and forevermore. The zeal of the Lord of hosts will accomplish this.[430]

Isaiah later writes, "For the Lord is our judge, The Lord is our lawgiver, The Lord is our king; He will save us."[431] These proclamations tell us that the kingdom's government will be centered on one person, who will be the final authority on judicial, legislative and executive matters of the kingdom, and that person will be Jesus Christ the Son of God.

THE NATURE OF THE GOVERNMENT

The nature of the government will be universal. That is, it will include governance over all nations and people. The prophet Daniel writes,

And to Him was given dominion, Glory and a kingdom, That all the peoples, nations, and men of every language Might serve Him. His dominion is an everlasting dominion Which will not pass away; And His kingdom is one Which will not be destroyed.[432]

The nature of the government will be righteous and just. Isaiah writes,

And He will delight in the fear of the Lord, And He will not judge by

what His eyes see, Nor make a decision by what His ears hear; But with righteousness He will judge the poor, And decide with fairness for the afflicted of the earth; And He will strike the earth with the rod of His mouth, And with the breath of His lips He will slay the wicked. Also righteousness will be the belt about His loins, And faithfulness the belt about His waist.[433]

The government will show lovingkindness based in truth toward those it governs. Isaiah reflects this as he writes, "And in mercy shall the throne be established: and he shall sit upon it in truth in the tabernacle of David, judging, and seeking judgment, and hasting righteousness." [434] The Psalmist writes, "Righteousness and justice are the foundation of Thy throne; Lovingkindness and truth go before Thee.[435]

The government will govern with an attitude of wisdom, understanding and knowledge. Isaiah states,

And the Spirit of the Lord will rest on Him, The spirit of wisdom and understanding, The spirit of counsel and strength, The spirit of knowledge and the fear of the Lord. And He will delight in the fear of the Lord, And He will not judge by what His eyes see, Nor make a decision by what His ears hear....[436]

While at the same time the government will rule with a rod of iron and will do away with the wicked. The prophet writes, "But with righteousness He will judge the poor, And decide with fairness for the afflicted of

---

[430] Isa. 9:6-7.
[431] Isa. 33:22.
[432] Dan. 7:14.
[433] Isa. 11:3-5.

[434] Isa. 16:5 KJV (King James Version).
[435] Ps. 89:14.
[436] Isa. 11:2-3.

the earth; And He will strike the earth with the rod of His mouth, And with the breath of His lips He will slay the wicked."[437]

THE PARTICIPANT MAKEUP OF THE GOVERNMENT

Throughout the historical record of the Scriptures, the millennial kingdom has been prophesied to be a place of peace, righteousness, and holy before God and designed for Israel's restoration, safety and a place of worship of their God. Other nations associated with the kingdom are said to be welcomed at the table, as the nation of Israel was to be a priestly nation—a testimony to the world. How do we know all this? Consider the following:

Genesis 19:6 states that if Israel will follow God, he will make them a kingdom of priests, a holy nation before God. This was all part of the conditional Mosaic covenant which the Nation of Israel failed to keep. Later the psalmist writes,

> The Lord says to my Lord: 'Sit at My right hand, Until I make Thine enemies a footstool for Thy feet.' The Lord will stretch forth Thy strong scepter from Zion, saying, 'Rule in the midst of Thine enemies.' Thy people will volunteer freely in the day of Thy power; In holy array, from the womb of the dawn, Thy youth are to Thee as the dew.
>
> The Lord has sworn and will not change His mind, 'Thou art a priest forever According to the order of Melchizedek.' The Lord is at Thy right hand; He will shatter kings in the day of His wrath. He will judge among the nations, He will fill them with corpses, He will shatter the chief men over a broad country. He will drink from the brook by the wayside; Therefore He will lift up His head.[438]

This is God's declaration that Christ will be the High Priest, forever in the order of Melchizedek. The point here is, God's future kingdom in any form will have a temple, priests and sacrifices, all for his honor and glory.

God goes on to tell us that everyone who is part of the first resurrection will serve as priests. It should also be noted that every New Testament saint is their own priest (1 Peter 2:4-5). Some may ask, why has God established it this way? Jeremiah 33:16-18:

> In those days Judah shall be saved, and Jerusalem shall dwell in safety; and this is the name by which she shall be called: the Lord is our righteousness. For thus says the Lord, 'David shall never lack a man to sit on the throne of the house of Israel; and the Levitical priests shall never lack a man before Me to offer burnt offerings, to burn grain offerings, and to prepare sacrifices continually.'

Does there need to be any other reason but because God has declared it to be so? If there is, we are missing the whole point of the Kingdom of God!

Remember the context of the tribulation period in relationship to the gentiles. Israel will serve its role as a testimony to the world through the 144,000 witnesses, and the response from some gentiles will be just as the prophet Zechariah pronounced ahead of time as he wrote,

> So many peoples and mighty nations will come to seek the Lord

---

[437] Isa. 11:4.

[438] Ps. 110.

of hosts in Jerusalem and to entreat the favor of the Lord. Thus says the Lord of hosts, In those days ten men from all the nations will grasp the garment of a Jew saying, 'Let us go with you, for we have heard that God is with you.'[439]

Then all the gentiles who come to God through the tribulation will come just as Isaiah announced.

Also the foreigners who join themselves to the Lord, To minister to Him, and to love the name of the Lord, To be His servants, every one who keeps from profaning the sabbath, And holds fast My covenant; Even those I will bring to My holy mountain, And make them joyful in My house of prayer. Their burnt offerings and their sacrifices will be acceptable on My altar; For My house will be called a house of prayer for all the peoples. The Lord God, who gathers the dispersed of Israel, declares, Yet others I will gather to them, to those already gathered.[440]

All this takes place under the context of God's prophets foretelling his intentions for the millennial period. The prophet Hosea writes,

Therefore, behold, I will allure her, Bring her into the wilderness, And speak kindly to her. Then I will give her, her vineyards from there, And the valley of Achor as a door of hope. And she will sing there as in the days of her youth, As in the day when she came up from the land of Egypt. And it will come about in that day, declares the Lord, That you will call Me Ishi And will no longer call Me Baali. For I will remove the names of the Baals from her mouth, So that they will be mentioned by their names no more. In that day I will also make a covenant for them With the beasts of the field, The birds of the sky, And the creeping things of the ground. And I will abolish the bow, the sword, and war from the land, And will make them lie down in safety. And I will betroth you to Me forever; Yes, I will betroth you to Me in righteousness and in justice, In lovingkindness and in compassion, And I will betroth you to Me in faithfulness. Then you will know the Lord.

And it will come about in that day that I will respond, declares the Lord. I will respond to the heavens, and they will respond to the earth, And the earth will respond to the grain, to the new wine, and to the oil, And they will respond to Jezreel. And I will sow her for Myself in the land. I will also have compassion on her who had not obtained compassion, And I will say to those who were not My people, 'You are My people!' And they will say, 'Thou art my God!'[441]

Can there be any doubt that both the Jew and Gentiles will be one with God in this final phase of the Kingdom?

Isaiah 62:4-5 tells us that Israel and God will be joined again in marriage, hence the reconciliation process will be complete. And the words Paul penned in his letter to all the saints in Rome will be fulfilled.

---

[439] Zech. 8:22-23.
[440] Isa. 56:6-8.
[441] Hosea 2:14-23.

For I do not want you, brethren, to be uninformed of this mystery, lest you be wise in your own estimation, that a partial hardening has happened to Israel until the fulness of the Gentiles has come in; and thus all Israel will be saved; just as it is written,

The Deliverer will come from Zion,
He will remove ungodliness from Jacob.
And this is My covenant with them,
When I take away their sins.[442]

In summarizing this section, a final thought is worth noting. Whatever God has planned for his people, the end result will be, they will be loved, justly treated, and happily serving and worshiping their God—forevermore!

EVENTS CLOSING THE MILLENNIUM

THE REVOLT

Revelation 20:1-3; 7-10 tell us that after the 1,000 years are over, Satan will be set free for a short time. He will immediately set about wreaking havoc once again, assembling an army from those living on the earth who refuse to submit to Jesus' authority. As Satan and his army of followers come to battle against God's saints, God will deliver his final blow against his enemies and will destroy them all in a single moment. Then he will casts Satan into his final holding place—the Lake of Fire, where the antichrist has already been for 1,000 years. This is Satan's final judgment.

THE PURGING OF CREATION

Second Peter 3:10 states, "But the day of the Lord will come like a thief, in which the heavens will pass away with a roar and the elements will be destroyed with intense heat, and the earth and its works will be burned up." The Apostle John expands on this thought by saying in Revelation 20:11, "And I saw a great white throne and Him who sat upon it, from whose presence earth and heaven fled away, and no place was found for them."

These events, when put together paint a picture that one day God will do away with the existing world system by purging it with great heat, leaving humanity in the presence of God with no place to go or hide, standing on nothing. This sets up the environment for the last Judgment of humanity and a time for God to establish a New Heaven and New Earth, free from any pollution, sin, or evil presence of any kind. A perfect final state of existence for his creation, clean, and redeemed from sin and corruption, and free from any curse.

THE GREAT WHITE THRONE JUDGMENT—REV. 20:11-15

This judgment will occur after the millennial kingdom. This can be seen in Revelation 20:5, which tells us that this judgment is not associated with the first resurrection but comes after the 1,000 years of Kingdom Rule.

Revelation 20:11 tells us that the place of this judgment will be somewhere suspended in space, most likely between the first and second heaven.

Who will be present or the subjects of this judgment? All the dead who were not part of the rapture or the first resurrection. The Scriptures explain it this way:

And I saw the dead, the great and the small, standing before the throne, and books were opened; and another book was opened, which is

---

[442] Rom. 11:26.

the book of life; and the dead were judged from the things which were written in the books, according to their deeds. And the sea gave up the dead which were in it, and death and Hades gave up the dead which were in them; and they were judged, every one of them according to their deeds. And death and Hades were thrown into the lake of fire. This is the second death, the lake of fire. And if anyone's name was not found written in the book of life, he was thrown into the lake of fire.[443]

According to this passage, the punishment or degree of punishment will be according to individual works. This seems to imply that even though the Lake of Fire is the final outcome for these dead, there may be an element of pain and suffering that accompanies it. This action would be according to how one treated others in everyday life, as judged by God's written or proclaimed standards. This would ultimately demonstrate God's justice and mercy, even to those who will be lost forever.

Why follow this line of reasoning? The simple truth is, it's a matter of commonsense. If everyone was going to be given the exact same punishment, both in place and degree, then why should God bother keeping track of everyone's deeds? If you're lost, you're lost, and if you're saved, you're saved. But this is not how the Scriptures presents God's justice. The saved will be rewarded for their deeds in heaven and the lost will be rewarded for their deeds in the Lake of Fire, the final resting place for all those without Christ. But in the end, it seems that all will fall under some varying degree of reward or punishment that will satisfy God's sense of justice (1 Corinthians 4:4-5; Romans 2:12-16; Jude v.14-16).

BEYOND THE END OF THE AGE

Revelation 21:1-5 provides us the following picture as to what will occur after the final purging and judgment of God's creation.

> And I saw a new heaven and a new earth; for the first heaven and the first earth passed away, and there is no longer any sea. And I saw the holy city, new Jerusalem, coming down out of heaven from God, made ready as a bride adorned for her husband. And I heard a loud voice from the throne, saying, 'Behold, the tabernacle of God is among men,' and He shall dwell among them, and they shall be His people, and God Himself shall be among them, and He shall wipe away every tear from their eyes; and there shall no longer be any death; there shall no longer be any mourning, or crying, or pain; the first things have passed away. And He who sits on the throne said, 'Behold, I am making all things new.' And He said, 'Write, for these words are faithful and true.'

A FINAL NOTE ABOUT CHRIST AS HIGH PRIEST

It is evident from previous passages that Christ will continue as our High Priest as a shepherd over his people. This is found in the proclamation, "Behold, the tabernacle of God is among men." (Rev. 21:3) What tabernacle is this declaration about? It is about a tabernacle that has always existed from the beginning. For the Scriptures tell us, "And let them construct a sanctuary for

---

Me, that I may dwell among them. According to all that I am going to show you, as the pattern of the tabernacle and the pattern of all its furniture, just so you shall construct it" (Ex. 25:8-9). The earthly tabernacle was a copy of the perfect one that existed in Heaven.

The Apostle Paul explains this further as he writes,

Now the main point in what has been said is this: we have such a high priest, who has taken His seat at the right hand of the throne of the Majesty in the heavens, a minister in the sanctuary, and in the true tabernacle, which the Lord pitched, not man. For every high priest is appointed to offer both gifts and sacrifices; hence it is necessary that this high priest also have something to offer. Now if He were on earth, He would not be a priest at all, since there are those who offer the gifts according to the Law; who serve a copy and shadow of the heavenly things, just as Moses was warned by God when he was about to erect the tabernacle; for, 'See,' He says, 'that you make all things according to the pattern which was shown you on the mountain.' But now He has obtained a more excellent ministry, by as much as He is also the mediator of a better covenant, which has been enacted on better promises.[444]

Paul clarifies this concept through these words,

But when Christ appeared as a high priest of the good things to come, He entered through the greater and more perfect tabernacle, not made with hands, that is to say,

not of this creation; and not through the blood of goats and calves, but through His own blood, He entered the holy place once for all, having obtained eternal redemption.[445]

The Apostle John sheds some additional light to this subject as he writes,

After these things I looked, and behold, a great multitude, which no one could count, from every nation and all tribes and peoples and tongues, standing before the throne and before the Lamb, clothed in white robes, and palm branches were in their hands; and they cry out with a loud voice, saying,

'Salvation to our God who sits on the throne, and to the Lamb.' And all the angels were standing around the throne and around the elders and the four living creatures; and they fell on their faces before the throne and worshiped God, saying,

'Amen, blessing and glory and wisdom and thanksgiving and honor and power and might, be to our God forever and ever. Amen.' And one of the elders answered, saying to me, 'These who are clothed in the white robes, who are they, and from where have they come?' And I said to him, 'My lord, you know.' And he said to me, 'These are the ones who come out of the great tribulation, and they have washed their robes and made them white in the blood of the Lamb. For this reason, they are before the throne of God; and they serve Him day and night in His temple; and He who sits on the throne shall spread His tabernacle over them. They shall hunger no

444 Heb. 8:1-7.

445 Heb. 9:11-13.

more, neither thirst anymore; neither shall the sun beat down on them, nor any heat; for the Lamb in the center of the throne shall be their shepherd, and shall guide them to springs of the water of life; and God shall wipe every tear from their eyes.'[446]

The ultimate conclusion is, there will always be a tabernacle for Christ to reside over as our High Priest. This is evident by its presence in the millennial kingdom, as testified to by John in his final writings. This is also supported through the psalmist who proclaimed in Psalm 110:4, "The Lord has sworn and will not change His mind, 'Thou art a priest forever According to the order of Melchizedek.'" Accordingly, the tabernacle that is present in the millennium, will also be part of the eternal state, where God's original tabernacle will be on full display in the realm of the New Heaven and New Earth.

[446] Rev. 7:9-17.

Bibliography

"A. H. Strong." *Christian Classics Ethereal Library.* n.d. https://www.ccel.org/ccel/strong; Internet (accessed November 26, 2018).

Aldrich, R. L. "An Outline Study on Dispensationalism." *Bibliotheca Sacra* 118 (1961): 134–135.

"Allegory." *Merriam-Webster's 11th Collegiate Dictionary.* n.d. https://www.merriam-webster.com/dictionary/allegory (accessed January 24, 2019).

Allen, Matthew. "Theology Adrift: The Early Church Fathers and Their Views of Eschatology." *Bible.org.* n.d. https://bible.org/article/theology-adrift-early-church-fathers-and-their-views-eschatology/ (accessed December 15, 2018).

Allis, Oswald T. *Prophecy and the Church.* 3. The Presbyterian and Reformed Publication Company, 1955.

Allis, Oswald T. "Prophecy and the Church. Philadelphia: Presbyterian and Reformed Publishing company, 1945." In *Things To Come*, by J. Dwight Pentecost. Grand Rapids: Zondervan, 1964.

"Allis, Oswald Thompson." *Biographical Sketch, 1916-2005.* PCA Historical Center. n.d. http://www.pcahistory.org/findingaids/allis/idex.html (accessed November 1, 2018).

"Anabaptist of sixteenth century." *Encyclopaedia Britannica.* Vol. 1. New York: Encyclopaedia Britannica, Inc, 1910.

"Anthony Hoekema." *Theopedia.* n.d. https://www.theopedia.com/anthony-hoekema (accessed November 9, 2018).

Aquinas, Thomas. "Sacred Doctrine." *The Summa Theologiæ.* Translated by Fathers of the English Dominican Province. Burns, Oates & Washburne, 1920.

Ashbaucher, Reid A. *Made in the Image of God: Understanding the Nature of God and Mankind in a Changing World.* 2 rev. Toledo: Reid Ashbaucher, 2017.

—. *The Christian Faith: A Quick Guide to Understanding its Inter-Workings.* 2. Toledo: Reid Ashbaucher, 2017.

Augustine. "Confessions." *Nicene and Post-Nicene Fathers.* Vol. 1. Edited by Philip Schaff. Translated by J.G. Pilkington. Compiled by New Advent by Kevin Knight. Buffalo, NY: Christian Literature Publishing Co, 1887.

—. "On Christian Doctrine." *Nicene and Post-Nicene Fathers.* Vol. 2. Edited by Philip Schaff. Translated by James Shaw. Compiled by New Advent by Kevin Knight. Buffalo, NY: Christian Literature Publishing Co, 1887.

—. "The City of God." *Nicene and Post-Nicene Fathers.* Vol. 2. Edited by Philip Schaff. Translated by Marcus Dods. Compiled by New Advent by Kevin Knight. Buffalo, NY: Christian Literature Publishing Co, 1887.

Augustine. "To Simplician on Various Questions (Augustine: Early Writings)." In *Letter and the Spirit* , by Wai-Shing Chau. New York: Peter Lang Publishing, 1995.

Baur, Chrysostom. "Theodore of Mopsuestia." *The Catholic Encyclopedia.* Vol. 14. New York: Robert Appleton Company, 1912.

Berkhof, Louis. *The Kingdom of God* . Grand Rapids: Wm. B. Eerdmans Pub. Co, 1951.

Blaising, Craig, and Darrell L. Bock. *Dispensationalism, Israel and the Church* . Grand Rapids: Zondervan, 1992.

Borsch, Frederick Hauk. *Many Things in Parables* . Philadelphia: Fortress Press, 1988.

Chapman, John. "St. Papias." *The Catholic Encyclopedia.* Vol. 11. New York: Robert Appleton Company, 1911.

Chau, Wai-Shing. *The Letter and the Spirit: A History of Interpretation from Origen to Luther.* New York: Peter Lang Publishing, 1995.

Clugnet, Léon. "St. Victorinus." *The Catholic Encyclopedia.* Vol. 15. New York: Robert Appleton Company, 1912.

"College of Sorbonne." *Wikipedia.* n.d. https://en.wikipedia.org/wiki/College_of_Sorbonne/ (accessed November 29, 2018).

Cooper, David L. "The Golden Rule of Interpretation ." *The Biblical Research Society.* n.d. http://www.biblicalresearch.info/index.html (accessed January 25, 2019).

Couch, Mal. "Progressive Dispensationalism: What Really Is It?" *Conservative Theological Journal* 3, no. 9 (1999): 258-260.

Criswell, W. A. "Why I Preach that the Bible is Literally True. Nashville: Broadman Press, 1969." In *The Interpretation of Prophecy*, by Paul Lee Tan. Winona Lake: Assurance Publishers, 1974.

"Daniel Whitby." *Biblicaltraining.org.* n.d. https://www.biblicaltraining.org/library/daniel-whitby (accessed November 21, 2018).

Darby, John Nelson. "Lectures on the Second Coming of Christ; Lecture II; Ephesians 1." London: George Morrish, 24 Warwick Lane, Paternoster Row, E.C.; Glasgow: R.L. Allan, 75 Sauchiehall Street; Dublin: F. Cavenagh, The Tract Depot, 32 Wicklow Street; Guernsey: J. Tunley, 104 Victoria Road, 1868. 33.

"Dispensationalism." *Theopedia.* n.d. https://www.theopedia.com/dispensationalism (accessed January 16, 2019).

"Dispensations." *Chafer Theological Seminary.* n.d. https://www.chafer.edu/dispensations (accessed January 28, 2019).

"Dogmatic Constitution on Divine Revelation." *Second Vatican Council.* November 18, 1965.
http://www.vatican.va/archive/hist_councils/ii_vatican_council/documents/vat-ii_const_19651118_dei-verbum_en.html (accessed January 19, 2019).

"E. W. Bullinger." *Theopedia.* n.d. https://www.theopedia.com/e-w-bullinger (accessed February 6, 2019).

"Economy." *Merriam-Webster's 11th Collegiate Dictionary.* CD ROM. 2003.

"Ernst Wilhelm Hengstenberg." *Encyclopaedia Britannica.* Vol. 13. New York: Encyclopaedia Britannica, Inc, 1910.

Farrar, Frederic W. *History of Interpretation* . London: Macmillan and Co, 1886.

Fuller, Daniel Payton. "The Hermeneutics of Dispensationalism." *Doctor's dissertation.* Chicago: Northern Baptist Theol. Seminary, 1957.

Gardner, Edmund. "Joachim of Flora." *The Catholic Encyclopedia.* Vol. 8. New York: Robert Appleton Company, 1910.

Gesenius, William. *A Hebrew and English Lexicon of the Old Testament.* Edited by Francis Brown, S. R. Driver, & Charles A Briggs. Translated by Edward Robinson. New York: Boston and New York Houghton Miffin Company, 1907.

Gigot, Francis. "Scriptural Glosses." *The Catholic Encyclopedia.* Vol. 6. New York: Robert Appleton Company, 1909.

Grimm, Wilke. *A Greek-English Lexicon of the New Testament.* Translated by Joseph Henry Thayer. New York: American Book Company, 1889.

Hippolytus. "On the End of the World." *Ante-Nicene Fathers.* Vol. 5. Edited by Alexander Roberts, James Donaldson, & A. Cleveland Coxe. Translated by J.H. MacMahon. Compiled by New Advent by Kevin Knight. Buffalo, NY: Christian Literature Publishing Co, 1886.

"Hodge, Charles." *New Catholic Encyclopedia.* n.d.
https://www.encyclopedia.com/religion/encyclopedias-almanacs-transcripts-and-maps/hodge-charles (accessed November 29, 2018).

Hodge, Charles. *Systematic Theology.* Vol. 3. New York: Scribner, Armstrong And Company, 1873.

Hoekema, Anthony A. *The Bible and the Future.* Grand Rapids: Willian B. Eerdmans Publishing Company, 1979.

Irenaeus. "Against Heresies." *Ante-Nicene Fathers.* Vol. 1. Edited by James Donaldson, and A. Cleveland Coxe Alexander Roberts. Translated by Alexander Roberts and William Rambaut. Compiled by New Advent by Kevin Knight. Buffalo, NY: Christian Literature Publishing Co, 1885.

"James Innell Packer." *Theopedia.* n.d. Https://www.theopedia.com/j-i-packer (accessed April 1, 2019).

Jamieson, Rev. Robert, Rev. A. R. Fausset, and Rev. David Brown. "Ephesians 1:10." *A commentary, critical and explanatory, on the Old and New Testaments.* Vol. 2. New York; Philadelphia; Hartford; Cincinnati: S.S. Scranton and company, 1873.

—. "Psalm 22:22." Vol. 1. New York; Philadelphia; Hartford; Cincinnati: S.S. Scranton and company, 1873.

Jerome. "Letters, 128." *Nicene and Post-Nicene Fathers.* Vol. 6. Edited by Philip Schaff, & Henry Wace. Translated by W.H. Fremantle, G. Lewis, & W.G. Martley. Compiled by New Advent by Kevin Knight. Buffalo, NY: Christian Literature Publishing Co, 1893.

"Joachim of Floris." *Encyclopaedia Britannica.* 11. Vol. 15. THA New Media, LLC. New York: Encyclopaedia Britannica, Inc, 1910.

"John Nelson Darby." *Wikipedia.* n.d. https://en.wikipedia.org/wiki/John_Nelson_Darb (accessed January 13, 2019).

Johnson, Paul. *A History of Christianity* . New York: Athenium, 1976.

Kasemann, Ernest. *The Spirit and the Letter in Perspectives on Paul.* Translated by M. Kohl. Philadelphia: Fortress Press, 1971.

Kelly, J. N. D. *Early Christian Doctrines.* Edited by rev. San Francisco: Harper & Row Publishers, 1978.

Kennedy, Daniel. "St. Thomas Aquinas." *The Catholic Encyclopedia.* Vol. 14. New York: Robert Appleton Company, 1912.

Kirsch, Johann Peter. "St. Hippolytus of Rome." *The Catholic Encyclopedia.* Vol. 7. New York: Robert Appleton Company, 1910.

Knowles, David. "The Evolution of Medieval Thought (Baltimore: Helicon, 1962)." In *The Letter and the Spirit*, by Wai-Shing Chau. New York: Peter Lang Publishing, 1995.

Lactantius. "The Devine Institutes." *Ante-Nicene Fathers.* Vol. 7. Edited by Alexander Roberts, James Donaldson & A. Cleveland Coxe. Translated by William Fletcher. Compiled by Advent by Kevin Knght. Buffalo: Christian Literature Publiching Co., 1886.

—. "To Simplician on Various Questions." *Ante-Nicene Fathers.* Vol. 7. Edited by Alexander Roberts, James Donaldson, & A. Cleveland Coxe. Translated by William Fletcher. Compiled by New Advent by Kevin Knight. Buffalo, NY: Christian Literature Publishing Co, 1886.

Ladd, George E. "Jesus and the Kingdom." *The Presence of the Future.* Grand Rapids: William B. Eerdmans Publishing Company, 1974.

Ladd, George Eldon. *The Gospel of the Kingdom* . Grand Rapids: WM. B. Eerdmans Publishing Company, 1959.

Lebreton, Jules. "St. Justin Martyr (Justin and Christian revelation)." *The Catholic Encyclopedia*. Vol. 8. New York: Robert Appleton Company, 1910.

Livingston, James C. *Modern Christian Thought*. 2. Vol. 1. 2 vols. Minneapolis: Fortress Press Publishing, 2006.

—. *Modern Christian Thought*. 2. Vol. 2. 2 vols. Minneapolis: Fortress Press, 2006.

Lizorkin-Eyzenberg, Eli. "Council Of Jamnia." *Israel Institute of Biblical Studies*. n.d. https://blog.israelbiblicalstudies.com/jewish-studies/jamnia/ (accessed January 23, 2019).

"Loraine Boettner." *Theopedia*. n.d. https://www.theopedia.com/loraine-boettner (accessed November 26, 2018).

Luther. *lectures on Romans (St. Louis: Concordia, 1972)*. Vol. 25, in *The Letter and the Spirit*, by Wai-Shing Chau. New York: Peter Lang Publishing, 1995.

Manson, T. W. *The Teaching of Jesus*. Cambridge: The University Press, 1931.

Martyr, Justin. "Dialogue with Trypho." *Ante-Nicene Fathers*. Vol. 1. Edited by James Donaldson, and A. Cleveland Coxe Alexander Roberts. Translated by Marcus Dods and George Reith. Compiled by New Advent by Kevin Knight. Buffalo, New York: Christian Literature Publishing Co, 1885.

Mattox, J. Mark. "Augustine 354—430 C.E." *The Internet Encyclopedia of Philosophy*. n.d. https://www.iep.utm.edu/augustin/#H7 (accessed December 1, 2018).

McInerny, Ralph, and John O'Callaghan. "Saint Thomas Aquinas." Vers. Summer 2018. *Stanford Encyclopedia of Philosophy*. Edited by Edward N. Zalta . n.d. https://plato.stanford.edu/archives/sum2018/entries/aquinas/ (accessed October 24, 2018).

Mendelson, Michael. "Saint Augustine." Vers. Winter 2016 . *The Stanford Encyclopedia of Philosophy*. Edited by Edward N. Zalta. n.d. https://plato.stanford.edu/archives/win2016/entries/augustine/ (accessed October 9, 2018).

Moore, Edward. "Origen of Alexandria (185—254 C.E." *The Internet Encyclopedia of Philosophy*. n.d. https://www.iep.utm.edu/ origen-of-alexandria/ (accessed December 1, 2018).

New American Standard Bible. The Open Bible Expanded Edition. New York: Thomas Nelson Publishers, 1985.

Oehler, Gustav Friedrich. "Theology of the Old Testament (New York: Funk and Wagnalls Pubs., 1883)." In *The Interpretation of Prophecy*, by Paul Lee Tan, translated by George E. Day. Winona Lake: Assurance Publicshers, 1974.

Origen. "De Principiis." *Ante-Nicene Fathers*. Vol. 4. Edited by James Donaldson, and A. Cleveland Coxe Alexander Roberts. Translated by Frederick Crombie. Compiled by New Advent by Kevin Knight. Buffalo, NY: Christian Literature Publishing Co, 1885.

Orr, DR. James, ed. "Sacrifice." *International Standard Bible Encyclopaedia.* Compiled by Inc. Biblesoft. Chicago: The Howard-Severance Company, 1915.

Packer, James. "Hermeneutics and Biblical Authority." *Themelios* 1, no. 1 (1975).

Papias. "Fragments, I." *Ante-Nicene Fathers.* Vol. 1. Edited by Alexander Roberts, James Donaldson, & A. Cleveland Coxe. Translated by Alexander Roberts, & James Donaldson. Compiled by New Advent by Kevin Knight. Buffalo, NY: Christian Literature Publishing Co, 1885.

Pentecost, J. Dwight. *Things To Come.* Grand Rapids: Zondervan Publishing House, 1964.

Peters, G. N. H. *Theocratic Kingdom. Grand Rapids: Kregel Publications, 1952.* Vol. 3, in *Things To Come,* by J. Dwight Pentecost. Grand Rapids: Zondervan, 1964.

Poncelet, Albert. "Lucius Caecilius Firmianus Lactantius." *The Catholic Encyclopedia.* Vol. 8. New York: Robert Appletion Company, 1910.

—. "St. Irenaeus." *The Catholic Encyclopedia.* Vol. 8. New York: Robert Appleton Company, 1910.

Portalié, Eugène. "Life of St. Augustine of Hippo." *The Catholic Encyclopedia.* Vol. 2. New York: Robert Appleton Company, 1907.

Preus, James Samuel. "Luther and the Old Testament. Translated by Eric W., & Ruth C. Gritsch. Philadelphia: Fortress Press, 1969." In *The Letter and the Spirit,* by Wai-Shing Chau. New York: Peter Lang Publishing, 1995.

Quanbeck, Warren A. "Luther's Early Exegesis." *Luther Today.* Vol. 1. Docorah, IA: Luther College Press, 1957.

Ramm, Bernard. *Protestant Biblical Interpretation.* 3 rev. Grand Rapids: Baker Book House, 1970.

Rome, Clement of. "First Epistle." *Ante-Nicene Fathers.* Vol. 9. Edited by Allan Menzies. Translated by John Keith. Compiled by New Advent by Kevin Knight. Buffalo, NY: Christian Literature Publishing Co, 1896.

"Rousas John Rushdoony." *Theopedia.* n.d. https://www.theopedia.com/rousas-john-rushdoony (accessed November 26, 2018).

Ryrie, Charles C. *Dispensationalism.* Chicago: Moody Publishers, 2007.

—. *Dispensationalism Today* . Chicago: Moody Press, 1965.

Sauer, Eric. *Dawn of World Redemption: A Survey of the History of Salvation in the Old Testament.* Grand Rapids: Wm. B. Eerdmans Publishing Company, 1964.

Scharf, Paul J. "Five Dispensationalists Who Changed My Direction." *Dispensationalpublishing.com.* n.d. https://dispensationalpublishing.com/five-dispensationalists-who-changed-my-direction (accessed January 31, 2019).

Scofield, C. I. *The Scofield Reference Bible.* New York: Oxford University Press, 1909.

Stallard, Michael D. "Anabaptists, Eschatology." *tyndale.edu*. n.d. https://www.tyndale.edu/wp-content/uploads/files/HIST5317-Stallard/HIST5317%20History%20of%20Eschatology%20Stallard%20Anabaptists.doc (accessed November 28, 2018).

Strong, Augustus Hopkins. *Outlines of systematic theology*. Philadelphia: American Baptist Publication Society, 1908.

Swanson, Dennis M. "The Millennial Position of Spurgeon." *Master's Seminary Journal* 7, no. 2 (1996): 191.

Tan, Paul Lee. *The Interpretation of Prophecy*. Winona Lake, Indiana: Assurance Publishers, 1974.

Terry, Milton S. *Biblical Hermeneutics*. New York: Eaton & Mains, 1890.

Thomas, Robert L. "The Hermeneutics of Progressive Dispensationalism." *Master's Seminary Journal* 6, no. 1 (1995): 78.

Victorinus. "Commentary on the Apocalypse." *Ante-Nicene Fathers*. Edited by Alexander Roberts, James Donaldson, & A. Cleveland Coxe. Translated by Robert Ernest Wallis. Compiled by New Advent by Kevin Knight. Buffalo, NY: Christian Literature Publishing Co, 1886.

Vos, Geerhardus. *The Teaching of Jesus Concerning the kingdom of God and the Church*. New York: American Tract Society, 1903.

"W. A. Criswell." *Wikipedia*. n.d. https://en.wikipedia.org/wiki/W._A._Criswell (accessed January 20, 2019).

Walvoord, John F. "New Testament Words for the Lord's Coming." *Bibliotheca Sacra* 101 (July/September 1944): 283.

—. *The Millennial Kingdom*. Grand Rapids: Zondervan Publishing House, 1959.

—. *The Rapture Question*. rev. Grand Rapids: Zondervan Publishing House, 1979.

Warfield, B. B. "The Millennium and the Apocalypse." *The Princeton Theological Review* 2, no. 4 (1904).

Waugh, Barry. "Author Biography Benjamin Breckinridge Warfield (5 November 1851 - 16 February 1921)." *The Southern Presbyterian Review*. n.d. http://www.pcahistory.org/HCLibrary/periodicals/spr/bios/warfield.html (accessed November 1, 2018).

West, Nathaniel. *The Thousand Years in both Testaments*. New York: Fleming H. Revell, 1880.

Whitby, Daniel. "A TREATISE of the True Millennium." In *A paraphrase and commentary on the New Testament: in two volumes*, by Daniel Whitby. London: Printed for Amſham and John Churchill, at the Black–Swan, in Pater-Noſter-Row, 1703.

Whitford, David M. "Martin Luther (1483—1546)." *The Internet Encyclopedia of Philosophy.* n.d. https://www.iep.utm.edu/luther/ (accessed November 29, 2018).

Wiersbe, Warren W. "Matthew 13:47-50." *The Bible Exposition Commentary.* Colorado Springs: Chariot Victor Publishing, 1989.

Wilkin, R. N. "Review of The Dispensational View of the Davidic Kingdom: A Response to Progressive Dispensationalism." Edited by Stephen J. Nichols. *Journal of the Grace Evangelical Society* (Theological Journal Library, Vol. 1-5. Faithlife Corporation product available from Logos.com.) 10, no. 18 (1997).

Subject Index

Scripture Index

Key: Books are listed in Alphanumeric order. Book page numbers follows any comma.

Illustrative Index